BIBLICAL CHRISTIANITY IN MODERN AFRICA

Wilbur O'Donovan

OASIS INTERNATIONAL LTD

ISBN: 978-1-59452-478-3
ISBN: 1-59452-478-5

Cover Design by Mainstream, Lancaster

Oasis International is a ministry devoted to fostering a robust and sustainable pan-African publishing industry. For more information, go to oasisint.net.

ABBREVIATIONS FOR THE BOOKS OF THE BIBLE

Unless written out in full, books of the Bible are abbreviated as follows:

Old Testament		*New Testament*	
Genesis	Gen.	Matthew	Matt.
Exodus	Ex.	Mark	Mk.
Leviticus	Lev.	Luke	Lk.
Deuteronomy	Deut.	John	Jn.
1 Samuel	1 Sam.	Romans	Rom.
2 Samuel	2 Sam.	1 Corinthians	1 Cor.
2 Kings	2 Kgs.	2 Corintnhians	2 Cor.
1 Chronicles	1 Chr.	Galatians	Gal.
2 Chronicles	2 Chr.	Ephesians	Eph.
Nehemiah	Neh.	Philippians	Phil.
Esther	Esth.	1 Thessalonians	1 Thess.
Psalms	Ps.	2 Thessalonians	2 Thess.
Proverbs	Prov.	1 Timothy	1 Tim.
Ecclesiastes	Ecc.	2 Timothy	2 Tim.
Song of Solomon	Song.	Titus	Tit.
Isaiah	Isa.	Hebrews	Heb.
Jeremiah	Jer.	James	Jas.
Daniel	Dan.	1 Peter	1 Pet.
Joel	Joel	2 Peter	2 Pet.
Zephaniah	Zep.	1 John	1 Jn.
Malachi	Mal.	Revelation	Rev.

Contents

Introduction

Africa is one of the most rapidly changing continents in the world today. The winds of change are affecting almost every sector of public and private life. Traditional practices and beliefs are being questioned and abandoned in many places. In other places, there is a strong effort to restore and renew traditional values and beliefs. Islam and Christianity are both claiming enormous numbers of converts in many countries. According to some estimates, Africa may have become the most Christian continent in the world by the year 2000 A.D in comparison with other continents. At the same time, Islam may have become the dominant force in politics and government on the continent.

Education, technology, globalization, urbanization, religious change and social change are touching the lives of people from Capetown to Cairo and from Dakar to Djibouti. The demand for democratically elected government instead of traditional or military leadership has brought a tidal wave of upheaval in many countries, especially among the newly educated and the young. The widespread use of western videos has changed the morality and values of an entire generation of young people in Africa. The roles of educated youth and the roles of women, both in society and in the church, are topics of active discussion in many places.

Along with the changes have come such great problems that no one seems to know what to do or where to start to solve them. Governments are caught up in political power struggles, war and endemic nepotism, while poverty, pollution, sickness, crime, unemployment, and the breakdown of traditional family life threaten to destroy the very core of existence of the people these governments control. What kind of future does Africa have? What, if anything can the people of God do for their native lands and peoples? Is the situation hopelessly out of control or is there anything that can be done for this large part of the world's population?

This book will attempt to look at the problems of modern Africa in a biblical perspective. Problems are not solved until people acknowledge them and face them openly, honestly and courageously. In this book, some of the immense problems confronting modern Africa will be discussed and analyzed. An effort will be made to see what God says about such problems in the Bible and to learn what God did at other times in history when similar problems threatened to destroy human society. If we understand what God did in the past it will help us to know what He can do today. The knowledge of what God did for His people in the past will help us to face the present great challenges with faith and courage. God does not change, and those who trust in God to solve their problems will make the discovery of what Daniel learned long ago: "the people who know their God will display strength and take action" (Daniel 11:32-NASB).

The problems of modern Africa are great, but they are not new. The history of mankind is a tragic story of problems caused by human beings and human sin. The Bible says, "there is nothing new under the sun" (Ecc. 1:9). There may be new inventions and new technology, but the problems resulting from sin have not changed. As a result, the wisdom and words of God are still the answers to the problems of modern Africa, just as they were to the people who lived thousands of years ago.

WHO AM I? A GAME OR A PROBLEM?

A game played by some people is called, "Who Am I?" One person in the group describes the characteristics of a famous person, and then says, "Who am I?" The rest of the group tries to guess who the person is who is being described. In Africa today, what can be a game for some has become a deep inner conflict for many people in trying to describe themselves.

The question, "Who Am I?" has become difficult to answer. No human being exists by himself or herself alone. Every person is a reflection of the influences of his or her culture, childhood experiences, parental training, education, beliefs, world view, and many other things. For the modern, educated person in Africa, these influences have brought two very different worlds together. On one side, there is the strong influence of a traditional rural African culture which has existed for centuries. On the other side, there is an increasingly strong influence from the beliefs, practices, values and world view of the modern, scientific, educated world of western Europe and North America.

Each of these influences has a strong attraction. Each world view exercises a strong influence on their thinking and decisions. These two world views are really quite different. Problems arise because of the inevitable conflict between two such different world views. Each type of culture has a very different set of values and a very different view of life itself. This can result in inner conflict and frustration for many Africans today. As a minimum, it almost always results in conflict between the younger and the older generation. This tension has brought a whole new world of problems to urban and educated Africans.

The traditional past says that clock time is not important. It is the event of the day that matters. However, young people soon discover when they attend university or find jobs in the city, that they must become very clock conscious if they want to pass their courses or keep their jobs. The same young person also discovers that in the academic or business world, it is "every man for himself." This is a strange and insecure feeling for a young person who has known the unconditional support, encouragement and participation of a caring extended family during their childhood years in the village.

What about basic beliefs and values? It can happen that one day a young person discovers that some of the people he or she admires most at school or at work hold very different beliefs and values than those he or she was taught as a child. Who is right? And who shall this young person believe and follow? When this young person returns to his village and home, there is often very little tolerance for new ideas among the older people. There may be conflict with parents, family members and respected leaders in the community over the views held by the young people. There is often the feeling that that the youth are simply in rebellion against the traditions of their people.

The young people have seen the value of education and modern knowledge. They have seen the benefits that such knowledge and education have brought to the modern world. The young person is caught in a conflict of values, traditions, beliefs and practices which make him or her wonder, "Who is right?" "Who am I?"

Inner conflict over identity and values is just one of many difficulties resulting from taking on the values, goals and ideas of the West. With modernity has come an enormous number of problems which seem to have no solution. On the community level, poverty, unemployment, crime, pollution, political instability, social injustice, homelessness, drug abuse, prostitution, the AIDS epidemic and the lack of such things as safe drinking water, waste disposal and affordable housing have become the scourge of the cities.

On the individual level, loss of traditional values, loneliness, sexual immorality, the breakdown of marriages and families, personal struggles for power and influence, psychological and emotional problems, violent tribalism, personal insecurity and even the temptation to suicide have become the plague of African cities.

In such an unstable and changing environment, what does God expect His on people to do? It is the intention of this book to bring an understanding of some of the major issues of modernity as they affect people in Africa today and to discover some of the ways in which God wants His people to deal with these problems.

From a human perspective, the situation often appears to be out of control. That is never God's perspective. We need a fresh view of Who God is, and what He has done in history. We need to see what He is still doing through His people today. We need to remember that there is no human problem too great for a God who can raise the dead!

God's solutions, however, are not usually easy. God does not provide "quick fixes" for problems that are as old as humanity. God's solutions also require a high level of personal commitment, sacrifice, courage and faith, as the true stories in this book will reveal. But God's solutions work, because God Himself is behind them and God has all power in the universe. Looking at examples from the past and the present, we will see how God's solutions work. We will see that even in seemingly impossible situations, "with God, all things are possible."(Matt. 19:26).

We will look at the lives of real people in history and in Africa today who have dared to believe in the God of the Bible. We need to be realistic, but we also need to have faith in the God Who made all things. It is the intention of this book that by learning what God has done in the past and what He is still doing in the present, many of God's people will hear His call to take part in applying the salvation of God to the practical problems of Africa at the beginning of the twenty first century.

Chapter 1

AFRICAN OR WESTERN: WHAT IS THE DIFFERENCE?

Joshua was a theology student at a Bible College in Nigeria. His parents and family lived in a quiet village about 200 kilometers from the Federal Capital. After his third year in school, Joshua decided to marry Sarah, the girl of his heart, with whom he had grown up in the village. The wedding would take place in his village, but Joshua wanted his friends from the Bible College to attend the wedding, including the faculty members who had come to respect Joshua for his abilities.

Some of the faculty members were expatriates from Europe and North America. Joshua had grown accustomed to their thinking and understood their western culture. When he had his wedding invitation printed, the invitation surprised both his fellow students and the faculty at his school. The wedding was scheduled for 10:00 a.m. on a day in June, just after Joshua's graduation. Following tradition in the West, Joshua indicated this on the invitation with the time for the wedding given as 10:00 a.m. SHARP. Knowing African tradition well, some of Joshua's Bible College friends found the invitation amusing. Did he mean what was printed? Or was it a joke? Did he really expect all his Bible College friends to appear in his village before 10:00 a.m.?

A few days before the wedding, Joshua's friends on the faculty had a discussion about what they should do, since they would be traveling together in a van. They knew that Joshua well understood the differences between African and western concepts of time. After some discussion, the teachers decided to take the invitation seriously. They gathered at the school promptly on the wedding day and planned to arrive in the village by 9:30 a.m. The staff was delayed by muddy roads, but they managed to reach the village at 9:55 a.m. They drove right to the church. The church the extended family, the clan or the tribe. This strong sense of community has a positive side and a negative side. The positive side is a caring, helping and sharing concern for one another. The negative side is tribalism, ethnicity, prejudice toward others and sometimes even tribal violence.

In sharp contrast to the African value of community, the important question in the West is usually, "What is good for me?" The person in the West often seeks his or her own freedom, privacy and individual recognition without reference to any community. In the West, people often purposely avoid the influence of others when making their plans and decisions. Except among teenagers and in certain ethnic communities, most western people cherish their individuality, uniqueness and differences from others. Westerners do not want to be bound by the traditions or opinions of other people. A popular saying in the West says that each person should, "do his or her own thing." This statement reveals that the person is not willing to be influenced or controlled by the desires, opinions or will of others.

SOME BAD EFFECTS OF WESTERN CULTURE

The demand for personal freedom without regard for the community in western culture is not based on something godly. It is the result of the pride, selfishness and personal rebellion of the sin nature of man. These are some of the most destructive forces in the world to peaceful human relationships. These demands do not tend to build a healthy cooperative community. When African people begin to embrace western culture and values, they find that these values have a bad effect on the unity of their own people. Western values tend to divide and separate the community instead of producing unity and cooperation.

When Africans move into the cities, many of them begin to adopt western values. In addition, there is a subtle assumption among many non-western people that, "West is Best." This comes from the fact that the West does offer many advantages in education, technology, health care and democratic government relatively free from political oppression. But is West always best for Africa? To answer this question, let us look at what is happening in western culture today.

The core values of freedom and individuality in the West have brought about the so-called "sexual revolution." By this is meant that men and women think they have the right to have sex with whoever will agree to it, whenever they want to do it. Among these people, there is no sense of wrongdoing in such behavior. They feel it is part of their right to freedom. Because of the "sexual revolution" the values and traditions of western people concerning sex have changed dramatically. Fifty years ago, virginity before marriage and faithfulness after marriage were held to be important values in the West. Divorce was considered to be a disgrace.

Today, these values have completely changed. Many unmarried people in the West do not think there is anything wrong with having sex with someone before they are married. Even after marriage, husbands and wives will often be unfaithful to each other, which is a continuation of their behaviour before marriage. Western people feel that no one has the right to tell them what they can or cannot do. There is no sense of accountability to a community to which people feel they must conform. To them, what is right is what they themselves think is right, not what is right according to the standards of any community. The only general exception to this attitude is found among Christians who feel a sense of responsibility to God and to the community of the local church.

The result of these attitudes about freedom and individualism in the West is horrifying. Marriages and families are breaking down at an alarming rate. Divorce is commonplace. Divorce is no longer considered to be a bad thing. Sexual immorality is found everywhere. Sexually transmitted diseases ("STD's") are multiplying at an alarming rate. More will be said about these problems later in the book.

The frightening thing is that this pattern is also becoming true in African cities. One reason for this is that many Africans moving into the cities have accepted western ideas about freedom, individuality and privacy. They do not seem to understand the dangers of embracing western cultural values. Because people in African cities are embracing western values and behaviour, marriages and families are breaking down with increasing frequency. Divorce is on the increase in the cities. Western videos, commonly available in the cities, have become a curse on marriages and families in Africa. The proof that this is true is seen in the rapid spread of AIDS and other STD's in African cities.

Another important result of the core values of individualism, freedom and privacy is that people do not have a collective sense of responsibility for what happens to others in their society. The rule of the cities is, "every one for himself." The results of this attitude are frightening. It has happened with increasing frequency in western cities that a person will be attacked by a criminal on the street in plain view of other people and others will just watch, as if they were watching a football match. Sometimes they will just turn away and completely ignore the situation.

This kind of behavior is rapidly spreading in African cities. People do not know one another and so they do not feel a sense of responsibility for one another. In the village there is no person who is ignored or uncared for within the ability of the community to care for that person. But in many African cities there are thousands of homeless, destitute people lying on the streets, uncared for and unnoticed by those who pass by. Another result of adopting western mentality is that close neighbors often hardly know each other. As in the West, urban society in Africa is becoming dangerously fragmented and isolated.

It is a great mistake to think that it is possible to have all the benefits of the West without having its great problems and dangers. As Africans increasingly adopt western values and behavior, the problems of the West will affect African society more and more.

There are other contrasts between the cultural patterns of the West and the cultural patterns of Africa that are causing problems in Africa today. The materialism and secularism of the West is capturing the hearts and minds of many city dwellers. Education and material wealth have become the "gods" of many people today.

Because many people have the idea that "West is Best," many African city dwellers want to appear western in order to be seen as modern or educated. This uncritical acceptance of western values is creating a serious breakdown in society. When African people uncritically accept western values in place of their own community values, they sacrifice some of the most valuable parts of their African culture. It may not be long before a majority of people in the cities become prisoners of the same self-serving values which have destroyed many people in western cultures. Inwardly they know that traditional African values such as living for the good of the community and putting people before programs and goals are really the right thing to do. But pride drives them to embrace western values so that they will be respected and successful in business or education.

From what has been said, it should be clear that there are some fundamental differences between what may be called basic African cultural values and what may be called basic western cultural values. These differences come from deeply held traditions and beliefs. Can we conclude that traditional African values are superior to western values and that Africans should forget trying to imitate the West? The answer is yes in some ways and no in others.

With respect to the importance of human relationships there is great wisdom in African tradition. It does not take much reflection to realize that relationships between people are much more important to happiness in life than education, wealth, projects, programs, and material things. It would be a great mistake to follow the western pattern of ignoring human relationships in order to achieve personal or material goals. On the other hand, there are benefits that can come to Africa through improved education, improved communications, improved city planning, improved health care and other benefits of western technology.

However, even some of the best community values of African culture are often corrupted by attitudes of tribalism, prejudice, political oppression, financial corruption and other evils because of the sinful nature of all human beings. In the matter of government, traditional rule by one family or one person is often corrupted into abuse of power and wealth as well as oppression of other people.

HOW SHOULD A CHRISTIAN RESPOND TO MODERN CULTURAL CHANGE IN AFRICA?

What is an African Christian to do? Which culture should he or she follow? The answer is that no culture in the world is free from the effects of sin (Rom. 3:23, Rom. 5:12). A Christian must learn to distinguish between things which are done just to make a person look good or seem modern and things which are done because they are right before God and good for other people. A Christian must learn to choose the ways of God rather than the ways of any particular culture. No culture is best. No culture is right in everything. There are things in every culture which must be rejected by the sincere Christian because they are not pleasing to God. There are also beneficial things which can be learned from every culture.

Western economic greed (an outgrowth of western individualism) is not pleasing to God (1 Tim. 6:10). Neither is tribalism and ethnic prejudice pleasing to God (James 2:9). A Christian must learn to choose his or her values from the Bible and not from his or her own culture. At times a person must reject some of the most strongly held values of his or her own culture, if he or she is to be pleasing to God. Separation from the world's system of values is an important part of holy living. The Bible says, "come out from them and be separate, says the Lord. Touch no unclean thing, and I will receive you" (2 Cor. 6:17). This is true regardless of what culture a person belongs to.

Here is a true story of an African girl who lost her testimony as a Christian and her close relationship with God because of her desire to have the benefits of living in the West and of getting a western education regardless of the way she had to dishonor God to get these things.

Deborah finished high school a few years ago. She did not get a good grade on her English language ability test. Deborah was considered to be a dedicated Christian. She led a Bible study and taught a Sunday School class in her church. She also sang in the choir. Deborah was unhappy because her family did not consider her to be a success as a result of her schooling. She found it difficult to accept herself, even though she often spoke to others in her Bible study about contentment with God's provision and acceptance of God's will.

After some time, Deborah was accepted into a commercial college in her city but she was still unsatisfied. A year later a friend of her brother won a lottery which offered him an opportunity to go to the United States as an American resident. According to the rules of the lottery, the winning person could also take his wife with him if he was married. The brother's friend offered to let Deborah use his lottery opportunity to let Deborah go to America as his wife! The plan was to sign the official marriage documents in a government office and then get a divorce after they were settled in the United States.

Deborah eagerly seized the opportunity and signed the necessary papers in the government office. She became the legal wife of her brother's friend even though she did not love the boy and did not want to be married to him. She then called her Christian friends together for a time of "celebration and praise to God for His provision for her need!" Her friends gathered and celebrated with her while Deborah calmly justified her actions using Scriptures such as Abraham's lie to Pharaoh about Sarah being his sister (Gen. 12:11-16)! When they got to the United States, Deborah and her brother's friend completed their hypocritical plan and were divorced, thus adding one sin to another.

We wonder what this girl was thinking? She had probably convinced herself that she was doing nothing wrong and that God would not care about her dishonesty and hypocrisy. How foolish it is when we deceive ourselves! How foolish to think that we can deceive God! How much more foolish is it to think that a holy God will bless a person who dishonors His holy name and His holy character! God sees our hearts (1 Sam. 16:7) and He judges us with righteous judgment. By dishonest behaviour and unholy decisions we dishonor the holy name of God and break our relationship with Him. One day when real trouble comes and we urgently need God to answer our prayers we discover that He won't hear us (Isaiah 59:1-2). Even then we rarely admit the fact that it is our own sins that have caused our problems. We begin to blame others and eventually to blame God. This is just what Adam did in the garden of Eden (Gen. 3:12). When we do this, we only hurt ourselves.

How much better if Deborah had chosen to live a life pleasing to God instead of choosing to love the things of this world. The Bible says, "Do not love the world or anything in the world. If anyone loves the world, the love of the Father is not in him" (1 John 2:15). How many other Christians make similar foolish decision as this girl made and live to regret it? Jesus said, "What good is it for a man to gain the whole world, yet forfeit his soul? Or what can a man give in exchange for his soul?" (Mark 8:36-37) Jesus said, ""No one can serve two masters. Either he will hate the one and love the other, or he will be devoted to the one and despise the other. You cannot serve both God and Money" (Matt. 6:24).

This story reveals the great danger and the great temptation which can come to African young people who embrace the values of the West at any cost. It is a clear reminder of the way in which many young people have made education, success or material things a god which they place before the true and living God. The first of God's Ten Commandments says, "You shall have no other gods before me" (Exodus 20:3). Jesus said the greatest commandment was to "Love the Lord your God with all your heart and with all your soul and with all your mind" (Matt. 22:37). If that is the greatest commandment and the greatest responsibility for human beings, then the greatest sin is to have other "gods" before God. How easily we deceive ourselves!

From what has been said, it should come as no surprise that when people in the cities begin to uncritically adopt western culture, their society begins to fall apart. This very thing is happening all over Africa today. Many problems in African cities are already out of control. We will examine some of these problems in this book. We will also suggest some possible solutions from a Christian perspective. However, before any solutions will work, Christians must determine to personally put away the hypocrisy, dishonesty, pride, immorality, materialism and godless attitudes of western culture. They must make the decision to put God first in life regardless of the consequences.

Some people say that you cannot always put God first in the selfish world in which we live. They say that holy living is an ideal in the Bible but it does not happen in real life. To show that holiness and sacrifice are choices which a Christian can make even in the face of great temptation, consider the following true story of an African evangelist.

Benjamin was a graduate of Bible College. He was also a very gifted and talented singer. He had made several cassette tapes of his music. After his graduation from Bible College, Benjamin felt a call from God to bring the gospel to unreached people in the northern part of his country. He set his heart on this goal and began to make preparations for this ministry.

A friend of Benjamin had taken an opportunity to leave his country and go to a European country to become the pastor of a wealthy church of his own people in that country. The friend became a respected and prosperous pastor. His congregation had plenty of money and they paid their pastor well. The friend decided that he would like to share his ministry with his friend, Benjamin. He wrote Benjamin a letter and told him about the financially successful ministry he had in Europe. He told Benjamin that he wanted him to join him in this ministry as a minister of music. He appealed to Benjamin's talents as a singer and musician. He told him that he thought Benjamin would be wasting his time and his talents by simply being an unknown evangelist at home. By accepting his friend's invitation, Benjamin could become a wealthy and famous Christian artist and sing all over Europe.

Benjamin wrote back that he felt that God had called him to his ministry of evangelism among unconverted people at home. Some time later, the pastor from Europe returned to his home country for a visit. Again he tried to persuade Benjamin to come and join him in his ministry. Benjamin thanked him for his invitation but still insisted that God wanted him to serve at home among the unreached.

Some time later, another friend invited Benjamin to his home. He told Benjamin that he had a special message for him. He told him that God was about to bless him very much. He invited Benjamin to go into another room in the house. There in the room was the most expensive and most beautiful sound equipment Benjamin had ever seen! The friend said that it had been donated to Benjamin for his ministry. Then the friend handed Benjamin an envelope. In the envelope was a large sum of money - more than Benjamin had ever held in his hands before. This too, the friend said, was being given to Benjamin to encourage him in his ministry. Benjamin began to wonder what was going on. He was amazed and confused.

Then the friend handed Benjamin another envelope. In this envelope was an airplane ticket to the European country where his other friend was a pastor. All at once Benjamin understood what the musical equipment and the money were all about. Quietly and calmly, Benjamin handed the envelope with the money and the envelope with the plane ticket back to his friend. He told his friend to thank his other friend for his generous offer but he could not accept the gifts. He could not leave the ministry God had called him to carry out among the unreached people in his own country.

Benjamin continues in his ministry of evangelism right up to the present time. Recently, God used this dedicated and humble young man to open up a whole new area of his country to the gospel of Christ and to establish an evangelical church where there had never been one before in that part of the country. Does Benjamin regret not taking his friend's invitation to go to Europe? "Not in any way" is his answer. "I would rather be in the center of God's will and have God's unconditional blessing on my life and my ministry than all the riches of the world." To show the dedicated character of this young man, not too long ago he sold the house which he owned and gave the entire price of the sale to his church to use in spreading the gospel!

Yes, holiness and unconditional commitment to Jesus Christ are not easy. But there are African brothers and sisters today at the end of the twentieth century who are willing to serve the Lord at any personal cost. What would happen in Africa if there were more young men and women like Benjamin who would not let the temptation to wealth, fame and importance stand in the way of their commitment to Christ? The answer is, Africa would be touched and changed forever. Are you ready to become a part of this company of the committed and to earn a reward from Christ that will last forever and ever?

SUMMARY OF CORE VALUES IN AFRICA AND THE WEST

A summary of twenty comparisons in core values between Africa and the West is presented below. Each of these comparisons has important significance in the way modernity is changing Africa. As these comparisons become part of the discussion later in this book, their importance will be studied in the light of the great changes taking place today, especially in the cities. These comparisons are not presented as absolute differences. They are presented as cultural tendencies in two different parts of the world. There will always be exceptions.

BASIC DIFFERENCES BETWEEN AFRICAN AND WESTERN CULTURAL VALUES

African Culture

1. Strong community values (group participation, group decisions)
2. Community identity
3. Community living style
4. Extended family emphasis
5. Holistic approach to life
6. Importance of the event
7. People oriented priorities
8. Real-life (situational) thinking
9. Preference for real-life learning
10. Spiritual world view
11. Emphasis on spoken communication
12. Emphasis on spoken agreements based on relationships between people
13. Respect for the elderly
14. Traditional inherited leadership
15. Death is a passing into the spirit world: (survivors must perform rituals)
16. Resolve conflicts through a mediator
17. Ritual response to spirit realities
18. Ritual approach to religion
19. Vulnerability seen as a weakness
20. Much interest in the spirit world

Western Culture

1. Strong individualistic values (individual decisions)
2. Individual identity
3. Private living style
4. Immediate family emphasis
5. Categorical approach to life
6. Importance of schedules and clock time

7. Task and goal oriented priorities
8. Abstract and academic thinking
9. Preference for academic learning
10. Scientific world view
11. Emphasis on written communication
12. Emphasis on written agreements based on policies created by committees
13. Respect for the educated
14. Elected (democratic) leadership
15. Death is a practical problem (survivors need counseling and support)
16. Resolve conflicts face to face
17. Intellectual response to spirit realities
18. Intellectual approach to religion
19. Vulnerability seen as a strength.
20. Little interest in the spirit world.

SUMMARY

Based on careful research and on the observations of many people, it is evident that the cultures of traditional Africa tend to be holistic and oriented to the extended family and the ethnic community. At the same time research suggests that the effects of urbanization and education are beginning to change these values in the cities. It is almost certain that things will change even more rapidly as more and more people move to the cities and are influenced by western cultural values.

Traditional African culture and western culture are built upon very different core values. Traditional African wisdom recognizes that the well being of the community strongly influences the well being of the individual. As a result, African traditional values emphasize the good of the community over the good of the individual. Western cultural values emphasize individual freedom and privacy as the most important human values. These differences are the cause of inner conflict for many city dwellers and the cause of many problems in the society. People who live in the cities today are often attracted by western culture, its material benefits and its emphasis on personal freedom. Although there are benefits in some elements of western culture there are also great dangers in some western values.

Christians in Africa today need to look to the Word of God rather than to the West to form their values in life if they want the blessing of God on their lives. This may mean they will have to reject some of the important values of their own culture and some of the important values of the West as well.

QUESTIONS FOR REVIEW, REFLECTION AND GROUP DISCUSSION

1. What is meant by the core values of a society?
2. Summarize some of the more important core values in Africa.
3. What are some of the advantages in African core values?
4. Summarize some of the more important core values in western culture.
5. What are some of the advantages of western culture?
6. What are some of the dangers of western culture for Africa?
7. What kind of problems are developing in African cities as a result of the acceptance of western values and western culture?

END NOTES

1. Herbert V. Klem, *Oral Communication of the Scripture: Insights From African Oral Art.* Pasadena: William Carey Library, 1982. p. 8.
2. Dorothy N. Bowen, 1984. *Cognitive Styles of African Theological Students And Implications of Those Styles for Bibliographic Instruction.* Ph.D. diss., Florida State University, 1984. p. 71.
3. Ibid. p. 71
4. Ibid. p. iii
5. Ibid. p. 128
6. Elie A. Buconyori, *Cognitive Styles and Development of Reasoning among Younger African Students in Christian Higher Education.* Ed.D. diss., Trinity Evangelical Divinity School, 1991.

Chapter 2

MEGAPROBLEMS AND A MIGHTY GOD

A recent criminal trial received much publicity in the newspapers and on television. The accused was a person with a police record, but the police had gone beyond the limits of their authority in arresting the man and the criminal court had mishandled the trial. There were accusations of brutality and injustice on the part of the police and the court system. The case was greatly aggravated by charges of ethnic discrimination and prejudice. The whole city was on edge. Over a small excuse, violent rioting broke out in one of the townships of the city. The rioting got out of hand. Many people were seriously beaten and hurt. Fires were started. Homes and shops were smashed, looted and burned. The police knew they should intervene and bring a stop to the violence but they were afraid to act because of the bad publicity over the trial.

During the height of the riots, a lorry tried to pass through the area where the rioting was taking place. The lorry driver had entered the area unaware of what was happening. The driver's business was unrelated to what was taking place in the riots. The lorry stopped at a traffic signal at an intersection between two streets. As the lorry stopped, the rioters surrounded the vehicle and dragged the helpless driver from his vehicle. They proceeded to mercilessly beat the driver, crushing his skull on the street next to his vehicle in plain view of everyone.

A person nearby had an amateur video camera. The person with the camera filmed the entire incident from beginning to end. The camera was brought so close to the action that it was easy to identify each of the persons involved in the brutal attack. A television network obtained a copy of the amateur video film and it was shown that evening on television news broadcasts all over the country. From the video film, it was an easy matter to identify those who attacked the innocent lorry driver. Yet the police and the government refused to arrest or charge the persons who had carried out the attack with the excuse that those responsible could not be held accountable because of the riot! Once again injustice was done. Once again an innocent person was bitterly tortured with no way to set things right. Only this time it had been witnessed by the whole nation.

In another country, more than three thousand innocent men, women and children were marched into a forest by an advancing army and shot dead, just to get them out of the army's way. No one was called to account. No one was made to pay for the lives of these innocent people.

These terrible true stories cause us to think hard about one of the many problems in Africa. There is a breakdown of justice, law and order in many places today. Innocent people are abused, tortured, raped and murdered every day and the offenders are not punished. Children starve to death or die on the streets of the city and no one sees or cares. Government officials use their power to torture their people and nothing is done. Heads of state order the death and torture of thousands of innocent victims and then are given protection and political asylum by governments of other countries where they live out their days in luxury on well-guarded estates. Justice is not done. The innocent are killed. The helpless are trampled. The guilty escape punishment.

PART I - THE PROBLEMS

Injustice is just one of many overwhelming problems that are destroying the African continent. Other problems are just as bad. There is poverty that is beyond imagination. There is open tribalism and tribal killing. There is rampant disease; in many cases with little or no medicine available to treat the disease. There is oppressive corruption among government officials. There are terrible economic problems and unemployment. There are huge levels of debt. There is fighting, killing and war in one country after another. There is a massive breakdown of marriages and families in the cities. There is more crime in the cities than anyone living can remember. The streets are filled with homeless and handicapped people. There is widespread prostitution. There is an epidemic of sexually transmitted diseases (STDs) greater than at any time in history. There is widespread despair, depression and hopelessness.

The news is bad. Where is God in a continent which some analysts say has become the most Christian continent in the world by the year 2000 A.D.? Where are the Christians who can change what is happening by their actions and by their prayers?

Has it ever been like this before? When things are really bad, it is quite natural to assume that things have never been this bad before. But that is not necessarily true. The history of mankind shows us that it has often been like this before. The truth is, there has never been a time when it has not been bad somewhere in the world. The location of the worst trouble has changed from one country to another but there have always been terrible problems and crises.

The difference is that today we are much more conscious of the problems in other parts of the world because of high speed communication such as television, fax and email. Many years ago people did not hear about the terrible things happening in other places. Today our ears are filled with bad news almost daily. We hear about terrible things happening on the world news every day. We hear bad news from our families or friends.

Bad news has a negative effect on our emotions and our state of mind. When we hear bad news, we become discouraged and depressed. We feel overwhelmed and lose hope. We lose the will to keep on doing good or even to keep on praying. We may even lose our faith that God is at work in our world. This is exactly what Satan wants to happen. That is just the way Satan tried to overcome Job in the Bible. The devil brought one piece of bad news right after another to Job until Job was overwhelmed by it all (Job 1;13-22, Job 2:7-10). The devil does the same with us today. He tries to crush our spirits with the burden of one piece of bad news on top of another.

What can we do about it? The answer is, we need to overcome bad news with the good news of what God has done in the past and is still doing in the world today. The Bible says, "Do not be overcome by evil, but overcome evil with good" (Rom. 12:21).

This applies just as much to good news versus evil news as it does to good works versus evil works. Yes, there is bad news in the world today. But there is good news in spite of the bad news.

The bad news is that sin is destroying a fallen world (Rom. 5:12). The good news is that Jesus has released us from our sins through His blood (Rev. 1:5). In addition, He has risen from the dead and is alive forevermore (Rev. 1:18). By His death and resurrection, Jesus has overcome the world (John 16:33), sin (Rom. 6:10-11), death (Heb. 2:9) and Satan himself (1 John 3:8). There is no power in all creation that can reverse this victory because Jesus is now seated at the right hand of God the Father in Heaven far above every power that exists (Eph. 1:20-21). All authority in heaven and earth has now been given to Christ (Matt. 28:18).

Has the world ever been as bad as it is now? To compare the present with the past, consider the following events from the time of Christ's birth.

"When they had gone, an angel of the Lord appeared to Joseph in a dream. "Get up," he said, "take the child and his mother and escape to Egypt. Stay there until I tell you, for Herod is going to search for the child to kill him." So he got up, took the child and his mother during the night and left for Egypt, . . . When Herod realized that he had been outwitted by the Magi, he was furious, and he gave orders to kill all the boys in Bethlehem and its vicinity who were two years old and under, in accordance with the time he had learned from the Magi. Then what was said through the prophet Jeremiah was fulfilled: "A voice is heard in Ramah, weeping and great mourning, Rachel weeping for her children and refusing to be comforted, because they are no more" (Matthew 2:13-18).

Think what this slaughter of innocent small children meant to each of the mothers and fathers of the quiet little town of Bethlehem. What parent could ever forget the terrifying memory of that day when Roman soldiers suddenly and brutally murdered their precious children right before their eyes? The truth is that injustice, brutality, and inhumanity has been with us for as long as man has been on earth. The Bible says, "the wages of sin is death" (Rom. 6:23) and so it has been for as long as human beings have lived on the earth.

The Bible tells us that very long ago, things were so bad that God had to destroy the entire earth because of the cruel violence of human beings toward one another. "Now the earth was corrupt in God's sight and was full of violence. God saw how corrupt the earth had become, for all the people on earth had corrupted their ways. So God said to Noah, "I am going to put an end to all people, for the earth is filled with violence because of them. I am surely going to destroy both them and the earth. So make yourself an ark of cypress wood" (Genesis 6:11-14). What follows is the story of how God permitted only 8 people to escape the greatest natural disaster in the history of the world, in a flood which destroyed the whole world of that day.

Yes, there are great problems in Africa today. But it is not a new situation. The sins of mankind have been with us for a long time. However, because of modern methods of communication, people today are much more aware of the effects of sin all over the world than they have ever been before. It has also been shown that some people imitate the evil things they see displayed on television because it plants ideas in their minds.

There are many more people living today than have ever lived. There are also many more people living in cities than have ever lived so close to one another before. Many of the people living in cities today do not know the people right next door to them. There is little left of the sense of community responsibility which the same people probably felt when they lived in their own rural village among their own people. We can conclude that although the same kinds of problems have always existed on earth, there are conditions today which make those problems even worse.

What we don't realize is that there is a lot of good news in the world today. God is very much at work. Good news has the opposite effect of bad news. Good news encourages us. Good news gives us hope and increases our faith in God. Good news motivates us to reach out to others with love and good works. The Bible says, "Like cold water to a weary soul is good news from a distant land" (Prov. 25:25). The trouble is, we don't often hear the good news.

Because of this, it is very important to share good news with others. The Psalmist said, "I will come and proclaim your mighty acts, O Sovereign LORD" (Psalm 71:16). In another place the Psalmist said, "I will . . . . proclaim what the LORD has done" (Psalm 118:17). The Psalmist wrote, "One generation shall praise Thy works to another, And shall declare Thy mighty acts" (Psalm 145:4 - NASB). The writer of Hebrews wrote, "Let us consider how we may spur one another on toward love and good deeds. Let us not give up meeting together, as some are in the habit of doing, but let us encourage one another" (Heb. 10:24-25).

How do we encourage one another? By doing just what these verses of Scripture tell us to do. We encourage one another by gathering together as God's people and sharing with one another the great and wonderful things God has done for us and for others. Perhaps we have seen God answer a specific prayer. We need to share this with other Christians to encourage them. Perhaps we have experienced God's special protection, guidance or provision in a certain situation. We need to share this with our fellow Christians. Perhaps we have heard about some of the exciting things God has done in another part of the world. We need to share this good news with others in the congregation. When we hear of the good things God is doing it will increase our faith and stir our hearts to pray more. When we pray, God will work in our lives and in the lives of others.

If Christians could hear the many things God is doing each day in this world, they would be greatly encouraged. They would be motivated to trust God to work in their own countries and their own lives. In this book we will relate some of the things which God is doing through His people to overcome the great problems in Africa today.

This book will examine some of the major problems of modernity in Africa and then discuss some of these problems in detail. It will not be possible to analyze all the problems listed below in a book of this kind. In some cases a biblical approach to solving the problem will be suggested. In some cases an example will be given of someone who actually used a biblical approach and saw God change the situation. Some of the more serious problems facing modern Africa are listed here.

(A) Cultural disintegration in the cities resulting from the collision of western and non-western values

(1) Loss of traditional values
(2) Loss of personal identity
(3) Fear and insecurity
(4) Hypocrisy, dishonesty and deception
(5) Loss of personal integrity

(B) The overwhelming problems of uncontrolled urban growth

(1) Overcrowding
(2) Crime
(3) Street people and homelessness
(4) Unemployment, prostitution
(5) Environmental pollution
(6) Lack of sanitation, clean water, adequate housing, good health care
(7) Drugs, alcohol and substance abuse

(C) The destructive effect of western video and the collapse of sexual morality

(1) The breakdown of families and family values and the growth of divorce
(2) The increase of pornography, sexual immorality and abortion
(3) The AIDS epidemic and other sexually transmitted diseases
(4) The drastic change in values of young people today

(D) Poverty and its many results

(E) Corruption and the mishandling of money, especially for development

(F) Injustice and the abuse of political power

(G) Materialism and Secularism

(H) The needs and challenges of today's youth

(I) The changing role of women in society and in the church

(J) Spiritual problems in the church today

PART 2 - THE GOD OF HEAVEN AND EARTH

Before we consider some of the specific problems above, it is very important for us to consider who God is and what God can do. For apart from God there is no hope for Africa and no hope for the world. Apart from God, human beings have sentenced themselves to hell on earth. Apart from God, the advances of modern technology and education will only lead to more efficient and effective ways to destroy one another.

Scientists make new discoveries in physics and chemistry and human beings use this knowledge to make atomic bombs which can destroy an entire city in one explosion, or nerve gas which can silently kill thousands of innocent people. Electronic engineers invent advanced computer technology and human beings use computers to guide ballistic missiles which bring destruction and death. Modern industry finds a way to make television available to the common man and those who produce TV programs find an easy way to draw people into pornography and sexual sin. It is possible that television and video films alone have done more than everything else in all of history to destroy the family and the moral values of whole nations. One of the popular themes of television in the West today is to display marital unfaithfulness and sexual immorality as acceptable social behaviour.

Heads of government hold summit meetings and make treaties only to have their agreements violated and broken. The United Nations forms organizations, agencies and commissions with the best of purposes only to have their plans ruined by corrupt officials who take for themselves the money provided to help needy people. Church leaders responsible for the moral and spiritual development of their people use their positions of leadership for selfish gain and political power. People marry and promise to love their partners for a lifetime only to betray them with adultery.

It is a dismal commentary on human history that human beings without God are able to corrupt and destroy everything they touch. We live in an amazing scientific age but the real things of life have not changed. Long ago the author of the book of Ecclesiastes observed, "What has been will be again, what has been done will be done again; there is nothing new under the sun" (Ecclesiastes 1:9).

Life would be a hopeless journey of despair if there was no God. But as Daniel said so long ago, "There is a God in heaven . . ." (Daniel 2:28). That simple fact changes everything. The truth that there is an omnipotent God who answers the prayers of His people provides hope to a hopeless world. The true and living God is very much concerned about the condition of mankind in this world. Beyond that, He has the power to change the terrible conditions of this world. If God's people are willing to act on His commandments and His promises, miracles of change can take place.

In the present age, God does not generally work apart from His people. The Bible says. "the people who know their God will display strength and take action" (Dan. 11:32 - NASB). Let us look at two true stories in history where God showed His concern for severe problems in the world and revealed His ability to do something about them in response to the obedience of His people. In each of these stories it is very important to observe that God used one of His own people to bring about the deliverance and help needed.

JOSEPH

The first story concerns a time when a devastating and long famine was about to destroy an African country (Egypt). The story is recorded in Genesis chapter 41.

> *"Pharaoh had a dream: He was standing by the Nile, when out of the river there came up seven cows, sleek and fat, and they grazed among the reeds. After them, seven other cows, ugly and gaunt, came up out of the Nile and stood beside those on the riverbank. And the cows that were ugly and gaunt ate up the seven sleek, fat cows. Then Pharaoh woke up. He fell asleep again and had a second dream: Seven heads of grain, healthy and good, were growing on a single stalk. After them, seven other heads of grain sprouted--thin and scorched by the east wind. The thin heads of grain swallowed up the seven healthy, full heads. Then Pharaoh woke up; it had been a dream.*
>
> *In the morning his mind was troubled, so he sent for all the magicians and wise men of Egypt. Pharaoh told them his*

dreams, but no one could interpret them for him. Then the chief cupbearer said to Pharaoh, "Today I am reminded of my shortcomings. Pharaoh was once angry with his servants, and he imprisoned me and the chief baker in the house of the captain of the guard. Each of us had a dream the same night, and each dream had a meaning of its own. Now a young Hebrew was there with us, a servant of the captain of the guard. We told him our dreams, and he interpreted them for us, giving each man the interpretation of his dream. And things turned out exactly as he interpreted them to us: I was restored to my position, and the other man was hanged."

So Pharaoh sent for Joseph, and he was quickly brought from the dungeon. When he had shaved and changed his clothes, he came before Pharaoh. Pharaoh said to Joseph, "I had a dream, and no one can interpret it. But I have heard it said of you that when you hear a dream you can interpret it." "I cannot do it," Joseph replied to Pharaoh, "but God will give Pharaoh the answer he desires." Then Pharaoh said to Joseph, "In my dream I was standing on the bank of the Nile, when out of the river there came up seven cows, . . ."

Then Joseph said to Pharaoh, "The dreams of Pharaoh are one and the same. God has revealed to Pharaoh what he is about to do. . . . Seven years of great abundance are coming throughout the land of Egypt, but seven years of famine will follow them. Then all the abundance in Egypt will be forgotten, and the famine will ravage the land.

"And now let Pharaoh look for a discerning and wise man and put him in charge of the land of Egypt. Let Pharaoh appoint commissioners over the land to take a fifth of the harvest of Egypt during the seven years of abundance. They should collect all the food of these good years that are coming and store up the grain under the authority of Pharaoh, to be kept in the cities for food. This food should be held in reserve for the country, to be used during the seven years of famine that will come upon Egypt, so that the country may not be ruined by the famine." The plan seemed good to Pharaoh and to all his officials. So Pharaoh asked them, "Can we find anyone like this man, one in whom is the spirit of God?" Then Pha-

raoh said to Joseph, "Since God has made all this known to you, there is no one so discerning and wise as you. You shall be in charge of my palace, and all my people are to submit to your orders. Only with respect to the throne will I be greater than you" (Gen. 41:1-40)

There are several important things to observe in this remarkable true story. First, God showed His character of mercy and concern for mankind in general by revealing the fact of the coming famine to an ungodly political leader (the Pharaoh) through two dreams. He did this so that something could be done to avoid a terrible disaster. Second, He chose a godly and humble man, Joseph, who was a forgotten slave in a prison, to provide a solution for the coming famine. He gave Joseph the wisdom to suggest a plan that would work, and the plan did work under Joseph's direction. Third, God made the political leader (Pharaoh) willing to appoint Joseph to such a high position of government authority that Joseph was able to carry out the plan God had shown him and thereby save the whole nation.

God was well aware of the problem in Egypt - long before human beings knew that such a problem was coming. Furthermore God planned to help them through this problem and provided both the wisdom about what to do and the right person to do something about it. Part of Joseph's qualification to fill this position was his faith in God and his own humility. After God had used him to preserve the lives of both the nation of Egypt and his own family, Joseph made an unusual statement of faith to his brothers. Reflecting on what they had done to him, Joseph said, "You intended to harm me, but God intended it for good, to accomplish what is now being done, the saving of many lives" (Gen. 50:20).

Joseph had already been faithful and obedient to God through 13 years of abuse and obscurity. Now he had to be ready and willing to do what God wanted him to do for the deliverance of Egypt. Although he did not know it at the time, part of God's plan included allowing Joseph to be sold as a slave by his brothers into Egypt.

The same thing can happen today. God can accomplish His purposes of deliverance in Africa. But He will wait until He has found a person (or a local church) of faith, humility and unconditional obedience before He works His miracles of deliverance. It is a very wrong idea held by some Christians that dedicated Christians should not be involved in government. The Bible teaches just the opposite. God chose to use some of His most dedicated servants in positions of high government authority (like Joseph and Daniel) to carry out His plans. Since God does not change (Mal. 3:6, Heb. 13:8), we must understand that it is still His will to use godly men and women of faith to bring about His solutions to problems today. What God seeks is a willing, available, humble person with a servant heart and a heart of faith. Perhaps God is speaking to you even as you read these words to become a part of His plan of deliverance for your country.

We can take courage from the story of Joseph. God knows the severe problems with which each of the nations of Africa is struggling, whether they are political, economic or moral problems. Furthermore, God can provide a solution to these problems - as great as the problems may be, if He finds obedient people ready to do His will. The question is: Will God find the humble, willing men and women of faith among His people through whom He can bring about His deliverance?

ESTHER

The second story tells us about a terrifying situation in which an evil government official planned to kill an entire race of people out of anger against just one person of that race! Unless God had intervened through the faithfulness and courage of one woman of faith, a whole nation of people would have been destroyed. The woman did her part and through her God saved the entire population of her people living in that country. He did this by simply keeping a king awake one night. The story is found in the book of Esther. This story especially shows how God can change the course of history without violating the free choices of human beings in spite of how evil those choices may be. The important points in this story are the courage and faithfulness of one woman and the faithfulness of God to respond to prayer and fasting by His people.

In the story of Esther, a proud, selfish and drunken king decided to display his beautiful wife before other men (Esther 1:10-11). This brought a family crisis (Esther 1:12-17). The crisis ended with the wife being put away (Esther 1:19). In the process of finding a replacement for the queen, an unknown Jewish orphan girl (Esther) was selected to become part of the king's harem of women (Esther 2:5-8). Out of the king's desire for her physical beauty, Esther was chosen to be his queen, even though she was a foreigner (Esther 2:17).

A selfish and evil official named Haman became angry when Esther's uncle and guardian, Mordecai, refused to bow down to him as he walked through the king's gate (Esther 3:1-2). It is quite possible that Mordecai intended to keep the ten commandments which warn God's people against bowing down to anyone but God (Ex. 20:4). The extreme evil in the heart of Haman was revealed in his decision not just to punish Mordecai but to kill all of the Jews in the whole empire (Esther 3:5-6)! Haman designed a clever plan which appealed to the king's pride and concern about safeguarding his throne. Through this plan Haman succeeded in getting an unchangeable law passed to kill all Jews in the empire on a certain day by the king's order (Esther 3:12-14). There was no way the Jews could avoid certain death - unless God Himself intervened.

Although the name of God is not mentioned in the book of Esther, God clearly did intervene in a most unusual way. It happened that Mordecai had saved the king's life some years before by exposing an attempt to kill the king (Esther 2:21-23). Mordecai had never been honoured for this. After the decree had been published to kill all the Jews, Haman constructed a gallows 75 feet high at his wife's suggestion, on which he intended to hang Mordecai (Esther 5:14). Meanwhile Mordecai asked his niece Esther to appeal to the king for the lives of the Jews. To do this without being invited could have cost Esther her life (Esther 4:11). Esther finally agreed. Perhaps she realized the truth of her uncle's words that she had been placed in the palace by God for just such a time as this (Esther 4:14). Wisely, Esther asked all the Jews in the capital city to fast for her for three days (Esther 4:16).

God heard and answered this prayer and fasting, as the next events in the story reveal. All God had to do was keep the king awake one night. The king asked for the historical records of the kingdom to be read because of his sleeplessness and as it was being read, he learned how Mordecai had saved his life (Esther 6:1-3). Meanwhile, Esther used her skillful abilities as a woman to appeal to the desires of men for good food, preparing two banquets for the king with Haman present. During the second banquet, Esther exposed the plot of Haman to kill the Jews, (Esther 7:6) and Haman ended up being hanged on the very gallows he had built to hang Mordecai (Esther 8:7)! Esther also persuaded the king to pass a second law which would permit the Jews to defend themselves from their enemies. Thus the lives of all the Jews in the empire were saved (Esther 8:9-11).

This amazing true story stands as one of the most unusual examples of the intervention of God in history. There are many lessons in the story. Perhaps the most obvious and powerful lesson is the fact that God fully understands the problems we face and He will respond to prayer and fasting to deliver His people, even in the most fearful circumstances. The truth of the Bible is this: There are no problems in this world which God cannot solve. If God can raise the dead, He can solve every other problem we can imagine.

But it is almost always His will to use ordinary human beings like Joseph and Esther to accomplish His will in history. God is the same today as He was 100, 1000 or 3000 years ago. He still answers prayer and He still performs miracles of national deliverance in response to prayer and fasting when He finds a person who will be completely faithful to Him no matter what it may cost. To be used by God, a person must be willing to give up his or her own desires. Jesus said, "If anyone would come after me, he must deny himself and take up his cross and follow me. For whoever wants to save his life will lose it, but whoever loses his life for me will find it" (Matt. 16:24-25).

SUMMARY

Africa has many great problems today. But "there is a God in heaven . . ." and this God is able to overcome every human problem which man's sin and Satan's power have brought into this sick world. We are overwhelmed with bad news every day. We need to overcome the discouraging effects of this bad news with the good news of Jesus Christ and the good things which God is doing in the world today through Christ.

God usually chooses to use His own people to bring His solutions to the problems facing the world. This has been His plan both in the past and in the present. The question is, are His people willing and prepared to be a part of His plan to solve the problems of their country, their tribe, their church, their family and their own lives? Or are they part of the problem because of living selfish prejudiced lives? It will cost Christians something to be used by God to help solve the great problems facing their countries but God is able to work miracles through His people. If there are problems it is not that God has failed us. It is that we have failed God. If His people are willing to believe Him and to obey Him, God is willing to intervene in the problems and needs of their country.

QUESTIONS FOR REVIEW, REFLECTION AND GROUP DISCUSSION

1. List five of the biggest problems in Africa today.
2. For each of the problems listed in question one, suggest some ways in which God might want individual Christians or local churches to become involved in helping to solve these problems.
3. What action can Christians take when injustice is the consistent pattern of the government of their country?
4. In what ways do radio and television often increase existing problems in the cities?
5. Two true stories from the Bible of God's intervention and deliverance during times of severe national crisis are presented in this chapter. Reflect on the modern history of your nation or another part of Africa and relate how God intervened to protect the nation from disaster.

Chapter 3

THE UGLY SIDE OF URBANIZATION

Urbanization is one of the major sociological changes taking place in Africa at the end of the twentieth century. Young Africans are moving to the city in large numbers hoping to escape the drudgery of the farm and the predictable routines of village life. Life in the cities sounds far more exciting and interesting than life in the village. They expect to find an easy life, lots of money, new friends and many services not available in the village. What they often find is something very different from what they expected.

Most cities are crowded, dirty, dangerous, impersonal and unfriendly. There is crime, disease, trash and a general lack of concern by people on the street for the welfare of one another. There are helpless handicapped people begging to survive and homeless people hoping for a handout. There is materialism, pride, lust, greed and selfish indifference instead of the gentle, supportive community the young person knew at home. There is hypocrisy, dishonesty, deception, corruption and tribalism at the workplace - if the young person is lucky enough to get a job. There is drug abuse and alcoholism, crime, strong temptation and impersonal selfish individualism in business and even in the church. Nights are filled with insecurity and fears of robbery, rape and break-ins. In short, the city turns out to be a very different place than the one he or she imagined. Even if the young person if fortunate enough to get a good job, his or her money seems to disappear over night with the high cost of housing, transportation, food, clothing, utilities and a thousand other expenses he never thought about in the village. Four recent true stories from four different African cities bring just the problem of crime in the cities into bitter focus.

A man was driving home from the international airport in the capital city one evening. The car in front of him slowed down and another car pulled up close behind him in such a way that the man could not pull out to pass or back up to move around the car in front. Some men jumped out of the car behind the man as his car came to a stop. Without even asking the man for the keys to his car, the men from the car behind dragged the man from the driver's seat and began to stab him again and again with a long knife. Finally they left him in a pool of blood and drove off in his car and in their own cars. Miraculously, the injured man did not die but his life was permanently changed by this terrifying experience. Needless to say, he never got his car back. He was grateful to still be alive.

In another city a man had driven into the business district of the city just before the 5:00 p.m. closing time of most shops. There were many people on the street. As the man got out of his car he was attacked by several men who beat him mercilessly and left him unconscious on the street as other people looked on with indifference or just turned away. The men took the little he had but left a memory which this man will never forget.

In a third city a group of young men sexually assaulted a woman in plain view of other people in a shopping mall. The young men took turns raping the helpless woman, yet no one called the police.

In a fourth city a man heard someone trying to break open the front door of his flat during the night. He came to the window of his room on the second floor of the flat to see what was happening. When the thieves saw the man appear at the window, they shot him in the face with a shotgun. The man never recovered.

URBAN GROWTH, UNEMPLOYMENT AND CRIME

Life in the cities can be very difficult and very dangerous. Yet in spite of this, people continue to move into the cities in large numbers, especially young people hoping to find a better life than they had in their rural homes. The statistics of urban growth are impressive. In the Global Report On Human Settlements published by the United Nations, the following statistics are given. In 1920 about 14% of the world's people lived in cities. In 1980 the percentage had increased to 40 percent. By the year 2025, it is projected that 60% of the world will live in cities (a total of 4.9 billion people). It is presently estimated that by the year 2000 half of the world's population will live in cities.[1] Thus the problems associated with urbanization will increase dramatically in the lifetime of most of those who read these words. For those who actually live in the cities this will not just be a statistic but a difficult personal reality.

The problems of the cities are great. One of the greatest of these problems is unemployment. Streets are filled with homeless people, handicapped people, beggars and wandering, jobless young people. Urban research has found that throughout the world, 40 percent of the urban poor are without jobs.[2] The same research found that 85 percent of urban growth between 1980 and 2000 is projected to take place in the less developed countries of the world.[3] Another study found that in 1950 there were only two cities in Africa with a population of one million or more people. By 1997 there were 37 cities with a population of one million or more.[4] These facts have serious meaning for Africa.

The combination of rapid urban growth and extensive unemployment makes the cities ripe for crime. Crime today is one of the most fearful realities of life in the cities. Burglary and thievery have become common in every large city. With the availability of guns in recent years, crime has become ugly and dangerous, as the recent true stories given above show. Thieves no longer simply slip their hands into the pockets of the unsuspecting passerby. It is becoming more and more common for thieves to point a gun in the face of an innocent person or even to shoot them first before taking their money and possessions.

CRITICAL PROBLEMS IN THE CITIES

Besides unemployment and crime, the other problems of modern cities are many. City planners are often years behind the population growth and need for public services. Cities are major sources of environmental pollution. This can come from factory smoke, motor vehicle exhaust gases, uncollected garbage, improper or non-existent sanitation and waste disposal, open sewers and general filth. All of these present major health hazards to those living in the cities. Shanty towns commonly spring up as people move to the cities without the means to build or purchase adequate housing. Shanty town areas are notorious for environmental pollution and the sickness and disease which accompanies such pollution. Lack of clean drinking water is a common problem in the shanty towns.

Clean drinking water is one of the most basic needs of human health. God has provided a way for people to have pure drinking water by means of the ultra-violet radiation of the sun's rays. Ultra violet radiation is not visible light but it is present in all unrestricted sunlight. Ultra violet radiation will kill all bacteria, viruses and other germs in water, provided the water is clear (not cloudy or muddy) and provided the water is given enough exposure to the sun. One simple way for rural or city people to provide pure drinking water for themselves is to lay out clear plastic bottles of clear water in the sun for a period of at least two hours. When this is done, the ultraviolet rays of the sun will kill the germs in the water which cause disease. It is only necessary to collect a supply of clear plastic bottles and to make sure the water is not cloudy or muddy. Experiments done by the World Health Organization show that in just one hour of such exposure to the suns rays, deadly bacteria and viruses such as typhoid and hepatitis are killed by the ultra violet rays of the sun.

The problem of dire poverty dominates most cities. There are more poor people, beggars, handicapped people, homeless people, street children, refugees, thieves and prostitutes than anyone cares to count. Schools are hopelessly overcrowded. Proper housing is hopelessly expensive. Ethnic and racial diversity produces tensions, and open violence of tribalism as people from each ethnic group desperately struggle to favor and help their own people. More will be said later in this book about a Christian approach to the problem of crushing poverty.

The impersonal and faceless reality of city life also encourages laziness and irresponsibility especially in government offices. The very institution (human government) which God established to help solve problems and maintain law and order (Rom. 13:1,4) has become the very seat of corruption, injustice, nepotism and public abuse. In many countries it is openly accepted that nothing can or will happen by the government until a bribe has been paid to the particular official concerned. This corruption has a continuing effect, where one problem produces another.

Attitudes of corruption, laziness and irresponsibility spill over into the church because Christian people do not see the examples of integrity in public life that would inspire or motivate them to work for change and improvement. As one person expressed it, "Everyone wants his share of the national pie. When a person gets into public office, he feels it is his right to take his share." This attitude leads to a socially sick handout mentality and an attitude of despising all forms of work. Even Christians have been so affected by this viewpoint that many of them think that normal work, especially manual work, is part of the curse which God placed on mankind. Nothing could be further from the truth of God. God placed Adam in the garden of Eden and gave him the command to cultivate the garden. All this took place before Adam fell into sin (Gen. 2:15).

It is therefore up to Christians to live out their lives in such a way that they expose and reject the godless attitudes of a sick society. The Bible says, "it is God's will that by doing good you should silence the ignorant talk of foolish men" (1 Peter 2:15). The apostle Paul wrote, "You yourselves know how you ought to follow our example. We were not idle when we were with you, nor did we eat anyone's food without paying for it. On the contrary, we worked night and day, laboring and toiling so that we would not be a burden to any of you" (2 Thess. 3:7-8). Paul went on to say, "We gave you this rule: "If a man will not work, he shall not eat. We hear that some among you are idle. . . . Such people we command and urge in the Lord Jesus Christ to settle down and earn the bread they eat" (2 Thess. 3:11-12).

There is a great need for the people of God to display a biblical example of hard work. The members of the local church must rebuke the godless attitudes of a corrupt culture by demonstrating a pattern of self-sustainability. It is up to God's people to show the way. There will be no help or proper example from a selfish society which is sick unto death with sin. The need for Christians to lead the way is made all the more urgent by the fact of shrinking foreign aid for Africa. The end of the cold war has meant that there is no longer an East-West competition for Africa. Money from North American and European governments is no longer being used to win African governments away from communism. It is up to African Christians to demonstrate how God wants their society to be responsible, hard working and self-sustaining.

OVERCROWDING INTHE CITIES

Many of the problems mentioned so far are the result of overcrowding in the cities. There are too many people and not enough jobs. There are too many people and not enough housing. There are too many people producing too much garbage and trash. There are too many people and too few sanitation and waste disposal systems to care for their needs. There are too many people and not enough schools. There are too many people and not enough water. There are too many taxis, buses and lorries, so there is too much traffic congestion and too much air pollution. There are too many people and too few health services. There are just too many people in the cities!

The problem is made worse by a prevailing attitude that one of the most important things in life is to have as many children as possible. This viewpoint is a carryover from the traditions and beliefs of African traditional religion where the continuation of the tribe and clan is seen to be the most important goal in life. In many traditional African cultures marriage is not primarily for the relationship between a man and his wife or wives but for the reproduction of children. These attitudes have been carried over into the Christian community as a result of a failure on the part of pastors and Bible teachers to present a biblical view of marriage and the Christian home. There is an urgent need in the churches today for biblical teaching on Christian marriage and Christian family life.

A CHRISTIAN PERSPECTIVE ON FAMILY PLANNING

Christians often support the view that a large number of children is the will of God by misinterpreting the command of God to "be fruitful and multiply and fill the earth" (Gen. 1:28). What exactly does the Bible say about the purpose of marriage? And what does the Bible say about the number of children which families should have? These are critical questions at this time of serious overcrowding in the cities.

First of all, the Bible is quite clear that the primary purpose of marriage is not the reproduction of children but the relationship between the husband and his wife. After the creation of man God said, "It is not good for the man to be alone. I will make a helper suitable for him" (Gen. 2:18). From this it is clear that the first purpose of marriage in the plan of God was to provide man with a companion and helper for life. There are many older people who marry who will never be able to bear children. However they have a great need for the companionship, love and help of a life partner. They will not lack God's blessing on their relationship just because they are unable to have children.

The Bible does teach that children are the normal blessing of God for marriage (Psalm 127:4-5). Children, however, are not essential to establish a marriage according to the Word of God (Gen. 2:24). There were godly people in the Bible from whom God withheld the blessing of children. For the godly woman without children, God offers this unusual word of encouragement, evidently referring to spiritual children. The Lord said, "Sing, O barren woman, you who never bore a child; burst into song, shout for joy, you who were never in labor; because more are the children of the desolate woman than of her who has a husband," says the LORD" (Isa. 54:1). Many single women, but especially those women who have faithfully served God in Christian orphanages, have proven the truth of this promise.

Concerning the command of God to "be fruitful and multiply and fill the earth," it is necessary to observe that this commandment was given only twice, under similar circumstances. The first time it was given was at the creation (Gen. 1:28). In this case the earth was without any human beings except for one man and one woman. The second time God gave this command was immediately after the flood of Noah (Gen. 9:7). Again the earth was without any human beings except for the eight people on Noah's ark. Those conditions do not exist today. It is inaccurate Bible interpretation to apply this command to God's purpose for marriage today.

Christian family planning is just what the words say. It is planning for the number of children and the spacing of those children according to the teaching of the Bible and the guidance of the Holy Spirit. It is responsible planning which will best suit the financial ability, health and welfare of the whole family, with special consideration for the health and well-being of the wife. It is a decision which should be made by both the husband and the wife together and not just by one or the other, since the Bible says the husband and his wife are to be united (Gen. 2:24).

What then is the biblical view of having children and the number of children which a couple should have? The answer is, the number which reflects spiritually responsible family planning. There are at least two guiding principles in the decision concerning how many children a couple should have and how they should be spaced. The first is the principle of responsible physical and spiritual care for the children which God gives. Concerning physical needs, the Bible says, "If anyone does not provide for his relatives, and especially for his immediate family, he has denied the faith and is worse than an unbeliever" (1 Tim. 5:8).

There are Christians couples in Africa who bring children into the world for whom they cannot properly provide even the basic needs of life. This is a serious issue of moral irresponsibility before God. God says that such a person is "worse than an unbeliever." Concerning spiritual needs, the Bible says, "Fathers, do not exasperate your children; instead, bring them up in the training and instruction of the Lord: (Eph. 6:4). The Bible also says, "Train up a child in the way he should go: and when he is old, he will not depart from it" (Prov. 22:6). When God gives a Christian couple children, they are obligated before the Lord to provide the needs of those children and to bring them up in the knowledge of the Lord.

A recent example of spiritual irresponsibility in bearing children reflects a situation that is repeated in many places. A certain Christian family has continued to have children when their resources have long been exhausted to care for their children. Several of the children from this family have run away from home. Some of these have gone to live with non-Christian families in the community where they will not be taught the truth of God. This couple and others like them are urgently in need of proper medical advice concerning responsible Christian family planning.

The second principle concerning the number of children which a couple should have and the spacing of those children, is the health and well-being of the wife. The Bible says, "Husbands, love your wives, just as Christ loved the church and gave himself up for her" (Eph. 5:25). It is a mark of selfishness and ungodly character when a husband insists that his wife continue to bear children or to bear them too close to one another, when it may be harmful to her physical or mental health.

The question of the role of the government in family planning and family life education has been vigorously debated in some African countries in the past few years. Along with this is the question of whether school children should be required to participate in government programs of sex education. The Bible makes it clear that Christian moral and spiritual training is a responsibility which belongs to Christian parents (Prov. 1:8, Eph. 6:4). God says it is something which should be done in the home (Deut. 6:6-7). No government on earth has the God-given right to take this responsibility away from Christian parents. Christian family life teaching and sex education are some of the most important moral and spiritual instruction which parents can give to their children. No Christian parent should give this responsibility over to the government. Governments which are involved in sex education almost always approach this subject from a non-Christian viewpoint rather than from the teaching of the Word of God. Such teaching can do great harm to the spiritual formation of a Christian young person who should form his convictions and standards from the teaching of the Bible.

THE NEED FOR CHRISTIAN FAMILY LIFE TEACHING

There is a great need for Christian family life teaching in the church. The family is the basis of human life and civilization. Many Christian marriages are in serious trouble today. Because of pride, shame and embarrassment, few Christians are willing to admit that they urgently need help in their marriages. To make matters worse, the subject of sex is never mentioned in many cultures, even though it was the Holy God who created the sexual differences between human beings. (Gen. 1:27-28) It was the same Holy God who brought man and woman together in marriage and said they were to become one flesh. (Gen. 2:24) It was God who said that the marriage bed must be held in honor by all. (Heb. 13:4)

Many Christian marriages are lived out according to cultural traditions rather than by the Word of God. How can marriages be happy when the purposes and plans of the Creator are not followed or are violated by the practices of a corrupt culture? In many African cultures women are considered to be of less value than men and in some cases of less value than children or even animals, even though the Bible says there is no difference in the value of men and women in the eyes of God. (Gal. 3:28) Wives are often treated as servants or even as slaves by their husbands.

Many African men think that marriage exists only to satisfy male sexual desires, and to produce children for the continuation of the clan or tribe. When marriages are based strictly on cultural patterns and not on the Word of God, there will never be the happiness which God intended for marriage, and there will be many problems. Unfortunately, that is the situation of many families in African churches today.

Marriage was established God. (Gen. 2:24) It is therefore only God who can teach human beings the right way to live out their marriage relationships. Every human plan that is different from God's plan is destined to failure and unhappiness. God has a plan for marriage. It is a plan that can be followed by people from every culture in the world if there is proper teaching from the Bible. There is a very great need in the church for Biblical teaching on the Christian principles of marriage and family life. It may be the greatest need in the African church today, along with the great need for the discipleship of new Christians.

THE EFFECTS OF URBANIZATION ON CHURCHES

Urbanization has dramatically affected churches. It is hard enough for those who attend urban churches just to cope with living in the city. For those who minister in urban churches, the sociology of the city requires a whole new approach to the ministry of the gospel. There are at least seven special characteristics of urban churches which make them different from rural churches.

1. Church member mobility. People move back and forth between the city and the rural village. The congregation is always in a condition of change. It is hard to set up on-going ministries in the local church since the congregation is always changing.
2. Finances. There is a greater potential for giving in urban churches but at the same time life in the city is much more expensive.
3. Counseling and family problems. The temptations and stress of life in the city create serious marriage and family problems. Urban pastors must be trained to deal with such problems.
4. Education level of the congregation. Many people in urban congregations are well educated. Pastors of urban churches require a higher level of education and better communication skills in order to meet the needs of their more educated church members.
5. Complex social and religious structure of the city. The presence of a multi-ethnic, multi-racial and multi-religious population in the cities presents a great challenge to the ministry of the local church.
6. The fast pace of life in the city. Traditional Africa is oriented to events and seasons rather than to clocks. By contrast, the pace of city life is fast and stressful and often controlled by clock time. Many adjustments are needed by those who are used to life in the village.
7. The social and physical problems of the city are overwhelming. This reality presents one of the greatest challenges to urban churches in Africa today. It is the intention of this book to give a Christian perspective to some of these enormous social and physical problems.

It is a temptation to look at problems such as those presented by urbanization in Africa with a reaction of despair and hopelessness. "What can anyone possibly do?" That would be a normal human reaction to a situation of such overwhelming magnitude, but that is not how a Christian should see such problems.

Before the world was created God knew what the conditions would be like in African cities at the beginning of the twenty-first century. God also knew how these conditions would affect Christians in terms of discouragement and despair. But God has all power in heaven and on earth. He created the universe out of nothing, just by speaking (Gen. 1:3, 6, 9, 11, 14, 24, 26). There are no human problems which God cannot solve including the problems of modern urban Africa. The words of Jesus ("What is impossible with men is possible with God" – Mark 10:27) are just as true in modern urban Africa as they were 2000 years ago in rural Israel because God is God and God does not change. This book will attempt to suggest an approach to some of these seemingly hopeless problems from a biblical perspective. The people of God, especially in the cities, urgently need to understand how God would have His people think about such problems.

THE EFFECTS OF URBANIZATION ON INDIVIDUALS

In addition to the enormous social and physical problems created by urbanization, there is a great problem concerning the effects of urbanization on the souls of individuals. City life can lead to major psychological and emotional problems. People moving to the city can lose many of their traditional values and their sense of personal identity. Young people living in the city often lose the all-important African core value of life in community. Sometimes they lose the traditional African value of respect for the elderly which is also an important biblical value. The Bible says the young are to, "Rise in the presence of the aged, show respect for the elderly" (Lev. 19:32).

Living in the city and being surrounded by godless people with godless values can bring temptation to materialism, secularism, greed, individualism and selfishness instead of Christian values of generosity, self-sacrifice, humility and support for the community. Working with people whose lives are dominated by hypocrisy, dishonesty, lying and corruption can lead to cynicism and indifference to the needs of others.

The temptation to conform to these godless and evil values of the city is an urgent call to the church for culturally relevant ministries of evangelism, discipleship, Bible teaching and counseling, so that Christians will not be overcome by the moral and spiritual temptations of modernity. The Bible says, "Do not conform any longer to the pattern of this world, but be transformed by the renewing of your mind" (Rom. 12:2). Nowhere is this exhortation needed more than in modern urban Africa.

SUMMARY

Urbanization is one of the major sociological trends in Africa in the twenty first century. The moral, physical, social, practical and individual problems associated with urbanization are very great. It will be one of the greatest challenges to the church in the twenty-first century to learn how to deal with these problems in a God-honoring way. The church must learn to seriously obey the teachings of the Bible and to rely on the power of the Holy Spirit more than it ever has in its history if it is to meet this great challenge and to help its people live a victorious Christian life in the midst of a corrupt, degraded and increasingly evil urban world.

QUESTIONS FOR REVIEW, REFLECTION AND GROUP DISCUSSION

1. How are unemployment and crime related to population growth in the cities?
2. What are some ways in which the local church could be of help to provide jobs for unemployed members of the congregation or job training for unskilled members of the church?
3. Why do crime and other problems increase more quickly in cities than in rural areas?
4. What practical steps could people take to reduce the risk of crime against themselves while living in the city?
5. What are some of the health risks for people living in cities?
6. What steps could people living in the city take to protect their health from health risks created by living in the city?

7. What is the biblical view of hard work?
8. What are some of the reasons why Christian family planning is needed by Christian families today?

END NOTES

1. United Nations Center For Human Settlements. The Global Report On Human Settlements, 1986.
2. Zanotelli, Alex. Facing Problems of Rapid Urbanization. African Ecclesial Review. Vol. 30 No. 5, October 1988, p. 280.
3. Ibid. p. 277.
4. Africa Ministry Resources. "The Church Leader In Africa" Vol. 7 No. 3 Third Quarter, 1997. p.1.

Chapter 4

CULTURAL CRISIS AND DEATH IN THE CITIES - CAN ANYTHING BE DONE?

Ndazi was a young man of eighteen. He had lived with his family in the village since he was born. He attended primary school in the village. He was not a good student but he had passed from one class to the next until he finished class seven. His father became sick with hepatitis during the year Ndazi was in class six, so Ndazi had to take over most of the farming for the family. It was hard work. The hard work did not help his grades in school. Most of the time he was too tired from farm work to stay awake in class.

One day Ndazi's friend Nuhu told him about life in the city. Nuhu had worked in the city for a year but had recently been released from his job. Nuhu's picture of life in the city appealed to Ndazi. Nuhu told him there were jobs where a young man could sit at a desk dressed in a shirt and tie and never have to pick up a hoe again. There were all sorts of interesting people and interesting things to see. There were places where you could eat food from other parts of the world. There were lots of pretty girls.

After Ndazi entered class seven his father recovered from his sickness. His junior brother, a year younger, had grown into a strong young man and Ndazi's father had also put him to work on the farm. Ndazi saw his opportunity to leave the farm for good. One day he told his father he had decided to move to the city. His father was unhappy and pleaded with him to stay and live in the village but Ndazi had made up his mind. As soon as school was over for the year he and Nuhu set out for the capital. He took along the little money he had.

For the first four weeks, Ndazi could not find a job. Finally he was given a job in road construction with a foreign company.

It was hard work - every bit as hard as the work on the farm. But on this job he could not sit down and rest when he wanted to as he did on the farm. If he did he would be fired. The little money he made was quickly used up buying food and helping Nuhu pay the rent for the one room flat where they lived.

One day one of Nuhu's friends, who worked in an office, invited the boys to his house to watch a video film. Ndazi had never seen such a thing in his life. He was fascinated. Later he learned that video films could be rented at a shop in the town. The boys spent hours in the video shop looking at the films that were available. On a certain weekend Nuhu's friend had to travel to another city. He invited the boys to spend the weekend in his house to guard the place against thieves. The man said the boys were free to watch video films on the man's TV and video player. The boys rented three video films that looked exciting, with pictures of partly dressed women on the cover. The films were very exciting indeed. The boys saw a man and woman doing something in the film they had never witnessed. That night, something changed in the hearts of both young men forever. Their innocence was gone.

It was not too many months later when Ndazi decided he wanted to try for himself what he had seen in the video films. One night he found a girl on the streets of the city who said she would be happy to do what he wanted to do - but it would cost him some money. With the money he had saved from his work he spent the night with the girl from the street. It was exciting alright but afterward he felt strange and alone and ashamed. A few weeks later he got sick but he had no money to get medicine. About the same time, Nuhu announced that he could no longer pay the rent. He was going to return to his father's home in the village.

Ndazi did not earn enough money to buy his food and also pay for the rent by himself. He thought about returning to his home in the village but he was too proud to face his father with his failure. He moved out into the street. The strain of his work each day was too much for him. His sickness got worse. At night he would sleep on the street under a cardboard box. He began to miss days at work because of sickness. At first his boss gave him a couple days of sick leave but later he was let go from his job for missing so many days at work.

Now Ndazi was desperate just to get money for food. He found that he could go into some of the shops in the city and put items in the shop under his clothes and leave without being caught. He would then sell the items cheaply on the street. He managed to survive for over a year this way. Thus began his "career" in shoplifting and petty thievery. One day, however he was caught stealing by a shop owner. The owner turned him over to the police. The police beat him and put him in a foul-smelling, rat infested city jail for a week. They released him with a severe warning. Now Ndazi was getting desperate. His sickness was also getting worse. Who could he turn to for help? He thought about taking his own life.

Modernity and the acceptance of western culture has brought serious problems to many people who move to the city. There is a dangerous absence of the cultural patterns and moral values which regulated and protected people's lives in the village. There is intense loneliness. There is temptation to see things and do things which would have been impossible in the village. Many are overcome by the shameless and widespread temptation to easy sex and are physically and morally destroyed by it. Some who never stole anything in their lives turn to stealing to survive. Young girls turn to prostitution in order to live. Even those with a strong Christian background are suddenly subject to temptations in a way they had never known in their lives.

URBAN ISOLATION

It is a basic assumption in Africa that people are taken care of by their own extended family or clan. This is the reality of the rural setting. It is rarely the situation in the city. It can happen that a person living in the city will have no extended family living nearby. People from other ethnic groups will often have little regard for the welfare and needs of people living right next door to them if they do not belong to their clan or tribe.

There can be intense isolation, fear, loneliness and difficulty for people living in cities. Young people come to the cities wanting to escape the drudgery of work on the farm and the boredom of a predictable traditional life. They expect to find a good job, a good salary, new friends and the physical benefits of city life. Instead what they often find is a poor job or no job at all, no true friends, no familiar life and the indifference or even hostility of other people. The security of a predictable life among their own people has been replaced by an unpredictable, insecure and often dangerous life among strangers who seem to care only for themselves. The excitement and appeal of the modern world is all there but there is something seriously missing.

In traditional rural Africa there is a certainty about who a person is and what that person's relationship is to everyone else in the community. There may not be much material wealth in the extended family but there is a certainty that so long as the tribe and clan exist, the person will always share in the food and care of his or her community.

This certainty brings with it a strong sense of security, encouragement and stability. The rural person knows that his or her physical, mental and emotional needs will always be met to the extent that everyone else's needs in the community are being met. The welfare of the individual is simply one part of the welfare of the community. If the community is blessed everyone shares in the blessings of the community. If the community suffers everyone shares in the suffering. The suffering becomes tolerable just because everyone shares it. It is hard to overestimate the importance of this sense of security and stability in the lives of rural people of the same clan or tribe.

Life in the city is often just the opposite. If a person is not part of an extended community of his or her own people in the city, a person can feel cut off from everything important. Isolation, loneliness, despair, insecurity and instability are evidences that there has been a serious loss of things that really matter. The effects of these changes can be deadly in individual lives. It is hard to overestimate the negative effects of this loss of personal security for those who move to the cities.

Men who have never been unfaithful to their wives and have left them back in their villages may invite other women to come and live with them. Boys who never thought about crime may turn to stealing in order to survive. Girls who were virgins in the village may turn to prostitution just to pay for clothes, food and rent. Young people get caught in temptations they never heard of or thought about. Children and adults may find themselves living in the streets just because they can not afford to rent a flat.

WHO WILL CARE FOR THE NEEDY?

African governments have not generally created systems of social welfare as western countries have done. One reason for this is the cultural reality of tribe, clan and extended family. It is correctly assumed that every group cares for its own. There may also be severe economic problems in the country which prevent the government from setting up a system of social welfare.

The present situation partly reflects the great differences between the core values of traditional Africa and the core values of the West which are being adopted in many cities. In the West, core values of individualism, privacy and mobility together with generally healthy economies have enabled western governments to create elaborate forms of government social security. These systems can include such things as unemployment insurance, government health programs, government funded job training, government retirement and pension plans, youth social and recreational programs and many other aspects of a government run "security net" which takes responsibility for those who have no other form of support or help.

These programs are supported through taxes. Such plans work as long as there are enough people paying taxes to keep the programs in operation. This, in turn depends on people having jobs. People can pay taxes only when they have a steady income. However, when unemployment is high or there is not enough industry or development in the country to provide jobs for people, the government is unable to set up such social welfare programs.

Many African countries find themselves in this situation. There is general poverty in the country. There is not enough basic industry or economic development to provide jobs for a large number of people. There is not enough income from taxes for the government to pay for a government-run social welfare system. In some African countries over half the population is without a job.

The result of this situation is a growing crisis in the cities. In many cities there are thousands of homeless people, thousands of street children, thousands of beggars, thousands of thieves and thousands of women who have turned to prostitution to survive. The situation is getting worse every day. In one African city, it is commonly said that 1/3 of the population employs another 1/3 of the population to guard them from the final 1/3 of the population!

Can anything be done in such hopeless circumstances? it is probably accurate to say that unless things dramatically change in the economic and political situation of Africa, nothing will improve unless the people of God take action. Saddest of all, even when a country has many natural resources and the potential for extensive industrial development (which is true in several African countries), the presence of a selfish or corrupt political leader can prolong a bad situation indefinitely.

If the government of a country cannot or will not help the poor is there anything the people of God can do in such a situation? We may not think so, but let us consider for a moment what God can do when He finds just one of His people with a heart completely committed to Himself. The following true story is given to illustrate what God did through just one couple because they were seriously committed to serve Christ. The point of the story is to see what might be possible if a whole group of Christians from one local church, or even all the Christians in one city, were to unite together to address the needs of the poor in their city.

Charles was a business man who owned several businesses. One day he had an appointment in the capital city. He drove to the place of his appointment in his Mercedes Benz automobile. Some street boys watched him as he parked his car. They approached Charles and asked if he would like to hire them to guard his car from thieves while he was doing his business. Being in a hurry, Charles disregarded the boys and went about his business. On returning from his appointment, Charles was shocked to find that his Mercedes Benz car had been stolen! When he asked the street boys what had happened, they dismissed his question and pointed out that he had not hired them to guard his car so how could they know what had happened to his car?

Although it was a bitter experience, the Lord used the theft of his car to cause Charles to begin thinking about the need of homeless street children whose only way to survive was through stealing - or "employment" as guards to prevent stealing! Over the next few months, Charles thought much about the hopeless condition of these children. Back in his home town he finally decided to begin a ministry of reaching out to such children in his area. It was difficult and dangerous work just to go to the places where the children were to be found. He began his ministry by bringing the children to the compound of the church where he was an elder.

Finally the numbers of children and their bad background became more than the church compound could handle. Charles wondered where he might continue this ministry, for the Lord had begun to touch a number of lives through his efforts to teach these young thieves, prostitutes, drug addicts and criminals about God's love and God's forgiveness in Christ. There was no place available for such a ministry. Finally after much prayer and heart searching, Charles and his wife Esther offered their own large home in the city to the Lord as the place for the ministry to continue.

In the course of time Charles and Esther brought over 100 children to live with them on the compound of their own private home! They built a school on the compound and a shop to teach the boys job skills. But it literally cost them everything they had. One by one they sold all of their businesses to care for the children's needs until there was nothing left. Finally one cold and awful night Charles cried out to the Lord for His help. He had given everything he had and there was nothing left to give. It was the low point of his life.

In the morning, a pick up truck appeared at Charles' door with a load of grain for the children from someone he didn't even know. From that day on, the ministry of this couple to street children has been sustained by the Lord in answer to prayer by the staff and the children. Impossible in Africa? It would seem so, but with God - and a heart of total commitment to Christ, all things are possible (Mark 9:23, Mark 10:27)). By the grace and provision of God, the ministry to these children has now expanded into 7 rural training and rehabilitation centers where more than 1500 children receive moral, spiritual and practical instruction and a new way of life! Many of them are finding a new hope to become productive members of their society and a new life in Jesus Christ. This ministry is also working hard to become self sustaining through the farm products, furniture and metal work they produce. The point is, if it can happen in one African country and in one place of need, it can happen in many other parts of Africa, if there are people like Charles and Esther who are willing to offer themselves sacrificially to God for His service.

WHAT COULD BE DONE IF CHURCHES WERE TO WORK TOGETHER?

If God can do such a thing through one dedicated Christian couple, what would happen if a number of people in every local church made a commitment to put the concern of Christ for the poor and needy before their own interests? The problems of the cities today are overwhelming to say the least. There is no way that any one person can ever solve such problems alone.

That is the way it is in a war. One person alone cannot win a battle against a foreign army. It takes an army, working together with skill and commitment, to overcome the enemy. Here lies the secret of God's plan to show His love to this sick world. It is not God's plan that His work should be accomplished by just a few dedicated people. It is His plan that the whole church should work together as a body to accomplish His salvation on earth. The famous hymn, "Onward Christian Soldiers expresses this truth. The hymn says, "Like a mighty army moves the Church of God."

One man cannot win a football match. It takes a coordinated team of 11 players on the field with each player doing his part with all his skill. So also in the work of God, one person cannot possibly do what needs to be done. The whole church must act together as a team or an army. The Holy Spirit gives spiritual gifts to every member of the true church so that this can happen (1 Peter 4:10). The Church is Christ's physical presence in this world. The Church is the hands, the feet, and the voice of Christ to the hopeless, helpless and needy people of this generation. By God's enabling strength, the people of God as a community of the Lord are able to do even more than a country's government can do. A government can provide social welfare plans and job training programs. But no government can offer a gospel of hope, peace, reconciliation, love and forgiveness as God offers to the world through Christ.

Think for a moment how often the news on radio and television speaks about some peace conference or effort to produce a cease-fire in some conflict. No sooner is one fire in the world put out but another one begins somewhere else. The problems of human beings begin right inside the heart and no government can change the human heart. Only God can change the human heart from within by the power of the Holy Spirit. That is why only the church can bring real hope and real solutions to the cities of Africa that will work and that will last.

All that people will ever know about the love and goodness of God they will have to see by observing God's people. They will have to see a visible demonstration of God's love through His people if they are to believe that God really loves them, especially if they have been bitterly hurt or abused. Let us imagine for a moment how a joint effort by local churches could actually solve the overwhelming problems of a particular city.

Suppose one local church in a city had a membership of 300 people. Suppose that 1/3 of the membership of that local church (100 people) were willing to commit themselves to the rehabilitation of the poor and needy in their own city in a manner something like the story just presented. Let us imagine that every such dedicated person or couple was realistically willing to reach out to just 2 needy people. What would happen?

Through that one local church 200 people would be helped. Each person's ministry to just 2 street children, or homeless people or beggars or prostitutes in that city would become a ministry to 200 such people through that one local church. Suppose there were 100 churches in the city with Christians who were willing to do the same thing. That would mean that in this one city alone, the people of God, without any help from the government, could change the lives of 20,000 needy people!

Such an effort would give these needy people something which no government could ever give them - a new hope and a new life morally, spiritually, and practically, along with the hope of eternal life with Christ in Heaven. This is an example of how

God works and the kind of solution God can bring to a seemingly hopeless situation even in a poor country. But the benefits of this kind of ministry would not stop with the 20,000 people who were helped.

Such a ministry as the one just described has an unusual power to duplicate itself. Out of gratitude for what has been done for them, some of the people who were helped to find a new life will want to become involved in helping other needy people like themselves. In simple language, love produces love. In other words, unselfish love has such an emotionally powerful effect on people's hearts that it motivates many of those who are helped to show the same kind of love to others.

This truth explains why Christians have been motivated to love and good works for the past 2000 years. When they come to really understand what God has done for them through Jesus Christ, their hearts are so deeply touched that they want to show their gratitude to God by doing something for others. The Bible says, "Christ's love compels us, because we are convinced that one died for all . . . . that those who live should no longer live for themselves but for him who died for them and was raised again" (2 Cor. 5:14-15).

No situation is hopeless with God. The problem is not what God can do. The problem is what we His people are willing to do. God does not generally solve problems for people apart from the active involvement of His own people. That is the truth taught in the Bible (Matt. 5:13-15, Philippians. 2:13). That is the reality seen in church history.

THE BIBLICAL BASIS FOR HOLISTIC MINISTRY

There is a great error in some Christian ministry today. Some people have the idea that when they have preached to people they have fulfilled the ministry of the gospel. That was not the pattern of Christ. That was not the pattern of the early church. Such a pattern is a serious departure from biblical Christianity. Kenyan professor George Kinoti has written,

"We (the church) failed to apply the gospel to the whole of life, limiting it to spiritual life only. We read the scriptures selectively, placing emphasis on those parts that talk about salvation and neglecting those parts that talk about justice, peace and material well-being. We . . . must seek to apply the whole of the Word of God to the whole of life" [1]

WHAT WAS THE PATTERN OF CHRIST?

Jesus healed people. He fed people. He cast out demons from people. He cleansed the lepers. He taught people. He counselled people. He encouraged people. He forgave people. In the garden of Eden He provided clothes for Adam and Eve. Jesus' ministry was to the whole person. It was holistic ministry. He ministered to the bodies, the minds, the emotions, and the spirits of people. His ultimate goal was that human beings might become whole persons by entering into a personal relationship with God. But for that to happen, He had to touch people at the point of their greatest need. That meant healing peoples' bodies, minds, emotions and relationships. Nothing opens people's hearts more than a loving ministry to their physical and emotional needs. In the historical growth of the Christian church throughout the world, the majority of the first converts to Christ in every community have come from people who were helped in ways they could understand, especially through medical ministries.

WHAT WAS THE PATTERN OF THE EARLY CHURCH?

The early church had the correct understanding of how the gospel should minister to the whole person. Here are the words of the apostle James. "Suppose a brother or sister is without clothes and daily food. If one of you says to him, "Go, I wish you well; keep warm and well fed," but does nothing about his physical needs, what good is it" (James 2:15-16)?

Here is the testimony of the apostle Paul. "They agreed that we should go to the Gentiles, and they to the Jews. All they asked was that we should continue to remember the poor, the very thing I was eager to do." (Galatians 2:9-10). Here is Paul's testimony to the Ephesian elders. "In everything I did, I showed you that by this kind of hard work we must help the weak, remembering the words the Lord Jesus himself said: 'It is more blessed to give than to receive" (Acts 20:35).

Paul was involved in bringing relief to the needy churches in Judea: In Romans 15:25-27 he said, "I am on my way to Jerusalem in the service of the saints there. For Macedonia and Achaia were pleased to make a contribution for the poor among the saints in Jerusalem. They were pleased to do it." The testimony concerning a sister named Tabitha was this: "In Joppa there was a disciple named Tabitha who was always doing good and helping the poor" (Acts 9:36). The Bible plainly teaches that a holistic ministry to human beings is the pattern of the New Testament. How is it to be done?

Every lasting work of God must be done by faith in God. The Bible says, "Without faith it is impossible to please God" (Heb. 11:6). We must do the work of God by trusting Him through prayer, not by trusting in ourselves. Prayer is the first and most important thing we can do to start a work for God.

HOW CAN MINISTRIES TO THE NEEDY BE ESTABLISHED?

Some who read this may wonder how an individual or a local church can get started in a ministry to the needy if they have never done it before. Many times Christians have the desire to do something for the Lord but they don't know quite where to begin. We can be encouraged if there is the desire to do what God wants even if we don't know what to do. We can learn what to do. God is the one who has put such a concern into the hearts of his people. Every lasting work for God begins because God pours out his love and compassion for the poor and needy into the hearts of his people. Romans 5:5 says "God has poured out his love into our hearts by the Holy Spirit, whom he has given us." It is the Holy Spirit who motivates us to love and good works. Philippians 2:13 says, "It is God who works in you to will and to act according to his good purpose." When God puts such a desire in our hearts, it is our responsibility to respond to His urging. He will not force us to act against our will.

If God is the one who raises up a ministry it is God who will sustain the ministry. Philippians 1:6 says, "He who began a good work in you will carry it on to completion until the day of Christ Jesus." Our part is to obey the urging of God's Spirit within us. We must also continue to pray and to carry out the ministry according to the principles of God's Word.

Recall what God did through Nehemiah, a cupbearer to a Persian King. He enabled this Hebrew servant of long ago to mobilize the people of God to physically restore the walls of Jerusalem and to spiritually restore the Lord's people. The same mighty God is at work today.

Recall what God did through St. Francis of Assisi. He founded a worldwide missionary organization and ministry to the poor. The same mighty God is at work today. Recall what God did through William Wilburforce, the British parliamentarian. God enabled this man, together with his co-workers, to abolish the practice of slavery in the largest empire in the world. This effort took a lifetime. There were years of discouraging and difficult work along with years of prayer. In the end, God gave success. The same mighty God is at work today.

It is through prayer, faith, hard work and patience that God will give success to the work He stirs up in the hearts of His people (Heb. 6:12). The most basic key to the success of any work for the Lord is prayer. We need to learn to pray and how to pray for the right things. For God's work to be accomplished in God's way, the primary emphasis in such a work must be prayer and the Word of God. Prayer overcomes many of the weaknesses of the sinful nature of man. Prayer also overcomes the opposition of Satan. The Word of God shows us God's way to help human beings whose lives have fallen apart. An emphasis on prayer and the Word of God will result in spiritual renewal and will have God's blessing.

Every effort to rescue needy people must make spiritual renewal its highest priority. As important as physical ministries are, they must not become the final goal of the ministry. Physical ministries must not be done without concern for the moral and spiritual needs of people. Physical ministries should be seen as one of the means needed to achieve the complete restoration of human beings. Physical assistance without spiritual renewal will only provide a bandage on a running sore. This is the reason why so many government programmes of rehabilitation fail.

The total restoration of a human being must involve helping the person find a personal, living relationship with God through Jesus Christ (John 17:3). It must also involve meeting their pressing physical needs. If the change is to last, the person must be changed from within by God's Spirit. In this way God will restore his own image in the person's life (Romans 12:2). The person being helped must be willing to make a commitment to God's truth and God's ways.

God is concerned about restoring His image in those who turn to Him for help. God is glorified when human beings reflect His loving and holy character. The Bible says the church is to be, "a people belonging to God, that you may declare the praises of him who called you out of darkness into his wonderful light" (1 Pet. 2:9).

It is only transformed individuals who can change a culture and a society. The error of communism and other human ideologies of reform is the assumption that a perfect social or economic system will produce a perfect society. These ideologies do not deal with the reality that all human beings are born sinners (Psalm 51:5). God must change people from the inside out for the society to permanently change for the good. This is why spiritual rebirth must be at the center of any lasting ministry designed to achieve rehabilitation of the needy. (John 3:3, 1 Peter 1:23)

Rehabilitation of the poor and needy involves the need to rebuild the lives of broken people. In addition to leading people into a personal relationship with Christ, Christians must seek to bring about the healing of their broken human spirits by enabling them to become self-sustaining persons who have a sense of self-worth, purpose and value in life. We must help them to restore broken relationships with other people, which are often at the root of their problems.

What then are the practical steps which an individual or a local church can take, in order to start a ministry to the needy in their community?

SOME SUGGESTIONS FOR HELPING LOCAL CHURCHES TO START PROGRAMS TO HELP THE NEEDY.

1. Form a committee to gather and share information. A local church can be challenged and inspired when it hears what God has done through other local churches and agencies. The church will be challenged when it learns about the actual needs in the city. It is important to know who is already being helped and who still needs help.
   a. Find out who are the most needy and where they are. Find out what their situation really is.
   b. Gather information on what others are doing or have tried. Include information on both their successes and their failures. If possible, also include information on what secular organizations are doing.
   c. Make a list of other organizations involved in ministries of rehabilitation and relief (including names, addresses and phone numbers) with detailed descriptions of what they are doing. This can promote cooperation and prevent unnecessary duplication of effort between individuals, churches and para-church organizations who are doing the same things.
2. Set up a strategy planning committee to work out a realistic plan of action for the local church or agency. This committee should include leaders of the local church and if possible, people from other organizations who are trying to do the same thing.
3. Have the pastor and elders publicly challenge the local church to individual commitment and involvement in the plan of action. A special group can be formed, such as a "company of the committed" who will begin to function as a team.
4. Distribute information to committed Christians about the actual steps they will need to take to become involved in helping people. Many people fail to get involved because they don't know what to do, how to do it, or who to contact. This step could include information on

   a. Job skills needed in the city
   b. Training facilities already available for job training
   c. True stories about how other people have carried out such ministries
   d. Materials and methods to use in Christian discipleship
5. There may be a need to deal with the government just as Nehemiah dealt with the Persian king and Joseph dealt with the Pharaoh. If so, there should be a committee to approach the government about cooperation with Christian efforts to help the needy and to advise the government about what Christians are doing.
6. It may be necessary and helpful for the local church or agency to set up a revolving loan fund to help needy people get established in a small business to make a living.
7. People in the local church with specific job skills can be challenged to volunteer some of their time to teach their skill to those who have no job skill at all.
8. Groups of churches or agencies may want to become involved in Christian literature, radio or television production in order to change the morally corrupt values which are destroying their society.

An example of a remarkable Christian ministry which has had great success under very difficult conditions in called, "Integrated Holistic Approach." This work is less than twenty years old, but it currently helps more than 42,000 people in Addis Ababa, Ethiopia through 52 different programs. The work has grown out of the dedication of a Christian Ethiopian woman with a great heart of compassion for the needy. For more information, contact Integrated Holistic Approach, P.O. Box 6889, Addis Ababa, Ethiopia.

SUMMARY

There is a growing crisis in the cities today. Modernity and the acceptance of western culture has brought profound cultural change and many personal problems to those who move to the cities. There is a dangerous absence of the cultural patterns and values which regulated and protected life in the village. The problems of the cities are many, including poverty, loneliness, insecurity, fear, loss of moral standards, homelessness, joblessness, sexual immorality, prostitution, breakdown of families and marriages, drug abuse, crime, suicide and much more.

God is able to solve even the most difficult problems concerning the poor and needy in the cities today. But He almost always uses His own people to carry out His works of mercy and compassion. For this to happen, God's people must have seriously dedicated and obedient hearts. They also need factual information on what is already being done and what needs to be done.

The church is the Body of Jesus Christ on earth. The church is the hands, the feet, and the voice of Christ to this sick and dying world. By God's enabling strength, the people of God can do much for the needy. The church can give people much more than any government program can give them. Christians can lead people into a new life where there is hope and restoration for the present life and hope for life after death with God in Heaven. Let the people of God in Africa today rise to the challenge in the Name of the Lord.

QUESTIONS FOR REVIEW, REFLECTION AND GROUP DISCUSSION

1. Give some reasons why city living can lead to isolation, insecurity, loneliness and temptation for youth moving into the city.
2. What kind of things could local city churches do to help young people like Ndazi, described at the beginning of this chapter?
3. What is meant by holistic ministry? In what ways was Jesus' ministry a holistic ministry? Why is holistic ministry very effective?
4. How can local churches become involved in ministries to street children, homeless people, drug addicts or prostitutes? What kind of people, what kind of information and what steps would be needed to establish such ministries?

5. What is the most important thing a church or an individual can do to enable God's work to move ahead and have success?

END NOTES

1. George Kinoti, Hope For Africa And What The Christian Can Do. Nairobi: Africa Institute For Scientific Research And Development, 1994. p. 2

Chapter 5

THE MOST COMMON PLEASURE AND COMMON PROBLEM IN THE WORLD

There is probably no desire that is stronger for most people than the desire for the opposite sex. Sexual desire was given by God to be used for blessing in marriage and for the reproduction of children. It is probably the most common pleasure and common problem in the world. As with so many things, the sinful nature of mankind has corrupted this good gift from God. Of the many stories that could be chosen on this subject, two stories have been selected in order to illustrate the great problem sex can be for many people, including God's people. It is not just ungodly people who get into trouble because of sexual desire.

"One day Dana, the prayer group leader planned an all-night prayer program for the youth and advertised it well in advance. On the assigned evening, however, only one girl (Ayanti) came. They waited for a while for the others to arrive. When no one else came, Dana went ahead with his program. They were alone in the house, although it had not been planned that way. Dana read the Bible and shared with Ayanti. After this, they began to pray together about different matters.

About midnight, Dana suggested that they should pray for one another by laying hands on each other. He began to pray, laying hands on Ayanti. During his praying, he began to caress her lovingly. After a while both of them were overcome with emotion and they began to kiss each other. Finally, they committed sexual immorality. Ayanti was overcome with guilt and went off to another part of the house and tried to commit suicide. Fortunately Dana found her and prevented her from taking her life."

The above situation which recently took place in an African country, has something in common with the following story from the Bible which took place 3000 years ago.

> *"One evening David got up from his bed and walked around on the roof of the palace. From the roof he saw a woman bathing. The woman was very beautiful, and David sent someone to find out about her. The man said, "Isn't this Bathsheba, the daughter of Eliam and the wife of Uriah the Hittite?" Then David sent messengers to get her. She came to him, and he slept with her. . . Then she went back home. The woman conceived and sent word to David, saying, "I am pregnant."*
>
> *So David sent this word to Joab: "Send me Uriah the Hittite." And Joab sent him to David. When Uriah came to him, David asked him how Joab was, how the soldiers were and how the war was going. Then David said to Uriah, "Go down to your house and wash your feet." So Uriah left the palace, and a gift from the king was sent after him. But Uriah slept at the entrance to the palace with all his master's servants and did not go down to his house. When David was told, "Uriah did not go home," he asked him, "Haven't you just come from a distance? Why didn't you go home?" Uriah said to David, "The ark and Israel and Judah are staying in tents, and my master Joab and my lord's men are camped in the open fields. How could I go to my house to eat and drink and lie with my wife? As surely as you live, I will not do such a thing!"*
>
> *. . . In the morning David wrote a letter to Joab and sent it with Uriah. In it he wrote, "Put Uriah in the front line where the fighting is fiercest. Then withdraw from him so he will be struck down and die." So while Joab had the city under siege, he put Uriah at a place where he knew the strongest defenders were. When the men of the city came out and fought against Joab, some of the men in David's army fell; moreover, Uriah the Hittite died" (2 Sam. 11:2 -17)*

David was a great leader of God's people. He had the high privilege of writing over half of one of the most beloved books of all time, the Book of Psalms. David was a man after God's heart, according to the Bible (1 Sam. 13:14). Yet this great and godly man not only fell into the sin of adultery, but skillfully tried to cover his sin by making it appear that the woman's husband, Uriah, had gotten his wife pregnant. When that plan failed, he committed the greatest sin a person can commit against another human being, which is to take that person's life. David made his sin of adultery very much worse by arranging for the death of Bathsheba's husband, Uriah . What two sins are more universally condemned by all people than the sins of adultery and murder? Yet David, the "sweet psalmist of Israel" committed them both! That was the beginning of a long series of painful consequences in David's family life.

Both of these true stories illustrate the enormous power of sexual desire and sexual temptation. In the first story from Africa, the two young people concerned had good intentions, coming together to spend an evening in prayer with other young people like themselves. They had no plan to engage in sex. Temptation came unexpectedly and caught them off guard. In the second story from the Bible, a great and godly king allowed his eyes to see what they should not have seen. From this momentary temptation came a tragic sequence of events which affected David and his family for the rest of his life.

In this chapter the expression sexual immorality will be used to refer to having sex before marriage. The term adultery will be used to refer to unfaithfulness by a marriage partner. According to these definitions Dana and Ayanti committed sexual immorality. King David committed adultery.

After God created Adam He made a beautiful creature for him of the opposite sex, presenting her to Adam naked (Gen 2:25). God immediately joined them together in a life-long relationship of marriage so that the great fire of emotional and physical desire of men and women for each other might be controlled and protected by marriage (Gen. 2: 22-24). Human beings simply cannot handle the intense emotional and physical desires of sex apart from the restraints planned by God through the institution of marriage.

The Bible speaks about the intensity of emotion connected with sexual desire. King Solomon, who had 1000 women, wrote, "love is as strong as death, its jealousy unyielding as the grave. It burns like blazing fire" (S. of Solomon 8:6). Contrasting the desire for money and the desire for the opposite sex, Solomon added, "If one were to give all the wealth of his house for love, it would be utterly scorned" (S. of Solomon 8:7). The fact is that for most people, there are few if any desires which are stronger than the desire for a partner of the opposite sex.

Some people feel that sexual desire and temptation are so strong that it is hopeless or impossible to resist. Obviously that is not true, since there are many people in history including some non-Christians, who have resisted temptation and have remained pure until they were married. Some Christians have even remained single and pure for a lifetime. However, remaining pure in thought as well as in action until marriage is not easy, especially in this generation which displays sex so openly. It requires the power of the Holy Spirit and a practical strategy for holy living. We will present a realistic strategy for sexual purity later in this chapter.

THE CONTEXT OF MODERN URBAN AFRICA

To develop a practical strategy for sexual purity we need to understand the cultural context of sexual temptation in modern urban Africa. In this chapter we will give an overview of this context. In the next chapter we will investigate the nature of that context in detail in order to understand what is taking place in urban Africa today.

Urbanization in Africa has brought many temptations to sexual immorality and adultery to those who move to the city. Unmarried people who move to the cities often do not feel the restraints of their traditional culture as they did in the rural villages where they grew up. In addition, there are a multitude of temptations in the city, such as easy access to sexually stimulating video tapes, cinema, magazines, disco clubs and morally loose companions. Living in the village has usually not prepared people to deal with the strong temptations of the city.

Married men are also tempted to sexual sin when they move to the city. In many cases they leave their wives and children in the rural village for some months or even years due to the costs of living in the city. Loneliness sets in and the same kinds of temptation which confront unmarried people also tempt the married person. Some married men who move to the city will have a woman who is not his wife come and live with him in the city unknown to his wife.

Secular music in the city can be a major source of sexual temptation. The people who own night clubs and disco's know this and use this fact to make their money. Much of the music popular with young people today is purposely designed by the composers to stimulate young people in rhythm and body movement as well as in words. Both men and women are easily aroused by certain kinds of music. Those who want to live pure lives before the Lord must make a decision to refuse to listen to this kind of music. If they are to protect their children, they must also have the courage to refuse to allow this kind of music to be played in their homes.

Another significant fact about the modern urban context is that sex crimes are often violent and often connected with murder. In the secular world the crime of rape often ends with the crime of murder. Here is a very sobering thought. The very act which is a deep expression of love, caring and unity between a married couple becomes one of the most terrible acts of violence and brutality known to man in the crime of rape.

God can forgive sin, including sexual sin, but there may well be horrible earthly consequences, such as a broken home, AIDS, an unwanted child, or some other result. The church must be faithful to clearly explain the results of sexual sin. Consider the following statistics about AIDS from a Ministry of Health Publication on AIDS In Ethiopia. "Over 1.2 million AIDS cases worldwide have been reported to the World Health Organization (WHO) as of December 1995. WHO estimates the actual number of cases to be about 6 million. In addition, WHO estimates that there were 17 million HIV-infected adults alive as of late 1994." [1] Of this number of people infected with HIV, 11 million of them are found in Sub-Saharan Africa! [2]

The Bible says, "The wages of sin is death" (Rom. 6:23). This truth applies to all kinds of sin in all cultures. Today it has a very specific application in the disease of AIDS. Those who get AIDS as a result of sexual sin will die. There is no known cure for AIDS. The church must teach her people to flee from sin at all cost. Jesus said it would be worth destroying part of your body to avoid sin if that would keep you from sin (Matt. 5:29-30). Unfortunately, physically destroying part of the body rarely solves the problem, because sin originates in the heart and mind (Mark 7:20-23).

PRE-MARITAL SEX

More and more young people in the West and in Africa are having sex before they are married. Very often this encounter is with a person they will never marry. In addition to violating the Word of God and the Will of God (1 Cor. 6:18, 1 Thess. 4:3-6), there is the obvious risk of an unwanted pregnancy. Even more than the risk of pregnancy, there is a high risk of being infected with a sexually transmitted disease (STD) which can lead to lifelong illness and even physical death.

Another great loss to those who commit sexual immorality is something which young people today rarely consider. It is the loss of a priceless once-in-a-lifetime experience. One of the greatest losses for young people who have sex before marriage is to give up their virginity to someone who may never become their marriage partner for life. God has so created human beings that a person will never forget the first time of having sexual intercourse. When it is reserved for the beginning of marriage, as God intended, it is an experience that brings great happiness and unity to a new husband and wife. To throw that once-in-a-lifetime moment away to momentary pleasure or lust with the wrong person is one of the most foolish things a person can do. Such a person will never be able to restore what he or she has lost.

God spoke of this experience as "becoming one flesh" in His creation of a wife for Adam (Gen. 2:24). Nothing in modern man's experience will ever change the way God created human beings. Those who make the foolish decision to waste that moment out of the will of God will have a lifetime to regret it. Those who reserve that moment to begin their marriage will be able to enjoy and renew that special experience each time they come together.

To those who have wasted that moment through sin, there is still good news in the gospel of Christ. God forgives sin (1 John 1:9). Beyond that, He helps those who have repented of their sin and desire to live a godly life. It will not be the same as for the person who has kept his or her virginity until marriage, but such a couple can still experience the grace and mercy of God (Prov. 5:18-19, Titus 2:11-14).

DELAYED MARRIAGES

The time-honored and God-honoring solution to a multitude of sex problems is godly Christian marriage. Yet many parents in Africa today delay or hinder their children's marriages for cultural reasons based on pride, which God opposes (1 Pet. 5:5). Parents insist on a large wedding feast and a big display before the extended family in order to maintain a good image before others. Young people think they must have a furnished house, a car and many other things before they can consider marriage. Is this God's perspective or man's pride? Such reasons may seem to make sense but they lack God's wisdom and God's blessing. Delaying marriage in this way leads to long engagements and very often to the couple having sex before marriage because their desires are strong.

Families who encourage their children to delay their marriages for the reasons given above only multiply the real problems of young people and push them into sexual temptation, which leads to sexually transmitted diseases, unwanted pregnancies and abortions. In addition, when young people give in to sexual temptation before marriage, their character and their wills are affected in such a way that it may later bring harm to their marriages. If a person has given in to temptation and been unfaithful before marriage, who is to say he or she will remain faithful after marriage?

Parents and relatives who discourage or prevent the marriages of their children for lack of what they consider appropriate financial means set their children up for sexual temptation. Such parents will share in the judgment of their children when their children sin against God as a result of a postponed marriage. Consider the following story.

Toma and Rachel are Christians who came from Christian homes. They became engaged while in high school and were engaged for 8 years. Rachel's parents wanted a large wedding to fulfill cultural expectations and to maintain their image in the community. This would take several years. The couple spent much time together alone. Toma's sexual desire got the best of him and he tried to persuade Rachel to have sex with him with the argument that it was not wrong because they were engaged and committed to marry each other.

At first Rachel refused him, but Toma used romantic persuasion and physical touching to arouse Rachel's sexual desires until she finally let him have sex with her. To his dismay, Rachel became pregnant. She could not face the shame of being seen pregnant by her parents. With Toma's help Rachel found a local person to perform an abortion. The abortion was done in a crude manner causing Rachel much physical pain in addition to the emotional pain and guilt she already had. But the worst was not over. After the abortion, she got a bad infection in her uterus.

The infection became serious, and Rachel required emergency medical treatment, which exposed the whole matter to her parents. Everyone in the family became angry and blamed everyone else for what had happened. Sadly, Rachel's suffering was not finished. The sickness lasted for several weeks and became a big expense. It left Rachel extremely weak and sickly.

It was some years later before Rachel finally married. After she got married she made the bitter discovery that the abortion and the subsequent sickness had left her unable to bear children. Rachel, her husband and her parents now bear the pain of Rachel's childlessness. In this situation who do you think God holds primarily responsible for these events?

Let us hear the Word of God: "Flee from sexual immorality. All other sins a man commits are outside his body, but he who sins sexually sins against his own body" (1 Cor. 6:18). Let parents hear an additional warning from God: "if anyone causes one of these little ones who believe in me to sin, it would be better for him to have a large millstone hung around his neck and to be drowned in the depths of the sea. Woe to the world because of the things that cause people to sin! Such things must come, but woe to the man through whom they come" (Matt. 18:6-7)!

UNFULFILLED MARRIAGES

There are many Christian marriages in which one or both partners are frustrated or unhappy much of the time. Just the fact of being a Christian does not guarantee happiness and fulfillment in marriage. According to Scripture, it was God's plan to make man as male and female (Gen. 1:27), clearly for the purpose of marriage (Gen. 2:22-24). It was God who looked down on the man He had created and said "It is not good for the man to be alone. I will make a helper suitable for him" (Gen. 2:18). Through the author of the book of Proverbs, the Lord said, "He who finds a wife finds what is good and receives favor from the LORD" (Prov. 18:22). These verses make it clear that marriage is God's plan for most people and that marriage is intended to meet many human needs. Why then are so many married people unhappy, unfulfilled and frustrated in their marriages?

Unfortunately there are more answers to that question than could be addressed in one chapter of a book of this kind. Surveys of married couples have been conducted to determine the major areas of conflict in marriages. Three areas of conflict which appear in many of these lists include disagreements over money, unfulfilled sexual relationships and conflicts over extended family responsibilities. Since this chapter has discussed issues related to sex and marriage, it is necessary to say something about sexual responsibilities in Christian marriage.

GOD'S PLAN FOR SEX IN MARRIAGE

It was God Himself who created mankind as male and female for the very purpose of sexual reproduction (Gen. 1:27-28) and sexual pleasure in marriage (Prov. 5:18-19). The apostle Paul, who personally recommended celibacy within God's will (1 Cor. 7:7-8) also wrote to his young pastor friend Timothy that it was a form of demonic spiritual deception that some people were forbidding people to marry (1 Tim. 4:1-3), supposedly for "spiritual" reasons.

Because sin has corrupted so many people in relation to sex, there is a widespread feeling among many people that sex is inherently something evil or dirty. Even some church theologians during the Middle Ages gave the impression in their writings that sex was somehow a degraded necessity of marriage. That is not the teaching of the Bible.

Let it be clearly understood that within the boundaries of faithful marriage, sex is pure, holy and good in the sight of God (Gen. 1:31, Gen. 2:22-25). Through the writer of the epistle to the Hebrews the Lord said, "Marriage should be honored by all"

(Heb. 13:4). Paul wrote, "since there is so much immorality, each man should have his own wife, and each woman her own husband. The husband should fulfill his marital duty to his wife, and likewise the wife to her husband. . . . Do not deprive each other (sexually) except by mutual consent and for a time, so that you may devote yourselves to prayer. Then come together again so that Satan will not tempt you" (1 Cor. 7:2-5). The author of Proverbs wrote, "May your fountain be blessed, and may you rejoice in the wife of your youth. A loving doe, a graceful deer-- may her breasts satisfy you always, may you ever be captivated by her love" (Prov. 5:18-19).

These verses make it clear that a regular, normal and enjoyable sexual relationship between a husband and his wife is both God's plan and God's will for every married couple. Sex was created by God. It is not something evil or corrupt unless it is used in a sinful way. Within the restrictions of marriage, sex is holy, pure and blessed by God. It is God's will for a married couple to enjoy each other on a regular basis for pleasure (Prov. 5:16-19), to avoid temptation (1 Cor. 7:2-5) and to bear children (Gen. 9:7). Failure to have a regular sex relationship in marriage is not the will of God. Such a failure can bring temptation and cause serious problems in the marriage.

Unfortunately such failures occur in many marriages, resulting in frustration, bitterness, loss of affection, and eventually in the temptation to commit adultery. It has been observed that wives will sometimes give sex to their husbands hoping to receive the affection and love which they need. Women, being more emotional than men, usually desire gentle affection and love more than sex. Men will sometimes give affection and attention to their wives, hoping to have sex with them and to receive the respect they need as the husband. The will of God is that each partner should understand their mate and give their partner what they need. Husbands need to give their wives love and gentle affection and not always demand sex. Wives need to give their husbands respect and regular sexual release.

God's solution to the problem of sexual temptation includes a loving marriage where husbands and wives meet one another's needs on a regular basis. For couples to fail to do this is to oppose the will of God. African marriages where wives regularly refuse to have sex with their husbands for months or years after a child is born are in urgent need of Bible teaching and Christian medical counseling.

Husbands who beat or abuse their wives urgently need to repent of this evil practice and to start doing the will of God. God's commandment is, "Husbands, love your wives, just as Christ loved the church and gave himself up for her" (Eph. 5:25). The word love in this verse is a translation of the Greek verb agapao, which means to love with a self-sacrificing, self-denying love. The same Greek word is used for the love of God when it says, "God so loved the world that he gave his one and only Son, that whoever believes in him shall not perish but have eternal life" (John 3:16). It is with this kind of love that husbands are commanded by God to love their wives. If husbands and wives would give one another what God commands and what their partners really needed, many serious problems in marriage would be avoided.

THE RESPONSIBILITY OF CHURCH LEADERS

The church in Africa today needs to take a strong stand on the Word of God concerning marriage, sex and the family. The church needs to demand sexual purity and faithfulness of its members and leaders before and during marriage. The church needs to speak out plainly about the responsibility of husbands and wives toward each other. The church needs to speak out strongly against those practices in the culture which undermine the institution of marriage. The church needs to openly and vigorously condemn a godless and evil society which mocks the Word of God. The church needs to be a place where the will of God is done in the lives of its leaders and members so that the world will see that the will of God is, "good, acceptable and perfect" (Rom:12:2). When church leaders compromise with the world's system of values, such leaders need to be disciplined and removed from leadership. It is time for the church to stand up and fearlessly speak for God to this evil and sexually immoral generation.

WHAT ARE THE CAUSES OF DIVORCE?

One of the main causes of divorce is adultery by one or both marriage partners. Unfaithfulness by a marriage partner is a betrayal of trust. It is a broken promise which leads to broken hearts and broken homes. The likelihood of adultery during marriage has increased because of the changing attitudes about sex before marriage. If a person does not feel it is wrong to have sex before marriage, it is likely that the same person will have less conviction about having sex with someone beside their marriage partner. This will especially be true if the marriage is in trouble.

Another common cause of divorce is selfishness by one or both partners. In the West today, people feel free to seek a divorce if "things are not working out." By this they really mean that they are not getting what they selfishly demand from their mate. They are not concerned with what they should give to their partner but only with what they want and demand. There are now laws in the West which support "no-fault" divorce. This simply means that the person filing for a divorce does not have to prove that he or she has been abused, mistreated, betrayed or deserted by his or her mate. "No fault" divorce is the ultimate confession of selfishness and sinful attitudes.

Together with the great increase in sexual immorality, no-fault divorce has begun to undermine the whole institution of life-long marriage in the West. [3] The emotional pain of rejection in a no-fault divorce can be almost as great as the betrayal of adultery. In all of this, it is the children of such marriages who suffer the most severe consequences.

No fault divorce laws encourage the very worst selfish and self-serving attitudes in human beings. They are public evidence of the danger in western core values of freedom and individualism. The practical outcome of no-fault divorce laws is that the number of divorces in America has tripled in the past 35 years. [4]

Another important cause for divorce is abuse or mistreatment. Men are generally more guilty of this than women because most men are physically stronger than their wives. Wife-beating is still commonly practiced in many parts of Africa. What sort of arrogant, twisted self-deception makes a man think he can beat his wife and still have a loving, responsive spouse? Wife-beating is the precise opposite of the biblical command that husbands should "love your wives, just as Christ loved the church and gave himself up for her' (Eph. 5:25).

Lack of commitment to make the marriage last is another serious cause of divorce. People entering marriage in the West today marry with little or no motivation to make their marriages last. When the laws of a government clearly support the practice of easy divorce, the motivation for the effort needed to make a marriage work has been taken away from those who plan to marry. There is an easy way out for them if they decide they want to end the relationship. The key question becomes, "What will please me?" rather than, "What will build permanence into this marriage?" or, "What will help my partner and help my children?" or, "What does God want?"

Reflecting the selfish and non-committal mentality popular today, even some churches have changed the words in their marriage ceremony. The traditional church ceremony of the past would ask the couple to repeat their vows ending with the words, "so long as we both shall live." In some places today, the vows end with the words, "so long as our love shall last." How long will that be? A year? Five years? Only commitment and unselfish effort will make a marriage last for a lifetime as God wants.

WHAT ARE THE RESULTS OF DIVORCE?

Divorce or permanent separation involves complete rejection. Rejection is one of the most difficult emotional experiences a person can have in Africa. Most people would rather die than be rejected by their own people. Divorce also involves great emotional pain as well as danger for the children of the marriage. It produces a destructive process which may continue in the children for several generations to come. The children of a divorced marriage carry their anger, grief and pain into their own adult generation and into their own marriages. Parents who divorce often have children whose marriages end in divorce.

Divorce involves the breakdown of a stable family unit - something which God hates (Mal. 2:15-16, 1 Cor. 7:12). Divorce destroys a family. Permanent family units are God's will and God's plan for a morally stable society.

Through divorce, the whole institution of marriage begins to fall apart in that particular family line. This pattern of increasing breakdown of marriage from one generation to the next is now being seen in the West. The anger, bitterness and pain of children who have watched their parents' love turn to hatred and divorce has also resulted in the greatest epidemic of illegal drug use in history among young people in the United States. Drug use and crime are related to the breakdown of the family. Young people seek an escape from the great pain and insecurity caused by a broken home. The children from most divorced marriages in the world bear emotional scars that last throughout life.

The above analysis may help us to understand what God meant when He said, "I, the LORD thy God, am a jealous God, visiting the iniquity of the fathers upon the children unto the third and fourth generation of them that hate me;" (Ex. 20:5-KJV). Those parents who show that they hate God by violating His will and by breaking His laws cause their children to suffer the consequences of their sin. In this way the sins of the parents are visited upon their children and grandchildren even to the third and fourth generation. Consider how many criminals come from broken homes.

WHAT IS THE CURE FOR DIVORCE?

The cure for divorce is commitment, unselfish godly love and the willingness to forgive. Biblical, self-denying love is the strongest medicine in the world for a sick marriage. We live in an age of instant gratification of desires. God is concerned about lifelong commitment regardless of emotions and circumstances. The timeless vows of Christian marriage state that one takes his or her marriage partner, "for better or for worse, for richer for poorer, in sickness and in health, until death do us part, so help me God." When Christians diligently keep these vows of commitment by the power of the Holy Spirit, marriage can last for a lifetime. Divorce is a profound public confession of selfishness and self-centered living by one or both partners.

Lifelong, stable marriages are based on commitment, faithfulness and self-sacrifice, not on emotions which change from day to day. For Christians, they are based on a conscious commitment to the will of God, which is life-long faithfulness (Mal. 2:14 -15). The dowry system in Africa was originally planned by many cultures to secure the permanence of marriage. Unfortunately it has become an excuse for greed by many people today. Even though faulty systems such as dowry may be used, permanence in marriage is always the will of God. The Bible says that God hates divorce (Mal. 2:16).

A STRATEGY FOR SEXUAL PURITY

It is only when a person's life is unconditionally committed to Christ and controlled by the Holy Spirit that temptation will lose its power. Even then, Christians must constantly be on their guard because temptation can come unexpectedly, as in the two stories at the beginning of this chapter. In addition to our own weakness, the devil also tempts God's people to sin (1 Peter 5:8). For these reasons, a Christian must actively plan a strategy for sexual purity in this unclean generation if he or she is to remain pure. The Bible speaks about the need to renew our minds in Christ (Rom. 12:2) and the need to bring every thought into captivity to Christ (2 Cor. 10:5). This has to do with the things we think about and the things we allow our eyes to see.

What sort of things should a person think about if he or she is to remain pure? We must think about the things of God. In Psalm 119:9 we read, "How can a young man keep his way pure? By living according to your word." Even though these words were written 3000 years ago they are still the only strategy for purity which will work in this present corrupt age. We must live according to the Word of God.

How can we live according to the Word of God? Where can a person get the strength to turn away from temptation? It can only be done by the power of the Holy Spirit. The Bible says, "those who live in accordance with the Spirit have their minds set on what the Spirit desires" (Rom. 8:5). The Bible says, "If we live by the Spirit, let us also walk by the Spirit" (Gal. 5:25). The Holy

Spirit can give a person the desire to be holy because God is holy. The Bible says, "it is God who is at work in you, both to will and to work for His good pleasure." (Phil. 2:13-NASB).

The Bible also gives us very practical advice on how to avoid temptation. First, we must pray before we ever enter a situation of temptation. Jesus said, "Watch and pray so that you will not fall into temptation. The spirit is willing, but the body is weak" (Matt. 26:41). He also taught His disciples to pray, "lead us not into temptation" (Matt. 6:13). When we pray in this way, God will help us avoid temptation.

Second, we must learn to discipline our eyes in what we allow them to see. Four thousand years ago, Job gave men a simple secret to avoid temptation. He said, "I made a covenant with my eyes not to look lustfully at a girl" (Job 31:1). We can control what we allow our eyes to see and what we do not allow our eyes to see. What we see or do not see will have much to do with whether or not we enter into sexual temptation. King David entered into temptation because he did not turn his eyes away from watching Bathsheba as she bathed. When people today look at sexually explicit films, videos or pictures, especially on the internet, they will be overcome with sexual temptation.

Third, we must physically leave the place of temptation. When Joseph was tempted by the wife of Potiphar to commit adultery with her, Joseph physically left the woman's presence (Gen. 39:11-12). In sexual temptation more than in most other temptations, it is almost always necessary to physically leave the person or place of temptation in order to relieve the intense power of sexual desire. This could mean leaving a cinema house, throwing away a magazine with the wrong kind of pictures, refusing to rent or watch a certain video, or refusing to be alone with a person of the opposite sex who is not your marriage partner. In the story at the beginning of this chapter, Dana and Ayanti entered into temptation because they stayed alone together in the house for the evening.

In the end, whether or not we are willing to flee from temptation will depend on who we most want to please. Do we want to please ourselves or to please God? Do we want temporary pleasure now with terrible consequences later or are we willing to "live according to the word of God" (Psalm 119:9) by waiting for God's perfect time to enjoy the pleasure of sex only in marriage? Those who choose to please God by living according to His Word will have the blessing of God on their lives both now and for all eternity. In the Bible story above, Joseph was willing to leave the presence of Potiphar's wife because he wanted the blessing of God in his life more than he wanted the short-lived pleasure of committing adultery with Potiphar's wife.

We can summarize the ways to avoid sexual temptation with ten practical and effective suggestions.

(1) You must know what God requires concerning your body (1 Cor. 6:18-20).

(2) You must decide that you want to please God more than yourself. (As Joseph did in the Bible - Gen. 39:9)

(3) You must pray to be kept from temptation situations (Matt. 26:41).

(4) You must understand and put into practice the way to avoid temptation situations (Men through what they see, women in wanting to be attractive to men and in believing what men tell them).

(5) You must understand the severe consequences of sexual sin (1 Thess. 4:6), which can include STD's, pregnancy, spoiling later marriage trust and happiness, losing the once-only treasure of giving away your virginity, and ongoing shame and guilt.

(6) Christian men must decide what they will and will not watch with their eyes and rigidly stick with that decision (Job 31:1). Such things as watching girls, watching erotic videos and films and reading erotic books will lead to overwhelming temptation.

(7) You must refuse cultural/financial pressure to postpone marriage. To do this you must recognize that sinning against God (by sexual immorality) has much worse consequences than offending your relatives over not having a big wedding. You must settle the issue, "Who will you fear most and obey first?" "Who matters most to please, God or parents?"

(8) You must physically flee the place of sexual temptation (2 Tim. 2:22) as Joseph did (Gen 39:12). You will almost never be able to resist temptation in the presence of intense sexual attraction. Hence you should avoid places like video showings, cinema, discos and other places where sexual temptation can be very strong.

(9) You must be very careful about physically touching the opposite sex or being alone with them, especially at night.

(10) You should pray for and seek a marriage partner among God's children.

SUMMARY

Sex is probably the most common pleasure and common problem in the world. It is one of the foundations of marriage, the means of having children and the means of helping to keep a husband and wife close to one another. Mankind has twisted and distorted this gift from God to such an extent that immoral sex has become the means of destroying individuals, marriages, families and even whole nations. Today pornography, pre-marital and extra-marital sex, sexually transmitted diseases, abortions, and divorces have become the moral cancers of modernity. These evil practices threaten to destroy the very foundation of modern civilized society. What is the solution?

The solution is that God's people must determine to live according to the Word of God and to refuse to tolerate any other standards in the church. The Church must insist on life-long commitment in marriage. In addition, as the voice of God to this present evil world, the Church must clearly expose and strongly condemn the evil practices being promoted today in the name of freedom.

Let all in Africa who cherish the most important things in life beware: Not only is West not best for Africa, in many cases West may be the Way To Death, at least as far as marriage and family are concerned. This situation is perhaps the most serious warning signal today about western core values of freedom and individuality. If the trend toward easy divorce continues and families continue to fall apart as they are now doing in the West, it will only be a matter of time before western civilization destroys African life. Let Africans who want to embrace the West and its values beware. God has so created the human race that life-long marriage, the family and the home are still the moral bedrock upon which every stable human civilization has ever been built. If that foundation is destroyed, the whole civilization will eventually collapse.

QUESTIONS FOR REVIEW, REFLECTION AND GROUP DISCUSSION

1. In what ways does the environment of modern urban Africa present many of the same temptations as the urban environment of the West?
2. In what way does secular music often present strong sexual temptation?
3. Why are TV and video such powerful instruments of sexual temptation?
4. What practical strategies can Christian parents adopt in order to protect their children from the temptation to watch sexually explicit video or internet pornography?
5. What are some of the problems which arise from delayed marriages?
6. What are some of the main reasons for unhappiness in many marriages?
7. Describe an appropriate marriage preparation and life training program which could be carried out for young people in a local church.
8. List some of the main causes for divorce today. What kind of things could the local church do to reduce the number of divorces in the Christian community?

END NOTES

1. Ethiopia Ministry of Health. AIDS In Ethiopia: Background, Projections, Impacts, Interventions. Government Publication, 1996. p. iv

2. Ibid. p. iv
3. Family Policy. Vol. 7 No. 1 Washington: Family Research Council, April 1994 p.
4. Ibid. p 1

CHAPTER 6

THE SICK SIDE OF SEX IN OUR SOCIETY AND WHAT WE CAN DO TO CHANGE IT

One of the major challenges to modern life in Africa is the challenge of how to stop the cancer of sexual degradation before it destroys the very society itself. This chapter will not be pleasant reading for many people but it is extremely important reading. Sexual sin and degradation is rapidly becoming one of the most deadly realities of modernity in Africa. If something is not done by the people of God to stop this cancer very soon, our children and grandchildren will receive a horrifying inheritance of evil in their generation. In this chapter we will discuss four extremely serious problems which are becoming a curse on Africa as they have become a curse in the West. These are pornography, sexually transmitted diseases, abortion and prostitution. The following recent true story illustrates the shocking destructive power of pornography.

Ted Bundy was executed in the United States for the rape and murder of a twelve year old girl whom he took from a school playground. He confessed to raping and murdering 23 women! In an interview with Dr. James Dobson of Focus On The Family, just one day before his death sentence was carried out, Dr. Dobson asked Bundy what had led to his life of incredible evil. His answers to Dr. Dobson were shocking and unexpected.

Bundy revealed that he had been raised in a "solid Christian home" with two loving parents and four brothers and sisters. It was nothing like the typical picture of a criminal from a broken home. Bundy described how he first began looking at sexually explicit magazines at the age of 12 and how these pictures got a tight grip on his thoughts. Gradually He became more and more addicted to worse and worse kinds of pornography. In Bundy's own words, "like other kinds of addiction, I would keep looking for more potent, more explicit, more graphic kinds of material." Gradually this ordinary young man from a good Christian home began to change into a violent, demon-possessed criminal. How could such a thing happen?

Bundy said, "You reach that jumping-off point where you begin to wonder if maybe actually doing it will give you something which is beyond just reading about it or looking at it." Bundy concluded by telling Dr. Dobson, "there are lots of other kids playing in the streets . . . who are going to be dead tomorrow . . . because other young people are reading the kinds of things and seeing the kinds of things that are available in the media today." [1]

It seems that human beings have found a way to spoil or ruin every blessing which God has given to man. Nowhere is this seen more vividly or horribly than in the area of sex. The gift which God has given to married people to unite husbands and wives and to bring children into the world has been twisted and degraded more than almost anything else in life.

PORNOGRAPHY

Pornography may be defined as pictures, videos, films or printed materials which were purposely made to stimulate people sexually. The power of pictures, videos, cinema films and even written stories, to stimulate people sexually is well known. Men are especially tempted by what they see with their eyes. Many kinds of advertising use this fact to attract interest in the products they want to sell. They do this by displaying beautiful women, often only partly dressed, together with their products..

Evil men well know the power of sexually explicit material and the weakness of men in particular to this kind of temptation, so they purposely produce it to make money. Along with illegal drugs, pornography is one of the biggest money-making businesses in the world today. In the United States alone, pornography is an 8 BILLION dollar per year business.[2] In a detailed study and investigation held in the United States in 1985, it was found that more than 85 percent of all commercially produced pornographic material in America was controlled by organized criminals. [3]

Pornography is also one of the most powerful addictions known to man. In 1985 and 1986, the United States Attorney General's Office held ten days of hearings on pornography. Many of the people giving testimony for these hearings were individuals whose lives had been destroyed through addiction to pornography.

Three thousand pages of testimony were included in the U.S. Government report. These testimonies prove beyond any doubt the extremely addictive power of pornography and its power to destroy marriages and families as well as human lives. It has been found that the majority of all convicted rapists have admitted to the use of pornographic material. Even more frightening, rapists have admitted to getting many of their ideas from the pornographic materials they have used. [4] A few testimonies from these hearings are given here to illustrate the great destructive power of pornography. The first two testimonies relate to the power of pornography as an addiction.

"I am a successful professional man, a management level employee with a large corporation . . . I have been a pornography addict for more than forty years. I was not born with this addiction. I was introduced to it at the age of nine." (There follows a graphic description of how another man led this man into pornography as a young boy) The man's testimony continues, "In addition to my sexual dependency on pornography at age 22, I began to experience problems with social behavior . . . There were periods when I was unable to concentrate my thoughts on anything other than mental images of sexually explicit material. . . . Over a three-year period I managed to collect more than 200 books, magazines and films."

This man concluded his testimony saying, "To be held in bondage to pornography is a terrible thing for a person to live with; and its grasp on people's lives extends to all levels of society-from truck drivers to ministers, judges and political leaders. . . . There are thousands, perhaps millions, of men and women just like me who have been enslaved by sexually explicit material, and their numbers continue to grow with the increasing availability of x-rated video cassettes. . . ." [5]

Another man gave the following testimony: "I do not believe males or females can watch this (pornography) . . . for long and ever expect to . . . form a normal sexual relationship with another person. . . . Today, at the age of forty-eight, with four children . . . I still struggle daily with the images, the thoughts, the yearnings, the lusts cultivated during those years of self indulgence in pornography. They are permanently embedded in my being. . . .The thoughts daily affect my relationship with my wife, my daughters and women with whom I come in contact, even in my church. I do not need expensive studies and educated experts to link involvement with pornography to the tremendous deterioration of family life and marriage breakdown in our land today." [6]

The testimony of the people in this report is a chilling reminder of the terribly destructive power of sexually explicit material on those who see it or read it. One additional testimony is given to illustrate the way in which pornography can ruin a person's soul and totally destroy a marriage.

"For more than thirty years I watched pornography destroy our marriage. . . . This obsession and addiction did not enrich our sex life. It robbed me of a loving relationship. . . . The hours spent with pornography definitely had an impact on our children. They did not view our family environment as being normal, even though they were not aware of his addiction. They were shocked when we announced plans of a divorce. They were all grown and in college." This former wife concluded her story by saying . . . "He was drawn to pornography even though I offered him a loving relationship and enjoyed sex with him before his involvement with pornography . . . I know for a fact that pornography destroyed our marriage." [7]

These testimonies are included because western video is making a great invasion in Africa today. Even though some of it is not openly evil, the overall effect is much worse than we may think. In many urban centers today, video stores are doing a big business. It is an easy matter to rent videos which have the morally destructive power of an atomic bomb. In these cities, the increase of sexual immorality, the increase in divorce and broken homes and the increase of rape are plain evidence of the power of pornography to destroy all that is good in God-given male-female relationships.

Western video is one of the most morally destructive force in African cities today. It is certainly one of the biggest reasons for the downfall of the family and the great increase in divorce in the West. Watching video or looking at pornography on the internet is an especially dangerous form of temptation because it can be done at home privately and in a seemingly harmless environment. The availability of pornography on the internet is one of the greatest curses of Satan in the twenty first century. Many, many Christian young men have become addicted to pornography by the internet.

Certain Muslim governments in the world have recognized the evil of this corruption from the West. To their great credit, they have forbidden the importation of western videos into their countries. If a Christian is to avoid being overcome by these temptations in modern Africa, he or she must actively refuse to watch those videos or to go to those places where sexually explicit material is available. The most morally dangerous places for a person today may well be a commercial video rental shop or a computer cyber café.

Youth are the most vulnerable to this kind of suggestion because of their recent physical maturity and accompanying strong sexual desires along with their curiosity about sex. A study done in the U.S. on 100 males and 100 females in the age range of 19 - 39 years old revealed the following statistics.

1. 91 percent of males and 82 percent of females had seen a magazine which depicted couples or groups engaging in sexual acts.
2. The average age of first exposure was 13.5 years.
3. A larger percentage of high school students had seen X-rated films than any other age group, including adults. [8]

It is hard to imagine the morally destructive effect that this kind of material has on the minds of young people. The effects are now being seen in Africa in the enormous increase of sexual immorality before marriage. A direct result of this has been the great increase in marriage and family breakdown. Another direct result has been the spread of sexually transmitted diseases (STD's) on a scale never experienced before.

The most frightening trend has been the change in moral values held by young people today compared with values held 40 - 50 years ago. A survey in 1985 in the United States found that 78 percent of young people between the ages of 18 and 29 believed there was nothing wrong with having sex before marriage.[9] This survey concluded that as a consequence of holding these values, "young people are paying the price for the recent sexual revolution which promised joy, liberation and good health but in fact delivered misery, disease and even death." [10]

Here were some of the results of this change in values among young people in the United States by the year 1985.

1. By age twenty, 81 percent of unmarried males and 67 percent of unmarried females had experienced sexual intercourse. [11]
2. A New York polling firm reported that 57 percent of high school students and 79 percent of college students had lost their virginity.[12]
3. For comparison, the researcher Alfred Kinsey reported that in the late 1940's only 3 percent of unmarried females had lost their virginity by age 16.[13] These statistics reflect a drastic change in values in the United States from the 1940's to the 1980's.
4. From 1965 to 1985 the percentage of illegitimate births to women 19 years of age and younger had increased from 15 percent to 51 percent. [14]
5. In 1984, 1,100,000 girls in the U.S. became pregnant out of wedlock. Of these pregnancies, over one third (about 400,000) ended in abortion, a 100 percent increase since 1972. [15]
7. Six years after 1984, a 1990 study by the U.S. Center For Disease Control and Prevention found that 75 percent of high school students admitted to having sex before they graduated from high school (as compared to 57 percent in 1984) and 40 percent said they were not virgins by the ninth grade. [16]

These facts have a sober and fearful warning for modern Africa. As people in Africa increasingly adopt western culture, values and especially video entertainment, it is certain that the moral death of the West is going to poison African life more and more.

THE CURE FOR THE CANCER OF PORNOGRAPHY: WHAT CAN BE DONE?

Many men and women in the West have been destroyed through the power of pornographic magazines, pictures, films and stories as indicated in the 3000 pages of testimony in the U.S. Attorney General's report mentioned above. A strategy for sexual purity was suggested at the end of chapter 5. The most important parts of this strategy are (1) Prayer (2) Rigidly guarding what we allow our eyes to see and (3) Physically leaving the place where temptation exists.

If a Christian is to avoid severe temptation, he or she must positively refuse to watch certain videos, attend certain cinemas or read those books and magazines with sexually exciting pictures or stories which inflame the mind and imagination. Christians must resolve before the Lord to forbid their eyes to look at such material. In addition, a Christian must refuse to go to those places where pornography can be seen.

The destructive power and easy availability of sexually explicit material is so great today that a person has to decide in advance how he or she is going to refuse this kind of temptation before it happens. When temptation comes, it may only be a matter of seconds before a person's eyes are caught. A Christian must understand that this kind of temptation is truly deadly poison which has the power to destroy individuals, marriages and whole nations. The battle will be won or lost in the first few seconds of exposure to such material. Either the person learns to say "absolutely no" to pornographic material or the person will be overpowered by this temptation as the true testimonies given above bear witness. There are many other tragic testimonies of church leaders who have been caught and destroyed by this powerful poison.

What about pornography in the society at large? Can anything be done? The answer is that more can be done than most people think. In the West, there have been a few courageous Christians who have worked hard through legal means to have pornography shops shut down or put out of business in their community. Other courageous Christians have worked through the parliament or legislature in their State or National government to pass laws which stop the distribution and sale of this kind of material. These efforts are hard work and they take a lot of prayer and cooperation among Christians from different denominations working together. With prayer Christians can succeed in publically fighting pornography because they are fighting against something which God also hates (1 Thess. 4:3-5). This is the kind of prayer and action that God has promised to answer and bless. Jesus taught us that through prayer we can cause the will of God to be done on earth as it is done in heaven (Matt. 6:10). Christians must pray, believe God, and act decisively if this great evil is to be stopped.

SEXUALLY TRANSMITTED DISEASES (STD'S)

If sexual sin with its terrible consequences is possible by those who follow the Lord, who can predict what is possible in a world of people who have no fear of God and no personal relationship with Him? The news is full of stories about sexual immorality, adultery, sexual abuse and rape almost every day, recently including even a president of the United States.

These sins have been present since human beings have been on earth but they are now reaching epidemic proportions, tearing apart families, homes and individuals. One specific result of such sins is that they have created an epidemic of sexually transmitted diseases (STD's). STD's are increasing in number and severity at an alarming rate each year. More young people are presently being infected by STD's each year than were stricken with polio during the entire epidemic of 1942 - 1953. [17]

Worldwide, the number and kind of STD's has dramatically increased in the past 35 years from five kinds in 1960 to more than 27 today.[18] Forty years ago the two primary STD's were gonorrhea and syphilis. In the early stages, each of these diseases can be treated with medicine. Some of the more recent STD's, including AIDS, cannot be cured with any medicine. An example of a recent incurable STD is the genital herpes virus. This disease causes severe pain and is a bitter reminder of the results of sin.

Among the STD's, none is more feared by most people than Acquired Immune Deficiency Syndrome (AIDS) caused by the Human Immunodeficiency Virus (HIV). There has been so much talk about the AIDS epidemic that many people have become confused. Although it is indeed possible for AIDS to be transmitted through infected blood transfusions and contaminated injection syringes, these two forms of transmission of the disease still only account for less than 5% of all cases of AIDS.[19] Besides this, governments are taking steps to eliminate HIV infection through blood testing programs in hospitals and rigid insistence on the use of sterilized syringes.

AIDS is also transmitted from pregnant mothers to their infants in the womb. The mother must have the disease herself for this to happen. But how did the mother get AIDS? The truth is that well over 90% off all AIDS is still originally transmitted through sexual sin. When people refuse to obey God, they must take the consequences of their actions. AIDS is the most widely known example of this fact. For the disease to spread, a person must have had sexual contact with an HIV infected person, except in the infrequent cases of contact with infected blood or syringes.

THE CURE FOR AIDS

AIDS is not a threat to normal sexual relations between a husband and wife who have kept themselves pure before and during marriage. The same can be said about contacting other STD's. If two people have remained without other sexual partners before and during their marriage as God commands that they should, the possibility of being infected with AIDS is left to infected blood or syringes. With care, these causes can be controlled or eliminated. This leaves a person who is the child of an AIDS infected mother as the only potentially innocent victim of the disease.

The projections for the number of cases of AIDS by the year 2000 A.D. are shocking. By 2010 A.D. AIDS will be the major cause of death in Africa.[20] By 1993, the following percentages of pregnant women were already infected with AIDS in various cities: In Lilongwe, 32 percent of pregnant women, In Kigali, 32 percent, in Kampala, 30 percent, in Lusaka, 25 percent, in Nairobi, 22 percent and in Harare, 20 percent. [21]

The reality is this: The more infected people there are, the more chances there are that taking part in sex outside of monogamous, virgin marriage will produce HIV infection. As the infection spreads and the number of infected partners increases, the possibility of infection and death from AIDS increases in every new act of sexual sin.

As a solution, most governments are recommending the use of condoms with sexual partners. However, as medical professionals know, condoms are not completely safe. Beyond that, many men refuse to use condoms. In plain language, teaching people to use condoms is not going to stop the AIDS epidemic. The only real protection from AIDS is complete sexual abstinence before marriage and complete faithfulness to one's marriage partner after marriage.

As if this news was not bad enough, most people are not aware of another AIDS-related danger in sexual sin. The medical fact is that if one of the partners has an STD other than AIDS, research has shown that it is much more likely that the person with the other STD will also be infected with AIDS if his or her partner has AIDS.[22]

As with every evil in this world, there is a way out, but it is God's way, not man's way. The only way the AIDS epidemic will be stopped is through a radical change of behavior. People must return to God's standard of virgin sexual purity before marriage and complete faithfulness after marriage, along with taking precautions about blood and syringes. Testing can be done to determine if mothers are infected with HIV. Drugs are also being developed which hold the possibility of protecting unborn infants in the mother's womb from the infection of the mother. The AIDS epidemic and the epidemic of other STD's can be stopped. The solution is widespread repentance from sexual sin and a return to God's standards for sexual behavior. No man-made solution is going to stop this epidemic. In addition, churches should require young people planning to marry to produce a very recent, valid medical certificate (less than two weeks old) that they are HIV negative.

ABORTION

Another worldwide epidemic of evil that has resulted from the great increase of sexual immorality has been the increase in the number of abortions. Abortion is the ending of a human life in the womb of the mother. Many different methods are used to perform abortions. In many places abortion is being practiced as a means of birth control. As King David added sin upon sin by arranging for the death of the husband of Bathsheba, those who practice abortion add sin upon sin when they add the murder of unborn babies to their sin of sexual immorality.

The Washington Post newspaper of January 23, 1983 in the United States, stated that "one in four pregnancies (in America) now ends in abortion, making it one of the nation's most commonly performed surgical procedures." If that was true in 1983, what must be true in the sexually immoral world at the beginning of the twenty-first century?

Since 1970, there have been more than 40 million abortions in the United States.

What does God think about life in the womb? Let us find out by reading what the Bible says. "This is what the LORD says -- your Redeemer, who formed you in the womb: I am the LORD, who has made all things " (Isa. 44:24). "For you created my inmost being; you knit me together in my mother's womb. I praise you because I am fearfully and wonderfully made; your works are wonderful . . . your eyes saw my unformed body" (Psalm 139:13-16).

These verses make it clear that God is very much concerned with and very actively involved with the formation of a new human being in the womb of a mother. For those who doubt that the unborn are persons, it should be observed in these verses how the Psalmist, by the inspiration of the Holy Spirit, refers to his life in the womb with the personal pronouns "I," "me" and "my." His body was not fully formed but that did not mean that he was not a person. The Holy Spirit is a person although He does not have a body.

Some people believe that human life and personhood do not begin until birth. This view cannot be supported either from science or the Bible. A baby in the womb is very much alive physically, mentally and emotionally as repeated experiments have proven. Babies are influenced both mentally and emotionally while in the womb. Before birth the baby gets its oxygen and food supply from the mother through the umbilical cord. However, the physical, mental and emotional functions of the baby are very much those of a living person. Birth only changes the environment in which the baby lives and the means by which he or she receives the essentials of life.

The genetic code which determines what every new human being will be is fixed for life at the moment of conception. These genetic characteristics, both physical, mental and emotional, continue throughout the person's life, being modified only by the environment. A totally new and unique individual is formed at the moment of conception. Body parts, including brain cells, become differentiated after just a few weeks of pregnancy. Bodily movements begin some months after this.

The testimony of the Bible is the same as science. God revealed through the angel Gabriel that John the Baptist had been, "filled with the Holy Spirit while yet in his mother's womb" (Luke 1:15 - NASB literal Greek translation). This clearly shows that John had spiritual life while he was in his mother's womb. The Bible says, "Surely I was sinful . . . from the time my mother conceived me" (Psalm 51:5), showing that from God's perspective, moral and spiritual life begin at conception and not at some later time. Concerning the prophet Jeremiah, God said, "before you were born I set you apart; I appointed you as a prophet to the nations" (Jeremiah 1:5).

Some people question the statement that abortion is the murder of a human being. The question of when human life begins is still vigorously debated. The real answer to this question has to do with the definition of life. The fact that a baby is inside the mother's body rather than outside her body has nothing to do with the presence of a human life. A baby is just as much a human being one day before birth as one day after birth. A baby may be born after 6, 7, or 8 months and still live to be a healthy adult provided there is medical help available for premature birth. Some babies are born even earlier than 6 months and physically survive in today's medical world.

The fact that a human life in the womb at two months is not as fully formed as a baby two months after birth is not an argument about life. It is a discussion about human growth and development. Does a child of 15 years old have more human life than a child of 2 years old? Life is a gift from God, whether it is life at 3 months in the womb or life at 30 years in the home.

THE JUDGEMENT OF GOD ON THOSE WHO PERFORM ABORTIONS

What does God think about those who perform abortions? First, here is what God says about shedding human blood in general. "For your lifeblood I will surely demand an accounting. . . Whoever sheds the blood of man, by man shall his blood be shed for in the image of God has God made man" (Gen. 9:5-6). Concerning an innocent person, here is what God says. "Do not put an innocent or honest person to death, for I will not acquit the guilty" (Ex. 23:7). "'Cursed be he that taketh reward to slay an innocent person" (Deut. 27:25-KJV). "But your eyes and your heart are intent only upon your own dishonest gain, and on shedding innocent blood" (Jer. 22:17 - NASB) "On your clothes men find the lifeblood of the innocent . . . Yet in spite of all this you say, 'I am innocent; he is not angry with me.' But I will pass judgment on you because you say, 'I have not sinned.' " (Jeremiah 2:34-35).

Humanly speaking, who is more innocent than an unborn baby? The man or woman who kills human life in the womb is sinning against God, the giver of life. That is the crime of murder. According to these verses, there are a large number of abortionists in the world who face a murder trial before God.

Here are some additional statements about those who shed innocent blood, especially the blood of children and babies. "They shed innocent blood, the blood of their sons and daughters, . . .and the land was desecrated by their blood. They defiled themselves by what they did" (Psalm 106:38). There are six things the LORD hates, seven that are detestable to him: haughty eyes, a lying tongue, hands that shed innocent blood" (Prov. 6:16-17). "This is what the LORD says: "For three sins of Ammon, even for four, I will not turn back my wrath. Because he ripped open the pregnant women of Gilead in order to extend his borders" (Amos 1:13).

In the West today, there is considerable argument made that a woman has some sort of legal "right" over the baby in her body.

On this argument, it is assumed that she has a "legal right" to end the life of her baby, if she chooses to do it. It is upon this argument that abortion has been made legal in the United States and in many European countries. This argument is both legally wrong and morally wrong. It simply reveals the sinfulness of the human heart.

First, the argument of the "legal right of the mother" is inconsistent and legally wrong. Just because the baby is inside the mother's womb does not give the mother a legal right to end the life of another human being. She certainly does not have the right to kill another person who just happens to be in her presence. A baby in the womb is another person. Its nutrition comes from the mother, but the baby is not the mother and the mother is not the baby. They are separate persons. If a woman was to kill a baby in a crib in her living room she would be charged with murder. In countries around the world, people do not have the legal right to kill other people just because they decide they want to end the life of that person. If they do, they are charged with murder. Hence abortion is murder by the very definition of murder.

Second, abortion is morally wrong. Murder is murder, wherever the crime takes place. Location is not the issue. The taking of human life is the issue. If a person kills a person in a house, in a field, in a car, or wherever, the person who commits the crime is charged with murder by every civilized government in the world. How then can it be considered less than murder to take the life of a person who happens to be inside a mother's womb?

The crime of murder is made much more serious and evil in the eyes of both God and man when a person takes the life of another person who is innocent, harmless or helpless, which is the case of every baby in a mother's womb. The Bible says, "You shall not murder" (Exodus 20:13). Human governments say the same and charge those who purposely take human life with the crime of murder. How then can willful abortion carried out by human beings be less than murder? This is a serious crime in the eyes of God. If God is holy and just, at some point He is going to demand a judgment on those who have performed abortions.

For those girls who have submitted to abortion and those who have performed abortions, there is good news in the gospel of Christ. God will forgive this and all other sins when there is true repentance (Matt. 12:31a, 1 John 1:9) Jesus came for the very purpose of forgiving and saving sinners (Luke 5:32).

WHAT CAN CHRISTIANS DO ABOUT ABORTION?

What is the solution to the growth of abortion as a practice? There is probably no solution apart from the action of God's people as recommended under the heading of pornography. If a nation's government makes this practice legal, the practice of abortion will continue to grow. The only solution is for the people of God to fast and pray, and then to rise up together and to demand that the government make laws against this evil practice.

Since there is such a great difference of opinion on this subject among different groups of people, the whole people of God from all denominations must determine to come together as one body when they present their case to the government. Even this will probably not succeed without strong prayer and fasting, because Satan himself (a murderer from the beginning (John 8:44) is the one behind this practice. God can work if His people will pray, fast and act. But they must act with determination and with the utmost cooperation and unity. It took a lifetime of prayer and hard work before the efforts of William Wilburforce in England resulted in the legal abolition of human slavery as a practice, but God finally gave this man and his associates success.

PROSTITUTION

Prostitution is sometimes called the oldest profession in the world. Over 3000 years ago, a prostitute named Rahab made the front page in the history of God's people (Josh. 2:1-21). Today, with the increase of poverty in Africa and with the decline of biblical values in relation to sex, prostitution is growing rapidly, especially in the cities. Although there have always been prostitutes, the present increase of this evil practice is based more on economics than on changing moral values. With no way to survive in a hostile urban environment, the only thing many girls can do to make money to pay for food, clothing and rent is to sell the use of their bodies for sex. Young girls come to the city and are offered money, food, housing and clothing by men who operate houses of prostitution. Little do these young girls realize the horrible life that is before them.

Prostitution is one of the more important social evils of modernity in Africa. Through prostitution the moral, spiritual, social and physical lives of men and women are degraded to zero. The growth of prostitution has the potential to destroy young people in the present and their marriages in the future. Through prostitution, STD's in general and AIDS in particular have become the scourge of the city and the scourge of Africa. It is an evil that must be addressed.

Statistics alone do not communicate the personal tragedy in the life of each girl who has been trapped by this vicious form of selfish indulgence by men with money. If we understand how prostitution usually comes about as a result of economic desperation to survive, we will get an important clue as to how to confront this evil in the cities. The following true story will help us understand how girls get into prostitution and how they can be rescued from it by the love of God and the commitment of His people.

Rebecca had an emotionally painful childhood. Her father and mother were divorced and her mother had remarried. There was a lot of tension in the home. Rebecca left home at the age of sixteen because she could not get along with her step- father, step-brothers and step-sisters. Because she had no real brothers and sisters she had to live alone after she left home. She was a high school drop-out. She had no money, no possessions and no job skill. She had no one she could turn to for help. She turned to prostitution as a way to survive on her own. She began to make a good bit of money from her "work."

During her years of living from prostitution Rebecca experienced many ugly things at the hands of evil men. She hated her life, but she did well financially because the men who used her paid her well. One night after she had been in prostitution for three years she had an experience which thoroughly frightened her. A man picked her up and took her for a ride in his car. He gave her a piece of fruit to eat. From that time until the next morning she could remember nothing. She woke up the next morning in a strange old house in a forest far from town. There was no one in the house. She ran from the house in panic and followed a dirt road until she came to a main road and was able to get back to town. She realized that she had been drugged so that she could be used in a Satanic ritual. She began to think about her life and realized that her way of "survival" might actually cost her very life. But there was no one to turn to for help.

Out of fear, she went to stay with another girl who was also a prostitute. The other girl had been contacted on the street by some Christian girls in the city who went out on the street one night a week to share the love of God with the girls they met. The Christian girls often came to visit the girls they had befriended. One day some of the Christian girls came to visit the girl Rebecca was living with and Rebecca met them. The Christian girls began to share with Rebecca how God loved her and wanted to forgive her sin and give her a new life. A few days later the Christian girls were visiting some other girls in the same "work" who were living nearby. Rebecca heard about it and went over to hear more of what the Christian girls had to say. At the end of the discussion, Rebecca asked the Christian girls how she could find God's forgiveness in her own life. The eagerness on her face was very evident.

The Christian girls operated a vocational training and rehabilitation center in the city. Rebecca asked if she could join the training. She realized it was the only way out of the life in which she was trapped. She worked hard at the training but years of living in harsh and difficult surroundings made it hard for her to get along with other people. She was stubborn, hardened and hot-tempered.

One day she became seriously sick. Another girl called one of the Christian ladies who was helping to rehabilitate Rebecca. Rebecca was in critical condition. She had lost 6 pints of blood because of an ectopic pregnancy. The Christian lady and her husband scoured the city and found some other Christians who were wiling to donate blood. She had surgery and her life was saved.

Seeing how much God really loved her through people who were strangers to her deeply touched Rebecca's heart. She began to understand that God's love was real (through God's people) and not just words. Even her own parents had not been willing to give her blood in her time of need. This experience brought a very great change in Rebecca's attitudes and values. She truly repented of the life and behavior in which she had been living. She decided that she would serve God herself in helping to rescue other girls from the street.

From that time to the present, Rebecca has become a partner in reaching out to street girls along with the Christian girls she first met. Although she is still young, she has become a real person of prayer with a great burden for other girls trapped as she was, especially the young ones who are forced into prostitution by necessity as she had been. The Lord has even begun to soften her heart and change her character from the hardness, stubbornness, and hot temper of her former life. Rebecca has learned that the living God is a God of forgiveness and a God of deliverance. She has also learned that God's love is expressed through His own people who reach out in love to others.

God can do the same for a multitude of other girls trapped in the same ugly life but it will take the love and commitment of other Christians who are willing to reach out to these unwanted and despised girls with practical evidence of the love of God. It will be of value here to relate how God first touched the heart of one of the Christian girls who originally spoke to Rebecca after she had moved in with the other prostitute.

Serawit was born and grew up in a middle class Christian family. Her parents loved and cared for her. She was secure in her parents' love and in the love of God. Serawit's parents encouraged her to be the very most she could be in life. The importance of education was taught to her from early childhood.

Eventually Serawit was able to attend the national university in her country. She majored in economics. When she graduated she was full of energy and enthusiasm about her future life. However, about that time the government went through a difficult time which created concern for everyone. During this time Serawit became involved in a discipleship training program and became part of a very active church.

Late one evening driving home from a dinner party with some of her family, Serawit saw something happen that made an impression on her heart and began a process in her life that lead to a ministry among street girls. A girl on the street with a very short skirt started running toward her car. For a few seconds Serawit and her family were confused but then they realized that the girl in the short skirt was trying to get the attention of the car behind their car which had a lone male driver. The man drove past the girl but the girl ran after him calling to the man.

At that moment, the whole tragedy of prostitution suddenly came into sharp focus for Serawit. She began thinking about her own secure, protected life and family relationships. She thought about her B.A. degree and her certainty of finding a good paying job with all her needs fully met. But what about this pathetic young girl on the street, trying to survive with the only thing she possessed - being a female? What could such girls hope for? What could they live for? What degrading experience would this young girl have to endure this very night with some gross, evil-minded man? As a female herself, Serawit wondered how these street girls must hate themselves. She thought about how they have to literally destroy their lives just to "survive" for a few more months or years. [Note: The highest percentage of AIDS (80 to 90 percent) is found among "commercial sex workers"][23]

Sometime later Serawit got a job with a Christian agency and enjoyed her work very much. The incident with the street girl did not leave her mind. She found herself praying that God would do something to rescue these pathetic young girls. She prayed that God would send some mature Christian girl with a deep knowledge of the Bible to help them find God's forgiveness and love. Serawit realized this would be a difficult prayer to answer. In addition to spiritual maturity, such a person would have to enlist the means to give these girls training to earn a living in an honorable way if they were to be permanently delivered from their hopeless way of life. That would be no small matter. Serawit felt she had none of the qualifications or resources needed to ever attempt such a ministry herself. Little did she realize that God intended to use Serawit herself to answer her own prayer.

One day Serawit shared her burden and concern for these pathetic street girls with the people in her discipleship Bible study group. The group began to pray about it. A friend in the group offered a suggestion that made Serawit think. Instead of being overwhelmed with the need of the estimated 10,000 prostitutes in the city, why not ask the Lord to open up an opportunity to contact and build a relationship with just one of them and then to love and pray that girl into a new life in Christ? As Serawit considered this idea over the next few days, the Lord brought her into contact with another Christian girl and her husband with the same burden and concern. Together Serawit and the other couple began to read articles and statistics about prostitution in their city and to talk to others who knew something about the situation.

As the three of them talked the matter over and prayed about it, the Lord gave them the courage and the will to go out onto the street together to seek to make contact with just a few girls. The other girl's husband promised to pray the whole time the girls were out on the street so that the Lord would lead them to the ones He had prepared. They also enlisted others to pray. On December 13, 1994 the two very nervous Christian girls made their first attempt to contact girls on the street as others prayed. God began to work. Relationships were built. Trust was established. But it was very hard.

Often the two girls would come home after an evening on the streets frustrated, discouraged and overwhelmed by what they would hear from the street girls. The world of street girls was an ugly, evil place. Some of the girls would indicate a desire to change but then the two Christian girls would find them back on the streets again a few weeks later. The two Christian girls realized that without serious occupational rehabilitation, there would be no lasting change. The street girls could make more money in one night from prostitution than they could in two weeks at any kind of casual jobs they might be able to find. Serawit and her friends cried out to the Lord for His help. In spite of their great difficulties, the Christian girls saw the Lord begin to touch the lives of a few girls through their love. Rebecca was one of these girls.

Then one day Serawit and her friend discovered how much God Himself cared about the street girls. They received word that a Christian foundation in another country had heard of their small efforts and was offering a grant of money to establish a vocational rehabilitation center for the girls! Now they could truly offer the girls a practical way out of their miserable lives. Slowly God has been answering their prayers. One by one, girls whose lives have been destroyed by circumstances and sin are being put back together by the love of God expressed through His people.

Even more important than the money they received to build a rehabilitation center, Serawit and her friends now realize that the key to success in this difficult ministry is the dedicated Christian partners in ministry God has given them as well as the many people committed to pray for them.

[Note: If you would like more information about this ministry or would like to be a help in some way, you can contact SIM Urban Ministries, P.O. Box 127, Addis Ababa, Ethiopia, or a similar ministry in West Africa called Evangelical Services Team, PMB 2009 Jos, Plateau State, Nigeria.]

SUMMARY

Modernity and the wholesale acceptance of western entertainment and values has brought some truly horrible problems to the cities of Africa. Such things as pornography, sexually transmitted diseases, abortion and prostitution have a grim power to destroy all that is good in families and in God-given male female relationships. These things are problems which will not go away apart from the intervention of God and His people. Human governments do not have the will or the moral and spiritual resources to solve such problems. Only God and His people on earth can bring about lasting change.

God is able to overcome these problems - but He chooses to overcome them through the intervention and involvement of His own people. The Church is the Body of Christ. The people of God are the hands, the feet and the heart of Christ for people who are trapped by the ugly sins of modernity. If God's people do not respond to His call to help others, there is a very grim future coming. It takes courage, faith, prayer and commitment to see God's deliverance take place. But the God who raises the dead is able to do "exceeding abundantly beyond all that we ask or think, according to the power that works within us" (Eph. 3:20). The question is, are we willing to let Him demonstrate His love and compassion through us and to allow Him to do the impossible?

QUESTIONS FOR REVIEW, REFLECTION AND GROUP DISCUSSION

1. What is the outcome of using pornography, in the lives of those who use it?
2. How does impure television and video contribute to the breakdown of the family?
3. What steps can the Christian community take to reduce the presence of pornographic material in the society?
4. Why have sexually transmitted diseases increased so much in the past 40 years?
5. What action could a group of Christians or a group of local churches take to help girls who have had an abortion or feel they must have an abortion?
6. What is the main reason why prostitution is on the increase in Africa?
7. What action could a local church or a group of committed Christians take, to help rescue prostitutes from their destructive way of life?

END NOTES

1. Bender, David and Bruno Leone. Sexual Values - Opposing Viewpoints. San Diego: Greenhaven Press pp. 139 - 144
2. Minnery, Tom. Ed. Pornography, A Human Tragedy. Wheaton, Illinois: Tyndale House, 1986. p. 31
3. Ibid. p. 40
4. Ibid. p. 39
5. Schlafly, Phyllis, Ed. Pornography's Victims. Westchester, Illinois: Crossway Books, pp. 160 - 165
6. Ibid. pp. 145 - 147
7. Ibid. pp. 86 - 89
8. Minnery, Tom, Ed. Pornography, A Human Tragedy. Wheaton, Illinois: Tyndale House, 1986. p. 42 - 44.
9. Mark, Allandra, and Mark, Vernon H. Medical World News. April 8, 1985. p. 156.

10. Ibid.
11. Teenage Pregnancy: The Problem That Hasn't Gone Away. New York: Guttmacher Institute, 1981.
12. Van Biema, David. "What's Gone Wrong With Teen Age Sex?" People, April 13, 1987, p. 112.
13. Kinsey, Alfred C. et. al. Sexual Behavior In The Human Male. Philadelphia: W. B. Saunders Co. 1948.

    Kinsey, Alfred C. et. al. Sexual Behavior In The Human Female. Philadelphia: W. B. Saunders Co. 1953.
14. Baldwin, Wendy. Adolescent Pregnancy and Childrearing - Rates, Trends and Research Findings. Bethesda, Maryland: NICHD, 1985.
15. Problems Born Of Teen-age Sex. Orlando Sentinel, January 31, 1987. p. E4
16. Bender David and Bruno Leone. Sexual Values - Opposing Viewpoints. San Diego, Greenhaven Press, 1995. p. 260
17. Ibid. p 41
18. Goldsmith, Marsha. Sexually Transmitted Diseases May Reverse The "Revolution" Medical News And Perspectives, 255 (April 4, 1986) p. 1665
19. Ethiopia Ministry of Health. AIDS In Ethiopia: Background, Projections, Impacts, Interventions. Government Publication, 1996. p. 6
20. Ibid. p. 17
21. Ibid. p.16
22. Ibid. p. 9
23. Ibid. p. 8

CHAPTER 7

MONEY: A GREAT EVIL OR A GREAT ENCOURAGEMENT?

John was a leader in his local church. He was respected by the church community. There was a need in John's area for agricultural development. A man representing a Christian relief agency for development visited John's church and felt that his organization could be a big help with the development needs of the area. A plan was created for development assistance over a period of 5 years. Everyone in the church was very excited about the plan. The man from the relief agency requested that someone in the church be selected to manage the development scheme. John was selected by the church.

The development projects were discussed by the church leaders and a 5 year plan was created which would benefit the whole area and increase the visibility of the local church as a helping community. Projects were begun and people were assigned various responsibilities in these projects. As promised, funds began to come from the relief agency. John, a man who had a salary of $150/month, was now responsible to manage over $500,000 per year. As supervisor, John was responsible for these funds and the final person to make decisions.

In the first year of the project things seemed to go well and everyone was satisfied. In the second year of the plan people in the church noticed that John began to change the supervisors on various projects. Some people observed that the new supervisors were all related to John's extended family in some way. The church members also observed that the newly appointed supervisors were becoming quite wealthy. Each one was building a new, large house for his family. Most of them were buying new cars, buses, grinding mills and other expensive equipment. They became abusive and impatient with the workers on their projects.

When John was asked about this he said that changes were needed to make the management of the projects run more smoothly. John became distant from the other church members. He became defensive when people questioned him about what was going on. After a while, the church elders requested a formal inquiry and audit of the whole development program. John strongly resisted this and refused to cooperate. Finally the church brought strong pressure to bear and an audit was scheduled. But on the day the audit was scheduled to begin none of John's appointed managers could be found. Each one had found an excuse to be absent. The audit was never carried out. The supervisors became more and more corrupt, getting into sexual immorality, drunkenness and stealing money and materials from the projects. The supervisors found ways to alter the records of their projects to cover up their stealing.

The matter became a hot controversy in the church, splitting the church into two factions. One faction consisted of those related to John or appointed by John to leadership in the projects. The other faction represented the rest of the congregation. Soon very hot words were being spoken and accusations were being made by both groups. The church split into two groups with each group trying to take legal action against the other. There was bitterness, resentment, and hot anger. The local church became a place of mockery to the rest of the community and completely lost its witness for Christ. All that was left were two groups of very angry, bitter people. While this was going on John made several trips out of the country to talk with representatives of the funding agency but the local church was never given an accounting of any of his trips or an opportunity to speak to the funding agency themselves. In the end, there were even death threats on both sides.

This tragic but true story directs our attention to one of the greatest challenges facing the church in modern Africa - namely, the responsible and wise use of money. Everyone knows that money is needed for many things and that many churches and groups of people in Africa have little money to accomplish the good they want to do. But that is not the end of the story. There is a God who can multiply the gifts given to Him by His people in such a way that miracles of provision for the Lord's work can happen. In this chapter we will look into how that can be done.

Unfortunately, money also brings one of the strongest temptations to sin in life. The Bible warns us about the destructive power of the love of money in the strongest possible language. The apostle Paul wrote, "People who want to get rich fall into temptation and a trap and into many foolish and harmful desires that plunge men into ruin and destruction. For the love of money is a root of all kinds of evil" (1 Tim. 6:9-10). In the true story above, a leader of the church was "plunged into ruin and destruction" by the love of money. Beyond that, the testimony and witness of the local church of which he was a part was totally destroyed. Let no one reading this think that the Bible has exaggerated the deadly power of the love of money.

Someone once asked the richest man in the world how much money was enough. With a little smile the man replied, "a little more." So it is with money, sex and power. Our desires are never satisfied. There is always something more we want or think we need to have.

Those who are consumed by the love of money have made money into a god. A god is something in which we put our hope or trust to help us in time of need. Thus money becomes a god in place of the true and living God because we trust in money instead of trusting in God to meet our needs. The Word of God warns people, "to put their hope in God, who richly provides us with everything for our enjoyment" rather than putting their trust in the uncertainty of money (1 Tim. 6:17).

This is what happened in the true story above. John had broken the first of the ten commandments (Exodus 20: 3) by making money his god. He had put another god, the god of money, before the true and living God and the god of money possessed him and destroyed him. Long ago Jesus warned His followers about this deadly false god when He said, "No one can serve two masters. Either he will hate the one and love the other, or he will be devoted to the one and despise the other. You cannot serve both God and Money" (Matt. 6:24).

At the time of giving the ten commandments, God added these words in reference to silver and gold: "Do not make any gods to be alongside me; do not make for yourselves gods of silver or gods of gold" (Exodus 20:23). The Lord said these words with good reason. Many Christians have lost their close relationship with God and have fallen into sin and disgrace through worshipping the gods of silver and gold.

Money has the power to do great harm when it is used in the wrong way. A large number of murders which take place in the world are related to the love of money. In the United States, it is estimated that as many as 75% of all murders are related to illegal drug traffic in some way. This drug traffic is directly related to the love of money because the selling of illegal drugs is one of the largest money-making businesses in the world.

Jesus said a lot about money, both the danger in it and the blessing possible through using money in the right way. We need to understand that money in and of itself is nether good or evil. It is simply paper, metal or other material which represents an accepted means of exchange for goods or services in a particular culture. It is needed for most things in the ordinary business of life.

Money also has the power to do great good to help people and to advance the kingdom of God. Money can be a great encouragement to the work of the Lord. Think about the following statement by the apostle Paul, inspired by the Holy Spirit: "Whoever sows sparingly will also reap sparingly, and whoever sows generously will also reap generously." (2 Cor. 9:6) Paul then goes on to say, "Each man should give what he has decided in his heart to give, not reluctantly or under compulsion, for God loves a cheerful giver. And God is able to make all grace abound to you, so that in all things at all times, having all that you need, you will abound in every good work. . . . Now he who supplies seed to the sower and bread for food will also . . . enlarge the harvest. . . You will be made rich in every way so that you can be generous on every occasion." (2 Cor. 9:7-11).

This is an amazing promise from God. The promise is that when God's people give generously to do the Lord's work, God promises to multiply what they have given far beyond their own means, to such an extent that, "in all things at all times, having all that you need, you will abound in every good work . . . so that you can be generous on every occasion." (2 Cor. 9:7-11).

For a recent example of what God can do through his own people regardless of the situation, consider the following true story from an African country where the economy is in very serious trouble.

A dedicated Christian brother was a University lecturer. This brother began to hold meetings with Christian students to teach them about living a more dedicated and holy Christian life. As time went by, more and more young people began to listen to the lectures of this man. Many of them began to recommit their lives to Christ. Part of their commitment meant giving God a tenth (a "tithe") of all that God had given them. Many people who rededicated their lives to the Lord through the preaching of this man began to give the Lord a tenth of all their possessions. Some even gave more, up to 50 percent or 75 percent of all they had.

The result is one of the most amazing chapters of church history in Africa today. In a few short years this renewal movement based on total commitment to Christ has grown into one of the largest churches in Africa. In a country where many people cannot afford to buy even the basic necessities of life this church has built a large college campus in the capital city. Many students from this denomination receive theological education at this school and are trained for the ministry of the gospel at very low cost. Why? Because the church receives large sums of money from outside the country? No. But because the members of this church have learned to give generously to the Lord for His work from what they have. God has blessed their faithful giving and multiplied their resources.

This denomination also has a local church with one of the largest weekly attendances in the world. This true story is an example of the words of the Apostle Paul which were quoted above, that . . . "having all that you need, you will abound in every good work . . . so that you can be generous on every occasion." (2 Cor. 9:7-11)

God blesses individuals and churches who give generously to the advancement of His work. When God blesses what they give he makes it grow beyond their imagination, regardless of the country, culture, or condition of the economy in that country because God is all-powerful and God is faithful. God keeps His promises, like the promise in Luke 6:38 "Give, and it will be given to you. A good measure, pressed down, shaken together and running over, will be poured into your lap. For with the measure you use, it will be measured to you."

He is the God of the resurrection. He is the God of the impossible. He is the God for whom no human situation is too difficult. It is up to his people to do what he asks them to do and then to discover with amazement what God will do.

This is not to say that God promises financial prosperity and wealth to His people if they just have faith. That is a false idea being taught in many places today. The apostle Paul said he knew what it was to be in need (Phil. 4:12). He said he had learned to be content with either a lot or a little (Phil. 4:12). None of the apostles of Christ died as rich men.

What God does promise is to meet out basic needs (Phil. 4:19). Jesus taught us to pray for our daily bread (that is, our daily needs) (Matt. 6:11). At the same time, the Bible warns us that "people who want to get rich fall into temptation and a trap . . . that plunge men into ruin and destruction" (1 Tim. 6:9). The so-called "prosperity gospel" popular in many places in Africa today is not Biblical Christianity. In James 4:2 the Bible says, "When you ask, you do not receive, because you ask with wrong motives, that you may spend what you get on your pleasures."

We can see from the true stories given above that money can be used to bring great blessing and great good to the lives of many people but it can also be the means of great temptation, sin and evil. The question is, what can be done so that it does not result in temptation, sin and evil as in the opening story of this chapter? Clearly there is a need for God's wisdom if money is to bring deliverance and not destruction.

In the next few pages, we will take an imaginative journey into what is possible when a whole community of God's people (for example a group of local churches or all the churches in one country) act together to do something for the kingdom of God.

WHAT ARE SOME BIBLICAL GUIDELINES FOR USING MONEY TO SOLVE PROBLEMS INSTEAD OF CAUSING PROBLEMS ?

THE PRINCIPLE OF TITHING

The beginning of a solution which God might provide for a particular need is the practice of faithful tithing to the Lord. Tithing means giving to the Lord the first ten percent of all that a person receives. This can be in the form of money, goods, food or anything a person has. Many Christians have learned the blessing that comes from faithful tithing. Tithing was required in the Old Testament (Lev. 27:30,32) and Jesus encouraged the same practice in the New Testament (Matt. 23:23).

For many dedicated Christians giving ten percent of what they have is just the beginning of their giving to the Lord. Many Christians have learned the blessing of giving a double tithe (20 percent) or even more. Some who have more resources discover that they can give 50 percent, 75 percent or even 90 percent of what God has given them and still have enough for their own needs.

The matter of giving to God is a matter of understanding the nature of money and all material things. A mature Christian realizes that everything he or she has belongs to God, not just 10 percent of his or her money. It is not a matter of, "this much belongs to God and this much belongs to me." It all belongs to God. Long ago King David recognized this truth in one of his prayers. David said, "O Lord our God, as for all this abundance that we have . . . it comes from your hand, and all of it belongs to you" (1 Chron. 29:16).

Consider the following promise made by God to His people, concerning tithing. Notice especially the reference to food. "Bring the whole tithe into the storehouse, that there may be food in my house. Test me in this," says the LORD Almighty, "and see if I will not throw open the floodgates of heaven and pour out so much blessing that you will not have room enough for it." (Malachi 3:10). Here God promises a direct response to faithful giving. The promise of blessing is general ("so much blessing that you will not have room enough for it."). This blessing may be evident in different ways. This is one of the only places in the Bible where God challenges His people to test Him.

A seminary student gave the following testimony from his local church about the blessing God promises to those who tithe. The story began about 20 years ago in a rural area of southern Ethiopia. The student wrote, "At that time, our people were deeply committed to following Christ and the commandments of His Word. Everyone in our local church practiced tithing. There was an abundance at our annual thanksgiving tithe conferences. The church used some of these gifts to set up a fund for needy people in the church. As a result, there were no needy people at all in our church at that time." [1] This example only referred to that student's local church. What effect would such a practice have on a community, a local government, or even a nation, if such a practice was followed by all churches in the country?

Unfortunately, this story had a sad ending. The same student reported the following sequence of events, which dramatically illustrate what can happen when relief funds from outside sources are not given wisely or not handled wisely by the church. The student wrote, "When the famine came, a very large amount of foreign aid money was given to bring famine relief to our church area. There were few guidelines on its use except to provide food. Even when the worst crisis of famine had passed the relief program was continued. Church leaders began to fight over the money. They did not devote themselves to the care of the needy. Because outside aid was being given to help the needy, many people in the church stopped tithing altogether and the church's own relief fund dried up. Today, very few people in my church tithe and there are many needy people in the congregation and in our community, even though the famine is past" [2]

This story reveals both the good and the evil that are possible through the right and wrong use of money and other resources. It reveals what is possible to meet human needs when the people of God do what God has commanded them to do with their money. It also shows the enormous power of the love of money to destroy people and to spoil the Lord's work. It shows what happens when financial help is given in the wrong way.

As we have seen, the first biblical principle to provide for the Lord's work and to meet human need is the principle of tithing. In the Old Testament the tenth part of a person's resources belonged to the Lord (Lev. 27:30). To fail to give a tenth to the Lord was to rob God of what belonged to Him (Mal. 3:8-10). When God's people did not give him a tithe the Lord said that His people were robbing Him and that they were under a curse (Mal. 3:9).

Those are strong words. They indicate that the matter of giving God a tenth of what we have is a matter of obligation, not something based on our emotions or generosity. Generosity begins after a tithe has already been given. In the New Testament Jesus taught that giving a tithe was still expected from the people of God (Matt. 23:23).

Tithing is God's way of supporting the local church and supporting other ministries for the Lord. This includes meeting the needs of the poor. For example, the apostle Paul took up a famine relief collection from the tithes of the churches in Macedonia and Greece in order to help those in need far away in the churches of Judea and Jerusalem (2 Cor. 8:1-7). This money was part of the tithes and offerings collected each week during the regular Sunday worship (1 Cor. 16:1-3).

Here is a simple way to understand tithing. In simple theory, it should only require ten people, each giving a tenth of their income or resources to the church, to provide the support for one full time pastor or Christian worker to live at the average level of the ten tithing people. The pastor or Christian worker should also tithe what he is given as well. In practice it will take more than ten people to support the local church because there are other expenses to be paid as well as the pastor's salary, such as the maintenance of the church building, the pastor's housing, and other needs. Twenty more people, each giving a tithe, should be able to provide for the church's upkeep. If there are more than thirty people giving a tenth of their resources, it ought to be possible to support other ministries as well as supporting the local church. This might include supporting an evangelist to unreached people, providing help for the poor and needy, supporting students in Bible school and other ministries, depending on the size of the local church.

Suppose there were 100 people in a church and all of them were regularly giving a tithe. This should leave the tithes of about 70 people to support other ministries besides supporting the ministry of that local church. What could be done with the tithes of these 70 people? They could be used for ministries such as missionary outreach, helping the poor and needy, supporting Bible schools and other good works to advance the Kingdom of God. In the Old Testament, when God's people were challenged to give their possessions and jewelry in order to make the furnishings for the

Tabernacle in the wilderness, God's people became so generous in their giving that Moses had to tell them to stop giving (Exodus 36:4)!! Enough was freely given to meet every need. This story reveals to us that it is well within the power of God's people to provide for very great needs when they give generously and willingly and when those gifts are handled carefully.

Suppose the members of all the churches in one community or city were faithfully tithing. Imagine there were 10 churches in the town, each with 100 members. There would be a total of 1,000 people in these 10 churches. That could possibly leave the tithes of about 700 people for ministries beyond the support of each local church! How much ministry to feed and rehabilitate the poor and needy could be maintained through the regular gifts of 700 dedicated Christians or even 300 Christians, assuming that some of these tithes would be used for other ministries? It is not hard to see how this simple plan of God could care for a multitude of needy people in those churches besides helping other needy people in the community outside the church.

It can be seen from this example that it should never be necessary for a local church or group of churches to depend on support from other sources to provide for its own ministry, even in poor communities. Most churches should also be able to provide help for other needs as well as their own. God intends for giving and tithing to be a community action by God's people. Such a community effort can produce much greater results than the efforts of just one person.

This is one secret of the great power of the church of Jesus Christ. As individuals we are weak and limited. But the whole Body of Christ acting together as a single community can do amazing things. The beauty of God's plan for the local church in Africa is that it fits the core values of community in Africa. Giving or working together as a community to accomplish a goal is popular even in the non-Christian African community. Jomo Kenyatta made the concept of "harambee" (working together as a community to accomplish a task) popular in the 1960's in Kenya. In Nigeria such efforts are often called a "launching." In Liberia, they are called "rallies." How much more should this practice be true for the church?

For Christians tithing should just be the beginning of giving to the Lord. The New Testament principle is that giving should be done generously and gladly (2 Cor. 9:6-7) according to the extent to which God has prospered and blessed a person (1 Cor. 16:2). Many people in the local church should be able to give more than one tenth because God has blessed them with more than they need. It is therefore not surprising that one of the gifts of the Holy Spirit is the gift of giving (Rom. 12:6-8). This means that some people have been given the ability by God to give much more than ten percent.

With people giving more than 10 percent of their income, much more money can be made available to do the Lord's work than what has been described in the example given above. When local churches give as God intends for them to give, miracles can happen in the most difficult situations found in Africa, just as it happened when Jesus fed the 5000. But there is a condition. It is the condition of a willing, obedient and generous heart on the part of every single member of the church. God can do it though His people but are the people of God willing to let God do it through them? There is also a need for great care and wisdom in handling and using the money which God's people give. Otherwise there will be temptation and sin due to greed and the misuse of money.

It is very important to understand that the principles just described apply to any church in the world, regardless of whether they have rich or poor members. Paul said that even though the members of the New Testament churches in Macedonia were very poor, they gave very generously for the needs of others even beyond their means (2 Cor. 8:1-4). The reason they were willing to do this is because they first gave themselves to the Lord (2 Cor. 8:5).

Wholehearted commitment to Christ together with strict accountability and safeguards for the handling of church money are the keys to generous giving in the local church. When the Lord's people are sure their money is being used for the purpose for which it was given they will be much more willing to give. The local church membership must insist on careful record keeping and strict accountability by church leaders for all donated money. Otherwise church money will be misused and people will stop tithing.

From these examples we can get a little idea of how much good could be done by a group of churches if all the members practiced tithing and demanded strict accountability. Tithing explains how the large African church mentioned earlier in this chapter had enough money to build a theological college in the capital city in spite of the bad economic conditions in that country.

THE PRINCIPLE OF JOINT COOPERATION AND MATCHING FUNDS

A second principle which can help the local church to use resources wisely to solve problems instead of causing problems is the principle of joint cooperation and matching efforts between those who give help and those who receive help. Briefly stated, the group receiving the help must contribute what they can to meet their own needs along with the help being given to them from outside sources. Two groups can do much more than one group can do alone, but those in the group receiving help must make a major effort to help themselves. The worst thing a person or a church can do is to offer help without requiring the person or group receiving the help to do anything to help themselves. If the people receiving the help do not make an effort to help themselves, it will create an endless self-defeating pattern of dependency and hopelessness.

The human body is an example of this. The whole body can do things which no one part of the body (such as a finger or an ear) can do but each part of the body must do what it is supposed to do for the whole body to work properly. For a finger to work correctly, the brain, the nerves, the heart, the blood and the muscles must all do their part. Even when these other parts do what they should the finger must still do its own part. The church is also a body, the Body of Christ (1 Cor. 12:27). When the church works together in joint cooperation and matching efforts, it can do much more than any one individual or one local church can accomplish by itself. The same thing is true in teamwork. A basic principle of teamwork is that a team can accomplish what one player cannot accomplish alone.

When those who are helped are required to help themselves, the people who are helped are given a sense of dignity and self-worth. Dignity and self-worth are qualities every person in the world wants to feel about himself or herself. The following true story illustrates this principle.

A teacher at an African Bible college visited one of his graduates who was a pastor. The young pastor was very zealous for the Lord. He was interested in establishing other churches in his area in addition to the one of which he was pastor. Unfortunately, the young man had no means of transportation. Because of this, the pastor took some of his small monthly income to pay for public transportation to the preaching points he had established. Some of these places were up to 100 kilometers away from his church. But the pastor was becoming discouraged because public transportation took so much of his monthly income. He needed a motorcycle.

When the teacher visited the pastor and his church, he challenged the elders of the church to provide a motorcycle for the pastor to do his evangelism. The elders were happy for the pastor's evangelism and zeal but they complained that they were already building a house for the pastor and his family and could not possibly do more.

When the teacher returned to his school he thought about the pastor and his good work for the Lord. He wrote a letter to the elders with this challenge: If the church would come up with half the money needed for a motorcycle for the pastor, the teacher would raise money for the other half. The elders were given only three months to make their decision and then the offer would be withdrawn. The elders rose to the challenge and collected half the money needed for the motorcycle within the three month limit. The teacher also did what he promised. The pastor got his motorcycle.

This pastor has now established several new churches in the area through his evangelistic efforts. Best of all, the church has the joy of knowing that they made this possible by their own extra effort. The principle of requiring those who receive help to make a significant effort to help themselves really works. It gives the person or group who is helped a sense of dignity plus the faith that God can help them accomplish their goals.

A bishop of the Methodist church in Kenya, Professor Zablon Nthamburi had this to say: "When people feel a sense of "ownership" . . . they are willing to give themselves to the task ahead, including full support of the church's ministries." [3] Professor Nthamburi goes on to state a conviction shared by many church leaders in Africa: "I believe that the church in Africa is endowed with the resources to support its own ministry." [4]

Another African Christian leader, Dr. Solomon Aryeetey, has this to say about the present trend in the West of supporting cross-cultural evangelists in Africa. "The model is simplistic. It attempts to address the problem (the need of support) but in the process it has the potential of killing the very same African initiative that it wants to bring about. For us, it is of the utmost importance that the enterprise be truly indigenous." [5] Dr. Aryeetey notes, "Our people are eager and zealous but we do not know how to go about it" [6]

Recognizing that the wise handling of money for missionary work is really a spiritual issue, Dr. Aryeetey observes that it cannot be correctly done, "without taking great pains to adequately undergird that attempt with biblical, prevailing prayer, accompanied by old-fashioned fasting." [7] He goes on to observe, "the Western missionary enterprise in Africa had a weakness . . . the area concerning teaching of a balanced biblical view of money and ownership. There was really no comprehensive, long term, deliberate strategy to so empower the churches that were planted that they would become truly and largely self supporting." [8]

An indication of the present dissatisfaction with overseas financial dependence among churches in Africa was revealed in the unified response against dependency expressed by a group of 89 African church leaders at a conference in Limuru, Kenya from 21-24 May 1996.[9] Dependency on foreign funding was described by several speakers at the conference as an addiction.[10] The consultation made a clear statement to the effect that requiring accountability with money was one of the most important keys in the process of achieving self-reliance in church finances. [11]

THE PRINCIPLE OF GROUP MANAGEMENT

A third guideline which will help to prevent corrupt people from using the Lord's money for their own purposes is the principle that financial assistance should always be managed by a widely representative group from the church and not by one or two people. The Bible says, "Plans fail for lack of counsel, but with many advisers they succeed" (Prov. 15:22). The key is having several people jointly responsible and accountable for the money. There is too much temptation for many people when it comes to handling money, especially large amounts of money. It is not wise to risk destroying a good work by putting one or two people in charge of handling all the money. This was clearly seen in the story at the beginning of this chapter. Group management by a mature group of church leaders fits the traditional African pattern of leadership in the village very well. There is wisdom from the past which can be a great help in the present when it comes to handling money and other resources which the Lord may provide.

MAKING TIME FOR WHAT MATTERS MOST

In this discussion about money and material possessions, there is another area of conflict between western and non-western values which must be considered. This is the conflict between the need to make money and the need to maintain relationships, especially a person's relationship to God and to his or her extended family members. One great weakness of western culture is the tendency to be goal-oriented at the expense of human relationships. Many westerners vigorously pursue their goals without regard to the effect that this has on their relationships to the people around them. As Africans in the urban environment become increasingly dominated by western values, the temptation exists to violate one of the most precious and important values of African life, the priority of people and human relationships.

Life in the modern African city demands money. Unlike life in the rural village where a man can often sustain himself and his family by what he produces on his farm the city dweller must depend on earning money to buy everything he needs. The compelling drive to make money can become a tyrant which rules every part of life. Even those relatives who still live back in the rural village expect their city cousins to have money. There is a false image in the minds of many people that people who work in the city will have plenty of money.

The pursuit of making money can become an all-consuming passion which changes the whole character of a person and his home. In many cases the wife will go to work just like the husband in order to provide enough money to live or to improve the family's standard of living. Instead of raising their own children many such couples give the care of their children over to relatives or even to hired employees at a day care center. In the process of trying to provide for their family in the city they lose the very relationships with their family that they are trying to maintain by their work. Husbands and wives become strangers to each other. Parents become strangers to their children. Even more seriously, Christians can lose their close relationship with the Lord and thereby lose the most important thing in life. Life in the city can very easily be dominated by the urgent demand to make money and to have a higher standard of living.

There is an interesting story in the gospels about two sisters who faced the needs of everyday life with two different priorities. Martha was a woman whose life was ruled by the urgent needs of the day. Her sister Mary knew about these needs but she made a decision to put the most important things in life first in spite of the needs. In Luke's gospel we read the following short story about Jesus' visit in the home of these two women. "As Jesus and his disciples were on their way, he came to a village where a woman named Martha opened her home to him. She had a sister called Mary, who sat at the Lord's feet listening to what he said. But Martha was distracted by all the preparations that had to be made. She came to him and asked, "Lord, don't you care that my sister has left me to do the work by myself? Tell her to help me!" "Martha, Martha," the Lord answered, "you are worried and upset about many things, but only one thing is needed. Mary has chosen what is better, and it will not be taken away from her" (Luke 10:38-42).

We must make choices about what matters most in life. We must decide whether we will allow the need of the moment to rule our lives or whether we will actively seek to maintain our relationship to the Lord and to those around us in spite of the problems which such choices may bring. In the story above Mary decided that the food and the dishes could wait. Listening to Jesus was more important. Do we realize that a higher standard of living will not necessarily make us or our children better people in God's sight? Do we realize that if we neglect our time with God each day in prayer and reading the Bible, the inner strength and peace of our life will be lost? Do we realize that the needs of our spouse or our children for our time and our attention can not be neglected without bringing life-long harm to the family?

Loss of the most important relationships in life can easily happen to the city-dweller who is forced into a life of schedules, time-pressure and the demand to make more money to survive. Perhaps for some families it would be better if they moved back to the village or the farm to save their marriages, their families and their own happiness in life. For all in urban Africa, it is a matter of making choices each day about what is really most important in life.

SUMMARY

Money can be the cause of great evil or great encouragement. It can be a burden or a blessing. This will depend on whether it controls our lives or is used for the good of others. For money to be a blessing to ourselves and others, God's people must be willing to do what God requires them to do with it and to use it with God-given wisdom.

The first principle to make money into a source of blessing is faithful tithing by the whole church along with strict accountability for the money given. Every local church in the world with more than thirty members should be able to support its own ministry and provide help to others as well if the members are obedient in the practice of tithing. A second principle is that a joint effort by more than one person or one group can accomplish more than one person or one group can accomplish alone. A third principle is that money given for ministry, aid or development should be managed by a representative group of mature leaders in the church rather than by one or two people. Those controlling the use of money must be held strictly accountable for the money under their control. If these biblical principles are carefully followed, the church can be used by God to do great works of love and mercy through their efforts even if they are poor and small in number.

Christians living in an urban environment must be particularly careful to set the right priorities in their lives. The demands to meet the needs of everyday life in a modern city can destroy the most important relationships in life.

When biblical principles are followed, God can do amazing things to provide for His work, to help the needy and to solve problems that seem impossible. The people of God must understand that God is "able to do immeasurably more than all we ask or imagine, according to his power that is at work within us" (Eph. 3:20). This will be true when God's people are willing to give themselves and their resources to the Lord.

QUESTIONS FOR REVIEW, REFLECTION AND GROUP DISCUSSION

1. In what way does money become a god for many people?
2. Why is it not possible to serve both God and money?
3. List some of the ways in which money can be used for good to advance the kingdom of God.
4. How does the love of money "plunge men into ruin and destruction" (1 Tim. 6:9)?
5. What is the meaning of tithing? Why does tithing have the possibility of doing such great good for God's work?
6. According to the teaching of Christ, is tithing something which God expects Christians to do today (Matt. 23:23)? What promise does God give to those who practice tithing (Malachi 3:10)?
7. What is the right way and what is the wrong way, to help people in need?

8. What practical steps should a church or a Christian organization take to ensure that money given for the Lord's work is not misused?

END NOTES

1. Testimony related in a term paper written for a course in Ethics at Evangelical Theological College, Addis Ababa, Ethiopia. 1995.
2. Ibid.
3. Zablon Nthamburi, "The Church In Africa: Making Its Way From Dependency To Self Reliance," *Missions Frontiers: Bulletin of the U.S. Center For World Missions,* January-February 1997. p. 18
4. Ibid. p. 18
5. Solomon Aryeetey, M.D. "The Road To Self Sufficiency In Africa's Missionary Development," *Evangelical Missions Quarterly,* January 1997, p. 34
6. Ibid. p. 35
7. Ibid. p. 37
8. Ibid. p. 38
9. "Historic Consultation On Self Reliance Held In East Africa," *Transition Notes,* August 10. 1996.
10. Ibid. p. 1
11. Ibid. p. 4

CHAPTER 8

THE PROBLEM OF POVERTY IN AFRICA

Poverty is one of the greatest problems in Africa today. Many cities have large shanty town areas filled with wretchedly poor people who lack many of the basic essentials of human life. Urban areas are overcrowded with homeless and displaced people, war refugees, handicapped people, beggars and abandoned street children. It is a situation which easily leads to despair in the hearts of even the most zealous crusaders for human needs. Can anything be done? What kind of perspective is needed to deal with such an overwhelming and depressing situation?

A recent true story will be given to illustrate the terrible condition of poverty for a great many people in Africa. Unlike the situation for most desperately poor people the story of this pitiful woman took a dramatic turn for good because of the totally self-sacrificing devotion of a few brave Christian people. The story of how this woman's life was rescued from hopeless despair can provide us with God's perspective on how to deal with crushing poverty in the cities.

Dinatu was married with two children. She was poor but she and her husband were able to survive on their small farm. In 1985 there was no rain in the area. As a result of the drought the farm produced nothing. The famine continued for three years. In desperation to survive, Dinatu was forced to leave the familiar surroundings of the little she had. Her husband left her. Carrying one baby on her back and leading the other by the hand, life suddenly became very dark for this woman. Survival was all that mattered. She moved into a government settlement area for victims of the famine.

Economic difficulties in the country brought problems in the famine resettlement area where Dinatu had settled with her children. The local people became angry that outsiders had been allowed to settle in their area and used harsh means to drive them out of the area. Dinatu moved to the capital city in hope of finding some help. What she found was a situation worse than she had in the refugee camp. She had no place to live and had to use scraps of cardboard and plastic to cover herself and her children from the rain and cold. She had no job, no family and no friends. She was reduced to begging to put something in her own mouth and her children's mouths.

After a time she met another man who lived in the street. She felt this man could provide some security for her and she began to live with him. Within a short time, however, this man left Dinatu for another woman in the area. Life had become very bitter for Dinatu. In her mind, if there was a God, He certainly didn't care for her in any way. Both she and her children were sick with TB. Dinatu was bitter with despair.

About this time she met still another man named Garba who showed an interest in her. In desperation she began to live with Garba. Garba was 29 years old and a former soldier. He came from a very poor family. He came to the city and began living in the street. He had no education or skill to get a job. He stole things to support himself and to support his drug habit. He was violent in his behavior and was always fighting. He was addicted to a local drug. He drank heavily and was a chain smoker. He was totally selfish in his behavior.

He made heavy demands on Dinatu. He took everything she and her children received from begging for himself and his addictions. When he got drunk he would beat her. He made Dinatu pregnant but did nothing to help support her children. As if this was not enough, Dinatu was tormented by evil spirits. Then in a blood test provided by the government, she discovered that she had AIDS. Her life was hell on earth. What hope was there for this woman? Unfortunately life was to get even worse for Dinatu before it got better. We will discover what happened to this woman later in the chapter.

THE PAINFUL REALITY OF POVERTY IN AFRICA

In his book, Hope For Africa, Kenyan professor George Kinoti reports, "One out of every three Africans does not get enough to eat. A study covering the period 1988-1990 showed that some 168 million Africans were victims of chronic hunger. This was an increase of 40 million people in just one decade. Tens of millions of African children suffer from malnutrition, which means retarded physical and mental development, disease, disability and death."[1]

Kenoti goes on to point out, "two thirds of the poorest 40 nations in the world are African, as are 8 of the poorest 10 nations." [2] There is a direct relationship between poverty and poor health. Kinoti observes, "poverty means disease. Disease means pain, inability to work and death." [3]

There are already serious problems of poor health in Africa due to the presence of tropical diseases and parasites such as bilharzia, malaria, hepatitis, dysentery and other things. Poverty and the poor nutrition which results from poverty makes this situation very much worse. When people lack proper food, their bodies become weak and unable to resist the diseases around them. God has created a natural immune system in the human body which can fight off many diseases, but this system only works properly when the body gets enough of the right kinds of food. Hence the need for proper food is one of the most urgent physical needs of modern Africa.

It can also be said that poverty is directly related to crime. If people do not have enough to eat, they steal to survive. When people become desperate for food and other necessities they will steal and even kill to get what they need. The great increase in crime in many African countries today, especially in the cities, is directly related to the problems of unemployment and poverty. If solutions to the problems of unemployment and poverty are not found, the problems of crime, suffering and poor health will increase at an alarming rate in the next few years.

What can anyone do in the face of such an overwhelming and discouraging situation as this? The answer is that no human being can solve or even understand such a great problem. Only God understands. But God also has the knowledge and wisdom needed to help His people do something about it.

Some people feel there is so much poverty in Africa that the situation is hopeless. That viewpoint shows a failure to understand the power of God or how God keeps His Word throughout history regardless of the time or place. God is not limited by geography, culture or difficult situations. His character and power do not change from one time in history to another. His promises do not depend on the country in which a person lives. He is not limited by conditions of extreme poverty. From a strictly human perspective, however, it is very easy to be overwhelmed with a feeling of hopelessness in the face of great poverty.

It is not being suggested that the problem of poverty can be overcome by the church. Jesus said there would always be poor people (Matt. 26:11). However, He also said there was something Christians could do for individuals even in the most extreme situations (Matt. 19:21).

The Bible teaches that even in the midst of seemingly hopeless situations, the love of God can be expressed through God's people in such a way that the hopeless are given hope and those who have given up on life can be given something to live for. One of the secrets of being able to do something about a hopeless situation is to work on one small part of the problem at a time rather than trying to solve the entire problem. Putting this into everyday terms, it means helping just one person or a few people at a time instead of trying to solve poverty in the whole nation. The secret is that if many people become involved in helping one or two people at a time, the sum of all their efforts will make a very big difference.

Consider the following five true stories where God used the generosity and love of a few extremely poor Christians to meet some urgent human needs and to open the hearts of their neighbors to Christ.

1. Members of a local church in a very poor community decided to look for older non-Christian widows in the community who lived alone and needed help. They believed that this was one way to respond to the Bible's command to care for widows and others who cannot care for themselves. They offered to help five widows with their housework. The offer was re-

ceived and the widows were amazed that people who were as poor as they were and who had no relationship to them were willing to help them. Each of these widows has since put her faith in Christ.

2. The pastor of a local church in a very poor area challenged his congregation with the following words: "You may not have much food, but you can share a small amount of sugar, rice, soap or something else with those who have less than you do." In response to what they believed God was telling them to do, the members brought small amounts of food during the week and put them into a common basket at the church. Each week the church gave the food basket to a very poor local non-Christian family. These families had an opportunity to see an expression of the love of Christ from people who were just as poor as they were.
3. A local church identified five families in the community whose homemakers were too sick to do housework. The church members helped them clean their homes, wash and iron their clothes and clean their yards. Most of these families have since become followers of Christ.
4. The church members of a poor rural community were surrounded by people of another religion. They considered themselves to be an oppressed religious minority. However, the pastor of the church encouraged the women of the church to investigate community needs. At the church service the next week, the women reported they had found twelve non-Christian women who each had only one dress. In the hot climate of the area, the women had to wash their dresses each day. If a woman had only one dress, she had to stay inside until the dress dried in the sun. The pastor asked if there were any women in the congregation who had three dresses who would be willing to donate one of them to one of the non-Christian women. Enough women volunteered to meet the reported need.

The non-Christian women were so impressed with this expression of love that they invited the Christian women to pray for them. Some even asked the Christian women to pray for their unborn children. This experience greatly increased the confidence of this rural church to continue to reach out in demonstrations of Christian love to their non-Christian neighbors.

5. In a rural community of poor people, there were no wells and the local people got their water from a polluted river. A visiting Christian with some experience in digging wells encouraged the church leadership to explore what they could do on their own to meet the need for water. At first the idea of successfully reaching water with a hand dug well was not well received. The people thought that the water level was too deep. However, with the outsider's encouragement and promise to help, the leadership decided to try. They rented some equipment which could be used to help dig wells by hand.

   They began to dig at the back of the church property. They struck water at 45 feet. There was a great celebration. Non-church members in the community, however, were not pleased. They thought that the church members would hoard the water for themselves. On the contrary, the church invited the community to share in God's blessings of their successful well. Soon, representatives from the community began to ask the church leaders if they would help them dig wells in other parts of the community. The church said they would help. In a little more than a year 15 wells were dug by hand. Through this expression of concern for the community, the church gained so much good will that when the church members invited the community to come to hear a message of God's love, the church was filled with non- Christian people from the community. [4]

THE ROLE OF THE CHURCH IN RELATION TO THE ROLE OF GOVERNMENTS

Human governments also have the authority to take actions which will help to relieve conditions of extreme poverty. The problem is that governments often do not make the right decisions or do not know what to do. Worse yet, many government officials are greedy, selfish and corrupt and are not willing to take the actions which would help solve the problems of unemployment and poverty. Such officials seem interested only in their own wealth, power and influence. At times, some governments even oppose those individuals and agencies which try to help.

Some years ago a Christian organization set up a very low cost feeding program for the hungry in one African city. Other Christians heard about the program and provided funds to expand the program into more than one feeding center in the city. When the organization providing the low cost food approached the government for permission to increase the number of feeding centers, the government refused to give permission. Not only did this government refuse to help the poor but it hindered those who were willing to help.

What can Christians do in a situation where the government not only refuses to help, but hinders those who are willing to help? The answer is, they can appeal to God in prayer. Christians are commanded to pray for their political leaders (1 Tim. 2:1-2). It is only the people of God whom God has promised to answer when they pray. The good news is that God has made specific promises about answering the prayers of His people (John 15:7, John 16:23-24). Since praying for government officials is something the Bible commands Christians to do, they can be sure they are praying according to the will of God when they pray for government officials.

Consider the promise God gives to His people who pray according to His will: "This is the confidence we have in approaching God: that if we ask anything according to his will, he hears us. And if we know that he hears us--whatever we ask--we know that we have what we asked of him" (1 John 5:14-15).

If God is truly God, and if it is God who has established the institution of human government as the Bible says He has (Rom. 13:1), then God is willing to answer prayers for government officials regardless of the country. The problem is, are Christians really willing to pray for their governments (1 Tim. 2:1-2)? Is the church willing to call the whole membership together to fast and pray, if the situation is really bad ((Matt. 6:16-18, Joel 1:14)? There are steps which God expects His people to take. He will not likely intervene until His people show they are serious about doing what He commands.

In the book of Joel, a locust plague was destroying the land because of the national sins of the people. God called on His own people through the prophet Joel to a time of national fasting and repentance so that the disaster could be avoided (Joel 2:15 -17). Some African countries today are in a situation of impending disaster just as great as the impending disaster on Israel in Joel's time. Where are the godly church leaders and church members who are willing to move the hand of God to heal their countries through national fasting and prayer? God is willing to answer when His people are willing to do what He calls them to do.

God may answer such prayers by changing the hearts of government officials. God changed the heart of a government official in the case of Nehemiah's appeal to the king of his day to release Nehemiah from his government duties so that he could return to Jerusalem to help his people rebuild the wall (Neh. 2:4-6). God may answer by putting a wise and godly man into a key government leadership position at a time of need. He did this when he put Joseph into a top leadership position in the Egyptian government just before a terrible famine struck the country for seven years (Gen. 41:41- 43). God then used Joseph to save the whole nation from the effects of the famine by wise planning (Gen. 41:33-36). God may answer prayer by removing an existing government official and replacing him with a better official. He did this when He removed an evil advisor named Ahithophel, who had betrayed King David, and replaced him with a wise man named Hushai the Arkite, who was loyal to David (2 Sam. 17:1-14, 23).

In some cases, God may answer by sweeping away an entire government. He did this in the case of the corrupt Babylonian government under the leadership of king Belshazzar in the days of Daniel (Dan. 5:22-30). Secular history tells us that Babylon was overthrown when the Medes diverted the course of the Euphrates river which flowed under the city of Babylon and the Medan army marched secretly into the city through the dry riverbed. In one night, the Babylonian government was overthrown by the hand of God (Dan. 5:30).

God swept away the corrupt government of a modern African country some years ago in response to prayer. The worldwide leader of the Anglican church, the Archbishop of Canterbury, called on Christians all over the world to pray for the removal of this evil dictator and his government. Six months later the dictator and his government were gone, driven out by the army of another country. In general, however, it is more likely to be the will of God to answer prayer for a government by changing the hearts of government officials or by replacing worthless officials with good officials than it is by overthrowing an entire government. These examples from the Bible show us that God is able to intervene in any situation, including situations in Africa today, even when the situation seems hopeless.

If God's people are willing to fast and pray with clean hearts, God is willing to intervene even if a nation is on the brink of disaster. It is not that God does not have power to solve humanly impossible problems. He waits for true repentance, obedience, humility and prayer from His people. Unfortunately, some church leaders are so preoccupied with establishing their own power and influence in the church that they have no time to do what God wants them to do to save the nation. When this is the case, perhaps the local church members need to fast and pray that God will first humble such church leaders even before they pray for their national leaders.

To many people, the situations in Africa today seem beyond the power of God to change. War, famine, starvation, disease, poverty, tribalism, corruption and many other evils seem to be hopeless problems to solve. What can God really do? It is worthwhile at this point to look at a situation in history which was as bad as any in Africa today. The following true story from the Bible reveals how God kept His Word and performed a great deliverance in a humanly impossible situation.

"Ben-Hadad king of Aram mobilized his entire army and marched up and laid siege to Samaria. There was a great famine in the city. . . . As the king of Israel was passing by on the wall, a woman cried to him, "Help me, my lord the king!" The king replied . . . "What's the matter?" She answered, "This woman said to me, 'Give up your son so we may eat him today, and tomorrow we'll eat my son.' So we cooked my son and ate him. The next day I said to her, 'Give up your son so we may eat him,' but she had hidden him" (2 Kings 6:24-29). How bad can a situation be that people would eat their own children?

It was in this unbearable situation that God acted according to His power and kept His Word. The story continues . . . "Elisha said, "Hear the word of the Lord. This is what the Lord says: About this time tomorrow, a seah of flour will sell for a shekel and two seahs of barley for a shekel at the gate of Samaria. The officer on whose arm the king was leaning said to the man of God, "Look, even if the Lord should open the floodgates of the heavens, could this happen?" "You will see it with your own eyes," answered Elisha, "but you will not eat any of it!"

Now there were four men with leprosy at the entrance of the city gate. They said to each other, "Why stay here until we die? If we say, 'We'll go into the city'--the famine is there, and we will die. And if we stay here, we will die. So let's go over to the camp of the Arameans and surrender. If they spare us, we live; if they kill us, then we die." At dusk they got up and went to the camp of the Arameans. When they reached the edge of the camp, not a man was there, for the Lord had caused the Arameans to hear the sound of chariots and horses and a great army, so that they said to one another, "Look, the king of Israel has hired the Hittite and Egyptian kings to attack us!"

So they got up and fled at dusk and abandoned their tents and their horses and donkeys. They left the camp as it was and ran for their lives. The men who had leprosy reached the edge of the camp and entered one of the tents. They ate and drank, and carried away silver, gold and clothes, and went off and hid them. They returned and entered another tent and took some things from it and hid them also. Then they said to each other, "We're not doing right. This is a day of good news and we are keeping it to ourselves. If we wait until daylight, punishment will overtake us. Let's go at once and report this to the royal palace." So they went and called out to the city gatekeepers and told them, "We went into the Aramean camp and not a man was there--not a sound of anyone--only tethered horses and donkeys, and the tents left just as they were."

The gatekeepers shouted the news, and it was reported within the palace. . . . So they selected two chariots with their horses, and the king sent them after the Aramean army. . . . they found the whole road strewn with the clothing and equipment the Arameans had thrown away in their headlong flight. So the messengers returned and reported to the king. Then the people went out and plundered the camp of the Arameans. So a seah of flour sold for a shekel, and two seahs of barley sold for a shekel, as the LORD had said.

Now the king had put the officer on whose arm he leaned in charge of the gate, and the people trampled him in the gateway, and he died, just as the man of God had foretold when the king came down to his house. It happened as the man of God had said to the king: "About this time tomorrow, a seah of flour will sell for a shekel and two seahs of barley for a shekel at the gate of Samaria" (2 Kings 6:24 - 8:16).

The lesson of this story is that God keeps His Word. No problem or person on earth can prevent God from keeping His Word. The same God who did this in the nation of Israel long ago is well able to keep His Word in Africa today. God is able to work miracles of love and compassion to overcome even disastrous national problems when His people come to Him in repentance, humility, prayer and faith.

Concerning hunger, consider the gospel story of a young boy with a small lunch and 5000 hungry men. This story is found in all four gospels to illustrate how God is able to multiply the little we have to meet an impossible human need. In this situation there were about 10,000 -15,000 people actually present, since the Bible tells us that there were "about 5000 men, besides women and children" (Matt. 14:21).

In this story, the human part of the solution to the problem was the willing and generous heart of one young boy. In John's version of the story, Jesus purposely challenged the disciples with the impossibility of the situation. He asked them, "Where shall we buy bread for these people to eat" (John 6:5)? Philip answered his question with the obvious impossibility of the situation: "Eight months wages would not buy enough bread for each one to have a bite" (John 6:7).

In Mark's version of the story, two other interesting facts emerge. First, the disciples of Jesus do exactly as we tend to do. They asked the Lord to just make the problem go away. "Send the people away" (Mark 6:36) they said to Jesus. But that is not how Jesus planned to solve the problem - then or now. In reply, Jesus said something that must have sounded totally impossible to the disciples. "YOU give them something to eat" (Mark 6:37). That was just what they did not want to hear! But that is exactly how Jesus planned to solve the problem!

So also today, it is God's will to meet the needs of the poor in the church through his people. It is also God's will to use responsible human governments to help meet the need of unemployment and poverty in a nation in response to the prayers of God's people for the government of that nation.

Jesus knows we do not have the ability or resources ourselves to meet the impossible needs of the poor in Africa but He still tells us to do it. Why? Because He is God, and He has the power to do what we cannot even imagine. He simply wants from us a willing and obedient heart as He found in the small boy who offered Jesus the little he had to feed the great crowd.

WHAT DOES GOD SAY CONCERNING THE POOR?

What does God expect His people to do concerning the poor? First, there is a need to understand how God thinks about the poor and needy. Second, there is a need to act on what God says. Let us read from the Bible how God feels about the poor and what He wants His people to do for them.

"There will always be poor people in the land. Therefore I command you to be openhanded toward your brothers and toward the poor and needy in your land" (Deut. 15:11).

"I know that the LORD secures justice for the poor and upholds the cause of the needy" (Psalm 140:12).

"My whole being will exclaim, "Who is like you, O LORD? You rescue the poor from those too strong for them" (Psalm 35:10).

"Do not let the oppressed retreat in disgrace; may the poor and needy praise your name" (Psalm 74:21).

HERE ARE SOME OF GOD'S COMMANDS CONCERNING THE POOR AND NEEDY

"Speak up for those who cannot speak for themselves, for the rights of all who are destitute. Speak up and judge fairly; defend the rights of the poor and needy" (Prov. 31:8-9).

"Defend the cause of the weak and fatherless; maintain the rights of the poor and oppressed. Rescue the weak and needy; deliver them from the hand of the wicked" (Psalm 82:3-4).

"When you reap the harvest of your land, do not reap to the very edges of your field or gather the gleanings of your harvest. Leave them for the poor and the alien. I am the LORD your God" (Lev. 23:22).

"Jesus answered, 'If you want to be perfect, go, sell your possessions and give to the poor, and you will have treasure in heaven. Then come, follow me' " (Matt. 19:21).

"Do not be afraid, little flock, for your Father has been pleased to give you the kingdom. Sell your possessions and give to the poor" (Luke 12:32-33).

Here Are Some Warnings To Those Who Don't Care For The Poor

"He who oppresses the poor shows contempt for their Maker" (Prov. 14:31).

"If a man shuts his ears to the cry of the poor, he too will cry out and not be answered" (Prov. 21:13).

Here Are Some Descriptions Of Godly People In The Bible Who Helped The Poor

"A wife of noble character who can find? She is worth far more than rubies. . . She opens her arms to the poor and extends her hands to the needy" (Prov. 31:10, 20).

"In Joppa there was a disciple named Tabitha who was always doing good and helping the poor" (Acts 9:36).

"Zacchaeus stood up and said to the Lord, 'Look, Lord! Here and now I give half of my possessions to the poor, and if I have cheated anybody out of anything, I will pay back four times the amount" (Luke 19:8).

"This is pure and undefiled religion in the sight of our God and Father, to visit orphans and widows in their distress, and to keep oneself unstained by the world" (James 1:27).

It is clear from these Scriptures that God is very much concerned about the condition of the poor and those in need. It is also clear that He expects His own people to do something to help them. We can only wonder what would happen in a village, a city or an entire country if the whole Christian community in that place took these words of God to heart and acted on them.

Here Are Some Promises For Those Who Minister To The Poor

"Whoever is kind to the needy honors God" (Prov. 14:31).

"He who is kind to the poor lends to the LORD, and he will reward him for what he has done" (Prov. 19:17).

"Toward your needy brother . . . Give generously to him and do so without a grudging heart; then because of this the LORD your God will bless you in all your work and in everything you put your hand to" (Deut. 15:9-10).

"Blessed is the man who fears the LORD, who finds great delight in his commands. . . . Even in darkness light dawns for the upright, for the gracious and compassionate and righteous man. Good will come to him who is generous" (Psalm 112:1, 4-5).

"A generous man will himself be blessed, for he shares his food with the poor" (Prov. 22:9).

"He who gives to the poor will lack nothing, but he who closes his eyes to them receives many curses" (Prov. 28:27).

"If a king judges the poor with fairness, his throne will always be secure" (Prov. 29:14).

"But when you give a banquet, invite the poor, the crippled, the lame, the blind, and you will be blessed. Although they cannot repay you, you will be repaid at the resurrection of the righteous" (Luke 14:13-14).

HOW SHALL THE CHURCH MINISTER TO THE POOR AND NEEDY?

It is quite clear from the Scripture references given above that it is the will of God for His people to minister to the needs of the poor and needy. The question is, what should be done and what is the best way to do it? These are questions which will require serious thought and discussion by each local church. As a starting point, the local church should have some sort of fund or program to help the needy right within their own congregation. One simple plan adopted by some churches is to have a special offering for the poor which is taken on special occasions, such as during the service of Holy Communion. This money is then given to the poor in the church by the church elders.

Another plan which some churches use is to have a regular time for the people in the congregation to express their needs during an appointed church service. After this time of sharing, an offering is taken specifically to meet these needs. The money is then given to the needy people by the church elders.

There are often other needs beyond financial needs. There may be a need for housing, a need for transportation to a certain place, or a need for special prayer or for medical help. There may be a need for fellowship for lonely older people (especially widows and widowers) who may not be able to leave their homes. If the church has a scheduled time when such needs can be expressed, it will provide an opportunity for others in the congregation to consider how God may want to use them to meet such needs.

THE PRINCIPLE OF EMPOWERMENT (HELPING PEOPLE TO LEARN TO HELP THEMSELVES)

There is a good way and a bad way to help needy people. The good way builds up the dignity and responsibility of the needy and gives them a sense of importance and value to God. The bad way degrades the needy and makes them feel dependent, helpless, hopeless and useless. What does God want people to do for themselves? What does God want outsiders to do for them so that such help does not make the poor more helpless and dependent?

In Proverbs 30:15 we read this interesting statement about begging and beggars: "The leech has two daughters. 'Give! Give!' they cry." Is it wise or compassionate simply to respond to the demands of the leech to give? The answer is no. Which is more caring and shows more godly wisdom? To give a man a fish to meet his need for food or to help him make a fishing net and to teach him how to catch fish for himself? It is easier and faster to keep on giving him fish. But that does not solve his problem. It does not cure the attitude of the leech.

It may be necessary to give the person fish for a short time while you are teaching him how to catch fish with a fishing net. You may need to provide him with the material to make the net. But once he has made a net the person should be given the sense of responsibility and dignity that he is really able to catch his own fish and to feed himself. This is a simple principle but it should apply to giving all kinds of help to the poor.

God is concerned with all the needs of human beings, not just with their souls. The hearts of people are made open to the love of Christ when they are helped at a point of physical need in their lives. In the history of missionary work down through the ages, it is a fact that most of the earliest converts came to Christ from among those who received medical or other physical help from the missionaries. The true ministry of Christ will always be an holistic ministry to the whole person. But the church must carry out such ministries with godly wisdom. God's people must help needy people to become self-sustaining. They should help them even to be able to help others rather than making them dependent on the help they receive. It is only when people begin to help others and to reach out to others rather than just thinking about their own needs and problems that people are truly helped and truly changed in a lasting way.

Listen to what the Word of God says on this subject. "He who has been stealing must steal no longer, but must work, doing something useful with his own hands, that he may have something to share with those in need" (Eph. 4:28). Notice how God says that the solution to the practice of stealing does not take place just when a person stops stealing. A permanent change takes place only when a person uses his own skill and energy to do something to meet the needs of other people who are needy like himself. This principle has many applications. In the matter of meeting the needs of the poor, it is essential for the poor person to take an active part in his or her own rehabilitation from poverty. Even more important, it is necessary for such people to become involved in meeting the needs of others who are as bad off as themselves. It is only when they begin to do this that a permanent solution has been found to the problem of poverty and need. How this works in real life will be seen as we continue the true story begun at the beginning of this chapter.

The rescue of Dinatu from hopeless poverty began in 1993. The end of a civil war in her country and a change in government led to a situation where there were many needy, displaced people in the capital city. Some of these people were soldiers who had been injured in the war. Some were war refugees and some were from families hurt by the war in different ways. A number of these people began to settle in temporary shelters on the street near the center of the city. Dinatu and Garba were among these people.

After a time there was a settlement of 48 groups of needy, displaced people living in makeshift shelters of cardboard, plastic and burlap sacks in one small area of the city. The condition of the people living in this place was very bad. Most of them were extremely poor. God put a burden of compassion for these people into the hearts of a group of Christians who lived nearby. The Christians began to discuss possible ways to help these helpless people. Out of this planning and discussion came a project to relocate and rehabilitate as many of these 48 groups as possible. Eventually the project became known as "New Life." The project name became an accurate description for what happened to these people as a result of the project.

The people to whom the project was directed were homeless street-dwelling people who survived by begging, stealing or selling a few small items on the street. Many of them were physically or mentally sick, especially with AIDS and TB. The initial condition of this group could be described as a form of living death from the perspective of a normal and stable human society. Every family unit was in serious trouble physically, economically, spiritually, mentally, emotionally and socially. There were no happy marriages, no employment and no proper family life. There was hunger and sickness. Anger, hatred, bitterness, disease, disunity, immorality and violence were the characteristics of these groups. There was a desperate need for the holistic salvation of God in each household. A resettlement plan was designed for the complete rehabilitation of whole family units, from their physical and economic needs to their emotional and spiritual needs.

The first step was to provide some kind of job training which would enable the people to sustain themselves in an honorable and fulfilling way. The next step was to provide a place to resettle the people in a healthy environment. The greatest challenge was to set the project up in a way that would give the people themselves the inner motivation to start a new and different way of life. Only an holistic approach to the need for rehabilitation could hope to bring success.

The land for resettlement was supplied by the government but it was not given in outright ownership. The plan was to have a trained builder teach one person from each household the needed construction skills to participate in the building of his own new house using his newly learned skill. The required training opened a door for the men to learn a skill by which they could make a living in the future. This training was purposely planned in order to create a sense of ownership of the project by the people. The street-dwellers could not become a part of the project unless they agreed to sign a contract to participate in the construction of their own homes and in their own job training. The goal of the project was to get the people involved in rebuilding their own lives. Thirty-eight of the forty-eight needy households agreed to sign the contract. In the end, thirty five households stayed with the project to the end and were given a new start in life.

The men were divided into teams, each using a different skill. One group did the masonry work, one group did the carpentry work, one group made concrete blocks, one group did the steel work and one group did the plumbing work. A relief agency provided the funds to buy the materials needed to build the houses and to cover other expenses. Three skilled builders were hired to train and supervise the construction workers.

Some men could not do some of the required building jobs because of physical handicaps. To provide for their rehabilitation, the handicapped men were taught to make toys for children so that they could make at least a bare living. The women of the project were taught how to make jewelry to sell. The initial materials needed to make the jewelry were provided by the relief agency. Once they began to sell the jewelry, the women had to use some of the profits to buy their own new materials to make more jewelry.

In the very first month of the project, the project fed the people and gave them fruit and vitamins because they had no money for food and most of them were seriously undernourished. After this initial help, they were required to use the money made from their labor to buy their own food. In the beginning the project provided 90% and the people provided 10% . The percentage of this subsidy was gradually reduced over a 2 - 1/2 year period until no more free food was given.

To create the motivation needed to participate in the project it was clear that there was a need for intensive individual counseling because of the severe mental, emotional and social needs of the resettlement group. A Christian counselor was assigned to the project. He was given specialized training in counseling homeless people and in counseling AIDS patients. The project leaders realized that the primary emphasis of the counselor's work must be to help bring the people in the project into a personal, praying relationship with God. Such a relationship would provide them with the spiritual strength needed to overcome the serious problems in their lives. It was clear that the key to success in the project was the mental, emotional and spiritual healing of the people.

The most serious problems were related to marriage and interpersonal relationships. It was not clear at times who was married to who. There was rampant sexual immorality along with a kind of informal marriage arrangement between various individuals. Many of these "marriages" lasted only 2-3 weeks. There was so much anger and hostility among some of the women that it was necessary to keep them off the compound while the building work was going on.

Since the street-dwellers had only known a subsistence day-to-day survival, they could not think in terms of planning for the future and they were not motivated to try to help themselves. This made it very difficult to work with them at the beginning of the project. The leaders of a nearby local church did not want to become involved with the project because "the people were too difficult to work with."

The small group of dedicated Christians who began the project found that it took a very high level of commitment in order to minister to the mental, physical and emotional needs of these people. There were severe needs in regard to mental and physical health, relationships, childbirth, marriage, family life, children's education, death and other realities of the human condition. In spite of these difficulties, those who had committed themselves to the project persevered to the end by the enabling power of the Holy Spirit (Rom. 5:5, Philippians 1:6, Philippians 2:13). Because of their deep and sacrificial commitment to God, God did a great miracle in this pathetic group of street people through their selfless love and faith.

The lesson from this story is that God will do the impossible in people's lives if there are truly dedicated Christians who will persevere with unselfish love, hard work, godly wisdom, prayer and faith in order to see God work a miracle of rebuilding broken human lives. Every Christian who participated in this project testified that he or she experienced the reality of the enabling power of the Holy Spirit. God works His miracles in human lives when we first give ourselves unconditionally to God. God gives supernatural grace and strength to us when we commit ourselves to obedience to His Word (Philippians 1:6). It does not happen any other way.

The second greatest commandment of God is this: "'YOU SHALL LOVE YOUR NEIGHBOR AS YOURSELF" (Matt. 22:39). Although this is God's commandment, it can only be consistently lived out by the power of the Holy Spirit, who comes alongside to help us as we make the decision to obey God. The Bible says, "it is GOD who is at work in you, both to will and to work for His good pleasure" (Philippians 2:13 - NASB).

The story of Dinatu and Garba shows us what God accomplished through obedient people. Garba had signed a contract to help build his own house through project New Life. However, his addictions and his violent behavior were more than the project could tolerate. Garba's behavior was so violent that he was dismissed from the project after one year. Dinatu could take no more and they were divorced. Before he was dismissed from the project Garba heard the Word of God in the Bible study meetings but he refused to listen or to follow Christ.

After he was dismissed from the project Garba passed through severe trials which finally broke him and brought him to genuine repentance. He came back to the project directors a broken man. His behavior showed a very great change in character. Even Dinatu was amazed by the great change in Garba's behavior. The project decided to take him back and give him another chance. Garba grew so much in his faith and changed so much in his character that he became a Sunday School teacher for new believers in a nearby local church. He also began to lead a weekly Bible study at the new housing site.

Dinatu became a dedicated Christian and began serving in the same local church. Because of the great change in Garba's life and in Dinatu's life, the couple was reconciled in their marriage. Garba has been greatly changed by Jesus Christ and he is now a witness to many people. Through the training he received in building his house, he now makes his living working as a mason in a block-making cooperative. Dinatu has been trained in making jewelry through the project and adds to the family income with her skill.

The true story of this couple, along with others in project New Life, is proof that there can be hope for the most hopeless people in the world. But there will not be hope until there are completely dedicated Christians who are ready to do the will of God. Salvation is a free gift from God but bringing that salvation to others can be the most costly thing in the world.

WHAT WAS THE FINAL RESULT OF THIS PROJECT?

Most of the people in project New Life have changed from a beggar mentality to a working mentality. Most of those in the project are now employed through one of the three cooperatives. There is a block-making cooperative among the men. There is a toy-making cooperative among the disabled. There is a jewelry making cooperative among the women.

The change in outlook among those living at the new housing site is especially evident among the children. Most of the school-age children are now in school and are doing well. Almost none of them were in school at the beginning. In the beginning the children were ashamed to speak about where they lived. There was little sense of family unity. Now the parents will celebrate birthdays, weddings and other family events. Most of those participating in the project have begun to take on the culture of the urban community around them. Some have even begun to reach out in hospitality to others, in some cases even inviting people from outside the community.

The group has elected their own local ruling council for the community. This council has started making decisions for the community on health problems, schooling, water supply, discipline, fines for things like fighting on the compound, damaging other peoples' properties and other offenses. The council also handles the rent for the houses and the utilities for the community.

There is a retail store run by the cooperative of the ladies who make the jewelry. The council carries out its own business with the government. Some of the adults are now taking adult education at primary and secondary level. One man has finished high school and is now the chairman of the council

There are about 25 people from the New Life community attending a local church. The greatest number of these are children and teenagers, thanks to the commitment of a very dedicated youth worker in the project. Most important, there are now 19 people from among the 35 households who have experienced a dramatic change in their lives through putting their faith in Jesus Christ.

It can be seen from this true story that there is a need for the church to become involved in a limited way in vocational rehabilitation programs for the poor so that such people can rebuild their lives in an honorable way. Considerable thought has gone into possible ways of helping people develop skills which will enable them to earn a living. The local church can benefit by studying what has been done by secular rehabilitation programs. An example of this would be the Job And Skills Program For Africa (JASPA) of the United Nations.

The church cannot bring investment and heavy industry into a nation. That is a function of the government. But the church can set up rehabilitation programs for people on an individual level which can include helping them to learn a job skill to earn a living. Helping people to become self-sustaining through projects of individual micro-industry is particularly suited to the church's task of making disciples for Christ. Skills such as commercial cooking, weaving, sewing clothes, furniture making, carpentry, plumbing, automobile repair, electrical repair, masonry, building and other practical skills can be taught to individuals one by one or in small classes by those in the church who have such skills. In this way needy people can be given skills which will help them to earn an honest living.

By sharing what they have, the people of God are able to give hope to a world that is without hope. The Bible says, "do not forget to do good and to share with others, for with such sacrifices God is pleased" (Heb. 13:16). Sharing, whether in a small or big way, encourages people and gives them hope. Sharing the good news of salvation in Jesus Christ gives the greatest possible hope to people without hope.

SUMMARY

Poverty is one of the greatest problems in Africa. This problem can be overcome within a local church. The church can even be the means of helping many poor people outside the church. When everyone in the church practices tithing and generous giving beyond the tithe, there will be resources to meet the needs of poor people in the church and even to help many people outside the church. In addition to giving money, the church should seek to use the skills and abilities of its members to help others find ways to make a proper living. Beyond meeting the needs of its own members, the church has a serious responsibility before God to pray for the government to take the right steps to meet the needs of the nation (1 Tim 2:1-2). Even in times of great difficulty, God can use the prayers of His people to save a nation from disaster.

To meet the needs of the poor, God's people must be willing to do what God has commanded them to do in the Bible. Jesus set the example for the church by ministering to the physical as well as the spiritual needs of people. He commanded His disciples to do the same thing (Matt. 10:8,42; Mark 6:37). Healing the sick, feeding the hungry, teaching literacy, providing job skills for the unskilled, counseling the hurting and restoring hope to the hopeless should all be a part of the ministry of the gospel of Jesus Christ. It is very important in helping the needy that help be given in such a way that people will become self-sustaining rather than becoming dependent. Those who are helped should also learn to reach out to help others in need. Churches and donors should require those who receive help to take an active part in their own rehabilitation.

QUESTIONS FOR REVIEW, REFLECTION AND GROUP DISCUSSION

1. How does poverty lead to crime, disease, despair and death?
2. How many of the ten poorest nations in the world are found in Africa? What does this fact mean for the Christian church in Africa?
3. What is a realistic way for a local church to approach the problem of poverty in the area where the church is located?
4. Make a list of what poor local church members can do for other poor people in the church congregation and poor people in the church's community.
5. What happens when help is given to poor people without requiring such poor people to do anything to help themselves?
6. What must poor and needy people learn to do if they are to experience a permanent change in their lives?
7. How can Christians find the motivation and the strength to do difficult tasks in relation to helping poor and needy people?
8. Discuss how members of a local church could use the people right within their own church to help unskilled people learn ways to earn an honorable living?

END NOTES

1. **George Kinoti,** *Hope For Africa And What The Christian Can Do.* **Nairobi: Africa Institute For Scientific Research And Development, 1994. pp. 15-16**
2. **Ibid. p. 16**
3. **Ibid. p. 17**
4. **Moffitt, Robert.** *Leadership Development Training Program, Level 2.* **Tempe, Arizona: Harvest, 1997. pp. 19-3 to 19-11.**

CHAPTER 9

POLITICS, POWER AND THE PROBLEMS THEY PROMOTE

The story of human governments and government leaders has been a weary story of power, pride, politics and problems for a prolonged period of time. Two thousand years ago Jesus commented on the current government officials of his day by saying, "The kings of the Gentiles lord it over them; and those who exercise authority over them call themselves Benefactors" (Luke 22:25). In other words, government leaders in his day used their positions of power to abuse, oppress and take advantage of those under their control. Publically they portrayed themselves as those who blessed and benefitted their people, but in reality they were selfish and corrupt. This is an accurate description of the way many government officials have acted down through history, including many government officials in modern Africa.

CORRUPT AND IMMORAL GOVERNMENT LEADERS

Many government leaders use their positions of power for their own personal gain. Many also live lives of gross moral evil. This can be seen in the life of one of the recent presidents of the United States. It can also be seen in the lives of some of those who went before him. Consider this commentary on the lives of the famous Kennedy family in America, of whom John F. Kennedy was a very famous American president in the 1960's. "It was not Joe [Kennedy] who was accused of rape in Palm Beach, Florida, not so very long ago. That was William Kennedy Smith, a cousin who was staying with his Uncle Ted, the Massachusetts senator at the time. . . It seems that the sins of the previous generations of Kennedys - and boy did they sin! - are now going to be paid for by this generation. The patriarch, Joseph Kennedy, publicly displayed his mistresses, cruelly humiliating the sainted Rose [his wife]. John Kennedy [the American president] behaved similarly, and he too, was never called to account. It is stunning now to contemplate his presidency. . . Here was a man who clearly felt that none of the rules, not even ones about co-mingling sex with national security, applied to him. Even so, the knowledge of his behavior is scant match for the dazzle of his smile. When you look at the old pictures of him, his charisma still triumphs over judgment." [1]

Compare this description of John F. Kennedy with the brief facts given in the gospel of Matthew about King Herod, a Roman political leader in the days of Christ. "Now Herod had arrested John and bound him and put him in prison because of Herodias, his brother Philip's wife, for John had been saying to him: "It is not lawful for you to have her." Herod wanted to kill John, but he was afraid of the people, because they considered him a prophet. On Herod's birthday the daughter of Herodias danced for them and pleased Herod so much that he promised with an oath to give her whatever she asked for. Prompted by her mother, she said, "Give me here on a platter the head of John the Baptist " (Matt. 14:3-8).

In this account of an evil political leader of long ago, John the Baptist had the courage to rebuke the man for his adultery with his own brother's wife. For this courageous act, John the Baptist was beheaded by order of the king, who did not appreciate having his secret sins exposed to the public (Matt. 14: 9-11).

It should not be surprising, then, that many political leaders in modern Africa have enjoyed less than an honorable reputation of character. One general description of such leaders is given in these words: "A Big Man who looks like this: His face is on the money. His photograph hangs in every office in his realm. . . . He names streets, football stadiums, hospitals and universities after himself. He insists on being called doctor or . . .'the big elephant' or . . . 'the wise old man' or 'the national miracle.' His every pronouncement is reported on the front page. He sleeps with the wives and daughters of powerful men in his government. . . . He scapegoats minorities to shore up support. He rigs elections. He emasculates the courts. He cows the press. He stifles academia. He goes to church. . . He blesses his home region with highways, schools, hospitals, housing projects, irrigation schemes and a Presidential mansion. . . . His enemies are detained or exiled, humiliated or bankrupted, tortured or killed. He uses the resources of the state to feed a cult of personality that defines him as incorruptible, all-knowing . . . and kind to children. His cult equates his personal well-being with the well-being of the state."[2]

In contrast to these discouraging descriptions of very real but very corrupt political leaders of modern and ancient history, the Bible describes another political leader of long ago who was a man of honesty, integrity and godly character. The man was Daniel, a captive Jew, who became the prime minister in each of four successive governments.

Just because a person is a government official does not mean that he or she must agree to the corruption, selfishness and moral evil of others in the government. The story of Daniel shows us that it is possible for a godly man to hold a very high position in a secular, corrupt government without becoming corrupt himself. Such a man can be a powerful witness for God to non-Christian government officials just as Daniel was. Daniel was an uncompromising witness for the true God to the kings under whom he served as prime minister. Consider this strong warning given by Daniel to King Nebuchadnezzar, who could have had Daniel killed for daring to speak such words: "O king, be pleased to accept my advice: Renounce your sins by doing what is right, and your wickedness by being kind to the oppressed. It may be that then your prosperity will continue" (Dan. 4:27).

The effect of Daniel's witness on King Nebuchadnezzar was dramatic. After God judged Nebuchadnezzar with insanity for seven years because of the king's pride (Dan. 4:28-32) we read these astonishing words written by the king himself in an open letter to his entire empire. "At the same time that my sanity was restored, my honor and splendor were returned to me for the glory of my kingdom. My advisers and nobles sought me out, and I was restored to my throne and became even greater than before. Now I, Nebuchadnezzar, praise and exalt and glorify the King of heaven, because everything he does is right and all his ways are just. And those who walk in pride he is able to humble" (Dan. 4:36-37).

Nebuchadnezzar was a man who had scorned the God of the Hebrews (Dan. 3:15) but finally he was broken before God in humility and reverence. This story concerning Daniel's witness to Nebuchadnezzar clearly shows us that there are times when it is God's will to put godly people into high government office. We will return to this story later in the chapter.

It is a fact that much of the suffering, poverty, injustice, war and oppression endured by African Christians today is directly or indirectly caused by evil governments or corrupt government officials. What is the common man to do? What are African Christians supposed to do when they are faced with the pride, power, political manipulation, tribalism, greed and corruption of some of the government officials who rule their countries? Even more difficult, what are Christians to do when these corrupt and selfish officials are not government leaders but the leaders of their own churches and denominations?! For indeed just about every denomination is plagued with the problem of proud, selfish, corrupt church leaders who use their power and position for their personal gain and not for the growth of God's kingdom.

As we have seen, the situation is not new in Africa or new in the modern world. The country which proclaims itself to be the most democratic nation in the world (America) has become just as corrupt as any other country of the modern world. The people of America have willingly elected some of the more immoral leaders of the modern age through democratic processes. The love of money, not the love of human beings and their needs, has been the basis on which many political decisions have been made in the West. If this is true in North America and Europe we can certainly expect to see the same thing in Africa, and we do.

SPIRITUAL WEAPONS TO SOLVE POLITICAL PROBLEMS

Is there anything Christians can do when there is corrupt and evil government leadership? Is there anything they can do when their churches are controlled by greedy and immoral men? The answer is yes. Christians may have to suffer persecution for their faith in Christ but there is something God wants them to do when evil leaders oppress and destroy nations. Most important, the church should not tolerate arrogant and corrupt church leaders. There are actions which the church can take which can change the situation. But God's people must understand that both in national governments and in church governments, corrupt officials do not give up their positions of power and influence without a fight. Renewal can be a long and difficult process.

It is very important for Christians to understand that the battle they fight is not a physical struggle but a spiritual war. The Bible says, "For though we live in the world, we do not wage war as the world does. The weapons we fight with are not the weapons of the world. On the contrary, they have divine power to demolish strongholds" (2 Cor. 10:3-4). What are the spiritual weapons with which Christians can fight to overcome strongholds of evil influence? What are the strongholds?

There are seven spiritual weapons mentioned in Ephesians chapter 6. These are truth, righteousness, the gospel of peace, faith, salvation, the Word of God and prayer. Some of these weapons, such as righteousness and salvation, can be considered defensive weapons since they are intended to protect the Christian. Others such as the gospel of peace, the Word of God and prayer can be considered offensive weapons because they can be used to overcome the forces of evil. The weapon of faith can be used both defensively to protect our minds and offensively together with prayer to overcome the works of Satan.

Concerning the weapon of prayer, God specifically commands us to pray for government leaders. Paul wrote, "I urge, then, first of all, that requests, prayers, intercession and thanksgiving be made for everyone-- for kings and all those in authority" (1 Tim. 2:1-2). Since God has given His people the command to pray for government leaders it should be clear that He intends to use their prayers to change things in the government which are wrong.

What are strongholds? In the Old Testament, a stronghold was a fortress. It was a place where people or soldiers could hide from the enemy or a place from which they could attack those opposing them without fear of being overpowered themselves. King David hid in a "stronghold" (probably a cave) in the Israeli desert when he was hiding from King Saul, and from the Philistines (as in

2 Sam. 5:17). For the true Christian God is his or her stronghold or fortress. The Bible says, "The LORD is my rock, my fortress and my deliverer; my God is my rock, in whom I take refuge. He is my shield and the horn of my salvation, my stronghold" (Psalm 18:2).

When we consider 2 Cor. 10:3-4 in the light of these uses of the word "stronghold" in the Bible, it is evident that the strongholds referred to in this verse are "places" (that is, institutions, or policies, or practices, or attitudes, or beliefs, or possibly individuals or groups of individuals) in which Satan or evil hides or from which Satan attacks the society for his own evil purposes. Thus an evil practice (such as bribery or female circumcision, or homosexuality) could become a stronghold of Satan. An evil government policy (such as the policy of ethnic genocide recently practiced by the Yugoslavian government) was a very powerful stronghold of evil. The fact is that many wars are powerful strongholds through which Satan is able to effectively carry out his evil purposes of death, suffering and destruction against mankind.

On a more personal level, an attitude of pride by an individual or a group of people can be a very effective and powerful stronghold of evil. For an individual or even a whole nation, a preoccupation with sexual lust or self-indulgence can become a stronghold of evil through which Satan can carry out his evil intentions to morally destroy individuals, to destroy the ministry of Christian workers, or to morally destroy whole nations. This strategy of Satan is working very effectively in certain parts of the world today, especially in the West.

Pride, the love of power and the love of money are probably the three most powerful strongholds of evil in the lives of political leaders and even in the lives of many church leaders. It was pride which brought the downfall of Satan according to the Word of God (1 Tim. 3:6) so it should not surprise us that pride should be such a powerful stronghold of evil in the lives of corrupt leaders today.

The devil has not changed in his character. He still brings some of his most effective temptation to human beings through pride. Perhaps the greatest danger of pride is that we do not take it seriously as we do sins in the area of money or sex. Pride seems harmless until we look at it closely. For example it was pride which destroyed the religious leaders of Jesus' day and brought Jesus' strongest words of condemnation. He actually promised the Pharisees they would go to hell for their pride (Matt. 23:33)! In the book of Proverbs we are told, "Pride goes before destruction" (Prov. 16:18).

If we think about this, it is not hard to understand the great evil that lies behind pride. Pride is the evil force behind tribalism, a great curse which has caused the death of literally millions of Africans in our generation. Pride is often what makes entire nations go to war with each other. Pride is the hidden reason for fighting and division in churches. Such fighting can destroy the witness of the church in a community. Pride is a powerful stronghold in the lives of many human beings and in many Christians as well. The Bible tells us over and over that God hates pride. (Psalm 101:5, Prov. 6:16-17, Prov. 8:13, Prov. 21:4, James 4:6). The Bible tells us that we must humble ourselves before God. (2 Chron. 7:14, Zeph. 2:3, James 4:10, 1 Peter 5:6).

Another stronghold of Satan in the lives of many people is the desire for power and the love of money. The desire for power and the love of money are the things which motivate many people in the present world system of values. This also includes the love of material things (materialism) and the love of self (1 John 2:16). The Bible warns us, "Do not love the world or anything in the world. If anyone loves the world, the love of the Father is not in him" (1 John 2:15). Another very powerful stronghold is sexual lust. How many church leaders in our time have destroyed their ministries, their marriages, their families and their ministries through sexual lust, immorality and adultery?

There are other strongholds which are very destructive. One of these is bitterness. The Bible warns us that bitterness will cause many people to be defiled (Heb. 12:15). Another stronghold is unforgiveness. Unforgiveness can bring the judgment of God on a person's life (Matt. 18:21-35). Unforgiveness will also keep our prayers from being answered (Matt. 6:14-15, Mark 11:25). The Bible says that anger, another stronghold, can give the devil a "foothold" in a person's life (Eph. 4:26-27, James 1:20). Jesus said that resentment (hatred of another person) is related to the intention to commit murder (Matt. 5:21-22). Thus resentment can be a stronghold in a person's life.

There are other powerful strongholds in which the evil purposes of Satan can hide. and from which his evil purposes against mankind can be effectively carried out. Such things as fear, self pity, hatred, doubt, jealousy, addictions, bad habits and broken human relationships can become strongholds of evil in people's lives.

The good news of 2 Cor. 10:3-4 is that these and all other strongholds of evil can be broken or torn down by the use of the spiritual weapons given to us in Ephesians 6:13-18. The weapon of prayer together with the weapon of faith is the most powerful force in the universe to break strongholds of evil in individual lives and even in the policies and practices of evil governments and evil government leaders. This weapon is powerful because God Himself has commanded it and God will answer such prayers of faith. Prayer moves the Hand that made the universe. Consider what God has commanded and what He has promised concerning prayer, in the following verses.

"This, then, is how you should pray: "'Our Father in heaven, . . . your kingdom come, your will be done on earth as it is in heaven" (Matt. 6:9-10).

"Watch and pray so that you will not fall into temptation. The spirit is willing, but the body is weak" (Matt. 26:41).

"Love your enemies and pray for those who persecute you" (Matt. 5:44).

"Pray for those who mistreat you" (Luke 6:28).

"I urge, then, first of all, that requests, prayers, intercession and thanksgiving be made for everyone--for kings and all those in authority" (1 Tim. 2:1-2).

"Ask and it will be given to you; seek and you will find; knock and the door will be opened to you" (Matt. 7:7).

"I tell you the truth, if anyone says to this mountain, 'Go, throw yourself into the sea,' and does not doubt in his heart but believes that what he says will happen, it will be done for him. Therefore I tell you, whatever you ask for in prayer, believe that you have received it, and it will be yours" (Mark 11:23-24).

"This is the confidence we have in approaching God: that if we ask anything according to his will, he hears us. And if we know that he hears us--whatever we ask--we know that we have what we asked of him" (1 John 5:14-15).

"the Spirit helps us in our weakness. We do not know what we ought to pray for, but the Spirit himself intercedes for us" (Rom. 8:26).

Who are the spiritual enemies of God against whom we must use spiritual weapons? We tend to think they are human beings such as corrupt government or church leaders. The Bible says that human beings are not the real enemy. As we just read, we are told to love and pray for our human enemies and for those who mistreat us (Matt. 5:44, Luke 6:28). The Bible says that our real enemies are evil spirits, that is, fallen angels and demons under Satan's control. Ephesians 6:12 says, "our struggle is not against flesh and blood, but against the rulers, against the authorities, against the powers of this dark world and against the spiritual forces of evil in the heavenly realms." It is because the real enemies are not human beings that human weapons of warfare are useless in this conflict.

Here is an example of why only spiritual weapons can finally overcome political oppression and problems of corrupt leadership. Suppose an evil leader finally dies or is put out of the government. This person will be followed by another leader. Experience shows that very often the new leader will be just as corrupt or even more corrupt than the person he followed. However, if the heart of an evil leader is changed (as a result of prayer) and the man is converted, there will be a great change for good in that country. How can an evil leader be persuaded to change from his evil ways? The answer is, God can work in the person's life in answer to prayer or through contact with the Word of God or the gospel of peace. Prayer, the Word of God and the gospel of peace are spiritual weapons.

For an example of how this actually happened in history let us see how God overcame the stronghold of pride in the life of the proud and defiant Nebuchadnezzar, King of Babylon. Nebuchadnezzar had abusively scorned Daniel's three friends with these words: "if you are ready to fall down and worship the image I made, very good. But if you do not worship it, you will be thrown immediately into a blazing furnace. Then what god will be able to rescue you from my hand?" (Dan.3:15).

To show the king His sovereign power, God proceeded to deliver Daniel's three friends from the fiery furnace right in front of Nebuchadnezzar's eyes (Dan. 3:24-26). God did this because the three Hebrew men had faith in God (Dan. 3:17) (a spiritual weapon) and because they had committed themselves to unconditionally obey the Word of God (another spiritual weapon) by refusing to bow down to any idol or graven image (Exodus 20:4, Dan. 3:17-18).

Nebuchadnezzar was greatly impressed with this display of God's power (Dan. 3:28). But he was still a proud and defiant king. He still had a stronghold of pride in his life so God continued to deal with him. The Bible says, "The LORD detests all the proud of heart. Be sure of this: They will not go unpunished."(Prov. 16:5). The Lord was about to punish Nebuchadnezzar for his pride and to destroy this stronghold in his life. The Bible records that, "Twelve months later, as the king was walking on the roof of the royal palace of Babylon, he said, "Is not this the great Babylon I have built as the royal residence, by my mighty power and for the glory of my majesty?" The words were still on his lips when a voice came from heaven, 'This is what is decreed for you, King Nebuchadnezzar: Your royal authority has been taken from you. You will be driven away from people and will live with the wild animals; you will eat grass like cattle. Seven times will pass by for you until you acknowledge that the Most High is sovereign over the kingdoms of men and gives them to anyone he wishes.' Immediately what had been said about Nebuchadnezzar was fulfilled. He was driven away from people and ate grass like cattle" (Dan. 4:29-33).

After seven years of insanity the stronghold of pride in Nebuchadnezzar's life was finally broken. At last the king confessed, "Now I, Nebuchadnezzar, praise and exalt and glorify the King of heaven, because everything he does is right and all his ways are just. And those who walk in pride he is able to humble" (Dan.4:37).

In a more recent example in Africa, God dealt with an arrogant church leader who had a stronghold of pride in his life. In response to prayer (a spiritual weapon) for this man, God allowed the leader's wife to give birth to a pitifully deformed child. The child has become a daily tool in the hands of God to break down the stronghold of pride in this leader's life.

THE POWER OF PRAYING FOR GOVERNMENT OFFICIALS

How should the people of God use the spiritual weapons of prayer and faith to pull down the strongholds of pride and other evils in the lives of corrupt political leaders and corrupt church leaders? First, they need to believe that God will answer such prayers because He has commanded them to pray this way (1 Tim. 2:1-2). This will enable them to pray strong prayers of faith which will have the effect of moving mountains of problems (Mark 11:22-24). Their prayers should be based on the promises and commandments of the Word of God (another spiritual weapon). Such prayers will be used by God to cause His will to be done in that government. This is exactly what God wants to accomplish through the prayers of His people.

Jesus taught His disciples to pray, "your will be done on earth as it is in heaven" (Matt. 6:10). Why would Christians be taught to pray for God's will to be done on earth if it was not God's intention to answer such prayers? Christians should therefore pray something such as the following for their government: "God, cause your will to be done through this government as it is done in heaven - whatever it takes to make that happen." It is so important that we pray for government leaders and officials that God does not leave it up to us to think of this. He commands us to do it (1 Tim. 2:1-2).

What would happen in a country if the people of every local church in that country were to devote one whole day each month to fasting and prayer for the government officials of their country? It is hard to predict exactly what would happen but it is unquestionable that something very good for the people of that country would take place. Concerning prayer, the apostle James tells us, "You do not have, because you do not ask God. When you ask, you do not receive, because you ask with wrong motives, that you may spend what you get on your pleasures" (James 4:2-3).

The point is this. If the people of God learned to pray for the right things, with the right motives, they would see God do unbelievable things in response to their prayers. One of the great secrets of the Bible which the devil does not want Christians to understand is that God really will cause His will to be done on earth in response to their prayers.

As an example of this, God has commanded us to make disciples of all nations (Matt. 28:19). This commandment shows us one part of the will of God. But to make disciples, people must go to other people with the gospel. Hence we are commanded by Christ to pray for people to do this. Jesus said, "The harvest is plentiful but the workers are few. Ask the Lord of the harvest, therefore, to send out workers into his harvest field" (Matt. 9:37-38). If we will obediently pray for such workers God will raise up people to carry out the Great Commission and this part of God's will can be done.

In another example, God had already revealed through the prophet Jeremiah that the Hebrew people would return from Babylonian captivity 70 years after their captivity had begun (Jer. 25:11-12, Jer. 29:10). Yet, when the time of captivity came to an end, God moved the man Daniel to pray that the Hebrews would indeed be restored to the holy city of Jerusalem (Dan. 9:2-3). In other words, God caused His will to be done in response to prayer even though God had already said that it would be done.

How do we discover God's will in other matters so that we will know how to pray for the will of God to be done? The answer is, by reading the Word of God. The Bible reveals the will of God to us for every part of life. The Bible will not give us an answer to every specific question we may have such as, "Should I travel to such and such a city today?" Instead, the Bible gives us principles and examples through stories of how the will of God applies to different parts of life. By following these principles and the examples of godly people, we will understand the will of God. In this way we will know how to pray about most situations.

Even when we don't know how to pray for a particular situation we have this amazing promise from God. "In the same way, the Spirit helps us in our weakness. We do not know what we ought to pray for, but the Spirit himself intercedes for us with groans that words cannot express. And he who searches our hearts knows the mind of the Spirit, because the Spirit intercedes for the saints in accordance with God's will" (Rom. 8:26-27).

It is the clearly revealed will of God that Christians should pray for their leaders. If we will do this we can have faith that God will answer such prayers. The apostle John said, "This is the confidence we have in approaching God: that if we ask anything according to his will, he hears us. And if we know that he hears us--whatever we ask--we know that we have what we asked of him" (1 John 5:14-15).

If we will obediently pray for government and church leaders as we are commanded to do and if our hearts are free from known sin when we pray (Isa. 59:1-2), God will do something to answer our prayers in spite of how corrupt such leaders may be. He may change the hearts or attitudes of such leaders, or He may bring judgment upon them for their evil doing, or He may remove them completely, but He will respond to our prayers in some way because He has promised to do it (John 15:7, John 16:23-24).

As much as possible, it is helpful to be specific when praying for government or church leaders. It is good to pray that they will be good leaders. It is even better to pray that they will be given the wisdom of God and the willingness to act on this wisdom, in order to care for the specific needs and problems in their administration. African governments have enormous problems in matters such as poverty, inadequate health care, unemployment, injustice and other things. In response to prayer, God can give leaders the wisdom to know how to deal with such problems and most important, the will to act in the right way. Leaders often know what to do but they do not have the will to do it because of their sinful desires. The Holy Spirit can give them the motivation to do what is right in response to the church's prayers. The Bible says, "for it is God who works in you to will and to act according to his good purpose" (Philippians 2:13).

Recently in one African country earnest prayer was made to God for the government to find a way to ease the problem of unemployment. After a few weeks the government came out with an unusual policy which encouraged wealthy nationals who had left the country to return for the purpose of making investments and setting up new businesses. The policy offered such attractive financial advantages to do this that many nationals who had left the country began to return to set up businesses. This in turn had the effect of creating jobs for people and easing the burden of unemployment and poverty.

It is also good to ask God to restrain government and church officials from their evil tendencies and corrupt practices and if necessary, to punish them if they persist in evil doing. If we fail to pray as we have been commanded, we will only have ourselves to blame for increasingly evil and oppressive practices by these officials.

In the case of corrupt church leaders, it may be necessary and right at certain times for church members to join together and remove such leaders if they refuse to repent of their corrupt practices. Leaders in the church of Jesus Christ are appointed by God to be servants, not to be kings. The apostle Peter wrote to church leaders in the following words, "Be shepherds of God's flock that is under your care, serving as overseers--not because you must, but because you are willing, as God wants you to be; not greedy for money, but eager to serve; not lording it over those entrusted to you, but being examples to the flock" (1 Pet. 5:2-3). When church leaders begin to use their positions for selfish purposes rather than as a way to serve God's people, such leaders need to be disciplined or removed. The church members should not tolerate corrupt church leadership.

SHOULD CHRISTIANS BE INVOLVED IN GOVERNMENT LEADERSHIP?

An important question in the minds of many Christians is whether or not it is right or good for a Christian to become involved in politics and government. There are two main viewpoints in answer to this question. On one side are those who point to the many problems which have been discussed in this chapter. They point out that politics in general is a corrupt and dirty business where the love of power, the love of money, dishonesty, bribery, tribalism, selfishness, immorality and many other corrupt practices seem to rule the lives of many government officials.

Some Christians warn that those who become involved in government are almost always corrupted or influenced in a negative way by the system of which they become a part. Hundreds of years ago a philosopher named Machiavelli observed, "power corrupts, and absolute power corrupts absolutely."

It has been the sad experience of some Christians of good intention that the temptations of power and money in government office have resulted in the loss of their Christian testimony and character. From the bad experiences of many Christians in government it would be wise for a Christian to be very sure of God's leading before seeking to become involved in politics. If a Christian is led by God into government leadership he or she should gather a group of mature Christians around him or her who will hold the Christian accountable for his or her actions in office and who will also pray regularly for that person.

The most important questions which a Christian seeking political office should ask himself or herself are these. Why do I want to run for this office? What will I accomplish that others are not able to do? Is my real motive personal ambition or the advancement of the kingdom of God?

On the other side of this question is the clear testimony of the Bible that God Himself placed certain people in very high places of secular government leadership at different times in history. God did this in order to accomplish His will for that government or for His own people.

Joseph was a foreign Jewish slave, sold on the slave market as household help to Potiphar, the captain of Pharaoh's guard (Gen. 37:36). Joseph was a man with no freedom, no rights, no reputation and no hope of anything in Egypt. Yet God placed this young man at the very top of the Egyptian government immediately under the Pharaoh himself (Gen. 41:41,44) in order to save Egypt from starvation and to provide a place of protection and expansion for God's people (Jacob's family).

Moses was the son of despised and enslaved Jewish parents in Egypt, yet God placed Moses in the home of Pharaoh's family. God enabled Moses to receive all the education, training and experience that was reserved for Egyptian royalty in order to prepare Moses for the task of leading God's people for 40 years in the desert.

Esther was an unknown but beautiful Jewish girl in a foreign land. She was an orphan who was being raised by a relative named Mordecai (Esther 2:7). Yet in God's sovereignty, this unknown girl became the queen of one of the largest empires in the entire world (Esther 2:17). God did this so that at the appropriate time this woman could be used by God to protect the entire Jewish nation from genocide by a crafty and wicked Persian government official named Haman (Esther 3:8-15).

Daniel was taken as a prisoner of war while still a young man (Dan. 1:1-6). Yet in God's sovereign plan this man became the most spiritually influential government official of ancient history and perhaps in all human history. This took place in spite of a carefully laid plan to take his life (Dan. 6:1-17). What other man in history has ever been appointed prime minister under four different world empires? Yet that is what God caused to happen to this most unusual man. More amazing still is the testimony of Daniel's political enemies about his character and integrity. Even his enemies could find no fault in him (Daniel 6:1-5)!

Throughout his long and unusual government career Daniel gave a powerful, effective, and absolutely fearless testimony to the living God and His holy standards. His personal testimony was so powerful that at least one of the kings under whom he served (Nebuchadnezzar) was converted to faith in the true God and wrote out the testimony of his conversion for the entire Babylonian empire to read (Dan. 4:1-37)!

It is clear from these examples in the Bible that it is the plan of God to have certain persons from among His own people to occupy the highest offices of government at certain times in history. It should be observed, however, that in each case mentioned in the Bible it was not through the effort of the particular individual concerned that the person came to occupy a position of high government leadership. Instead, it was the hand of God through circumstances which brought that person into power in each case.

This fact should be a guideline and a warning to Christians who seek high government office through the political process. As Daniel himself observed, it is God who puts His people into positions of government authority and also removes them (Dan. 2:21). If Christians try to secure such positions for themselves they run the risk of personal ruin by entering an area of very great temptation and corruption just as Machiavelli said long ago. God alone will choose those of His people whom He wants to run world governments and God alone will determine the way to put them into that position.

Some years ago, a senior Christian military officer was installed as Head of State of the most populated country in Africa. The general did not seek this position. It came about through a selection by the ruling military council. This man ruled his country for nine years and became the most beloved leader of his nation since its independence in 1960. He was removed from his office by a military coup de tat, although in God's sovereignty, he was not personally harmed by the coup. These circumstances revealed the hand of God since most Heads of State are killed as a result of coup plots to overthrow their government.

This man went on the get a phD degree in Britain. Many times he was asked by his people to return to his country and run for political office. Instead, he chose to return to his country in the 1990's to lead an interdenominational prayer movement for national spiritual renewal. The story of General (Dr.) Yakubu Gowan of Nigeria is a modern example of the hand of God for the spiritual good of a nation. If you would like more information you can contact the organization called, "Nigeria Prays" at P.O. Box 586, Abuja, Nigeria.

Apart from prayer, what else can the common Christian do to influence the government of his or her country for good? The answer is that every Christian is called upon by God to be "salt and light" in the society in which he or she lives (Matt. 5:13-16). In the days of the New Testament, salt was used as a preservative to prevent spoilage of food. Christians today can exercise an influence against sin and evil in their societies through prayer and through making their voices heard by the public on issues of good and evil.

Light helps people to know where they are going in the dark. In many countries the lives of Christians may be the only way that non-Christian people will ever know what is truly the right thing to do or the right way to live. Jesus said the lives of His people are "the light of the world" (Matt. 5:14-16).

It is God's plan that Christians should live out their lives and their civic responsibilities in a manner which will bring praise to our God and Savior, Jesus Christ. The apostle Peter long ago wrote, "Live such good lives among the pagans that, though they accuse you of doing wrong, they may see your good deeds and glorify God on the day he visits us. Submit yourselves for the Lord's sake to every authority instituted among men: whether to the king, as the supreme authority, or to governors, who are sent by him to punish those who do wrong and to commend those who do right. For it is God's will that by doing good you should silence the ignorant talk of foolish men. Live as free men, but do not use your freedom as a cover-up for evil; live as servants of God" (1 Peter 2:12-16). These words summarize the way in which individual Christians should relate to the difficult problems of politics, power and the national problems which they promote.

SUMMARY

Those involved in political leadership in every country of the world are subject to great temptations to use the power and influence of their positions for personal gain. The love of power and money and the pride of national recognition has destroyed the moral and spiritual lives of a great many people in government leadership and even in church leadership. It is easy to feel that the situation is hopeless, but that is not the perspective of the Word of God.

God commands His people to pray for government leaders regardless of whether they are Christians or not. Since God has commanded this, it is clear that He intends to use the prayers of His people to bring about changes in government officials and government policies through such prayers. The prayers of Christians for their leaders can bring about a change of heart from evil to good. Their prayers can reduce temptation for such officials or the complete removal of such officials. Most important, the prayers of Christians for their governments can hinder Satan and his demons from carrying out their plans of evil for that government and that nation.

God sometimes places one of His people into a position of high government leadership in order to accomplish God's will in that nation. Christians, however, should be very careful about seeking political office for themselves. Such positions can lead to great temptation and moral problems. If a Christian does have clear leading from the Lord to seek political office, he or she should surround himself with a team of committed prayer partners. All Christians in every society are called on to live holy, helpful and obedient lives in their community and their country in order to be salt and light for God in the presence of a sinful and selfish world.

QUESTIONS FOR REVIEW, REFLECTION AND GROUP DISCUSSION

1. What kind of problems exist in your country due to the influence of corrupt government officials?
2. What would be the difference in the way Christians should respond to corruption in government officials and the way they should respond to corruption in church leaders?
3. Which of the seven spiritual weapons listed in Ephesians 6:14-18 could be most effectively used by Christians to bring about change in corrupt government officials?
4. Why do you think God commands Christians to pray for government officials?
5. What do you think God does in response to the prayers of His people for government leaders?
6. What are the three or four most powerful strongholds of evil in the lives of political leaders and church leaders?
7. If a Christian feels led by God to enter politics, what should that person do to protect himself or herself from temptation?
8. Make a list of the kind of things Christians can do in order to influence the societies in which they live for God and for God's standards of holiness.

END NOTES

1. International Herald Tribune Newspaper, September 2, 1997, p.8.
2. Harden, Blaine, Africa: Dispatches From A Fragile Continent.

CHAPTER 10

WOMEN IN MODERN AFRICA AND IN THE CHURCH

The role of women in society and especially the role of women in the church is a subject of considerable discussion in modern Africa . It is almost certain that the recent changes in western culture concerning attitudes towards women is affecting Africa in an important way. The subject of "women's liberation" has become a major issue in the West in political and popular discussion. The church is well aware of this discussion and great changes have taken place in churches and church policies in the West as a result of this debate. Such questions as whether or not women should be ordained to the ministry or whether women should be church leaders and church elders are serious issues of discussion in the West today.

The debate has now come to many parts of Africa, especially in the cities. The churches in Africa are certain to be affected by this debate. In addition, most women in Africa are very much aware that there is still a strong cultural pattern of male dominance in most of Africa. This has often resulted in unfair treatment of women by men and it has made the subject of the role of women an important topic of discussion. The following true story illustrates a common pattern.

A Christian girl named Lydia wanted very much to get married. The only offer of marriage she had came from a non-Christian man in her village. Lydia realized she was disobeying God to marry an unbeliever but she liked the man and decided to married him anyway. Lydia's parents tried to stop the marriage but did not succeed. The man was a teacher. He had a low view of women.

After the birth of 4 children the marriage began to deteriorate. There were many arguments over money. The husband began to drink heavily and wasted much of the family income on drinking. Lydia and her husband began to quarrel seriously. Without much fellowship or a good spiritual foundation, Lydia began to develop many spiritual problems. Her husband would often beat her severely. She wanted to leave him but she realized that she had no way to support herself and her children. Eventually her husband got a scholarship to Russia and was away for seven years. Lydia began going to a witch doctor to enquire about her husband. Because of their long separation both partners were unfaithful to each other.

When her husband did return their financial problems continued. They were made worse by living far from their home area. The couple had moved to the capital city and were again struggling financially. Life became very difficult. Then one day Lydia's husband abandoned his family completely without telling anyone where he was going. Later he wrote to her but gave no address. Still later she learned that her husband had committed suicide. Lydia was a broken and destitute woman. It was only later when she again became active in a Bible teaching church that she received any help or encouragement in her life. Yet even today, Lydia's life and the lives of her children are painfully scarred from her bitter marriage. Lydia experienced the grief that comes from disobeying God by marrying an unbeliever. She also experienced the pain of a cultural pattern of harsh male dominance.

As in many secular discussions, there are extremes of viewpoint concerning the role of women in the society. One extreme is found in North American and European cultures today. Another extreme is found in some African cultures. There is a strong movement in the West today to encourage women to do everything that men do in the society including participating in the army as combat soldiers. There are strong political organizations, such as the National Organization of Women (NOW) in America who promote legislation to give women access to all areas of private and public life, especially those formerly dominated by men. Some of the women most active in this movement have been described as "feminists." This refers to the desire of these women to have equality with men in all areas of life and to refuse to be dominated by men in any situation, including the home.

The other extreme viewpoint is found in many parts of Africa and in other non-western cultures. In some of these cultures women are still considered to be of much less importance and value than men. In some African cultures women are regarded with less value than certain forms of property, such as cattle. In other cultures, women are treated by men in the same way as children are treated. In still others, women are regarded as the slaves of men. Dr. Danfulani Kore, the former principal of Jos ECWA Theological seminary in Nigeria, carried out six years of research with 34 ethnic groups in Nigeria in order to discover the prevailing attitudes on a wide range of issues concerning marriage and male-female relationships.[1] What Dr. Kore discovered was not encouraging to most women in Africa.

Dr. Kore writes, "The study indicates that all 34 tribes have a very high concept of men. He is regarded by many ethnic groups as a king, a boss, and even as a semi-god." [2] In contrast to this, Dr. Kore found that, "The majority of the respondents indicated that the concept of women is quite inferior. She is looked upon as the source of sexual satisfaction for men. . . . Some husbands . . .view them as 'incomplete human beings.' Even some religions consider women as inferior to men. There is much to be desired from the biblical point of view regarding the image of women in most Nigerian cultures." [3]

It is clear that there is an urgent need for Christians today, both men and women, to understand the teaching of the Bible concerning women and God's plan for women in relation to men if God's will is to be done on earth as it is done in Heaven (Matt. 6:10). Unfortunately this subject more than most others has been dominated by culture, conflict and tradition rather than by the teaching of the Bible. This makes it difficult for Christians to think and act as God would have them think and act.

It is important to remind ourselves that God is the one who created mankind. Only God knows what is best for the human beings He created. If we want God's blessing on our lives and our churches, it is very important that we be willing to put away the prejudices of culture, whether they are western or non-western, and submit our behavior and attitudes to the Word of God. Any other viewpoint will not result in God's blessing. Instead it will result in social disorder, harm to individuals and the judgment of God.

One example of the folly of submitting to the pressure of culture can be seen in the recent experience of the feminist movement in America. This movement has politically succeeded in encouraging women to take part in all aspects of military activity. This has resulted in women being placed on American naval ships and on the front lines of fighting with male soldiers. This unnatural pressure to urge women to do what has always been done by men has brought major problems and scandals to the military forces. There are now many complaints from women in the United States military forces of sexual assault, rape and sexual harassment by men.

It is obvious that God created men and women with a natural sexual attraction and desire for each other. If men and women are required to live together in what is clearly an unnatural situation it should not be surprising that the strong sexual desires of men will result in sexual abuse of women in those situations. This is a a good example of the teaching of the Bible which says that, "the wisdom of this world is foolishness in God's sight" (1 Cor. 3:19).

THE BIBLICAL VIEW OF MEN AND WOMEN

We need to start at the beginning and see what the Bible teaches about God's creation of woman. What was the plan of God concerning the female half of the human race? We read in Genesis chapter one that God created man in His own image. The Bible says, "So God created man in his own image, in the image of God he created him; male and female he created them" (Gen. 1:27). This statement shows us that at God's creation, there was no difference in importance or value between men and women. They are both created by God. They are both created in His image.

The same idea is repeated in the New Testament concerning the value and importance of men and women in the church of Jesus Christ. Paul wrote, "There is neither Jew nor Greek, slave nor free, male nor female, for you are all one in Christ Jesus" (Gal. 3:28). In another place Paul observed, "In the Lord, however, woman is not independent of man, nor is man independent of woman. For as woman came from man, so also man is born of woman. But everything comes from God" (1 Cor. 11:11-12). It is also clear in the New Testament that Jesus Christ came to earth to suffer and die for the sins of all human beings, both men and women (John 3:16, 1 Pet. 2:24).

From these verses, the biblical view of men and women is clear. God created them both in His image. They are of precisely equal importance and value to God, not because they are male or female, but because they are human beings. If we place a greater importance on either men or women we are challenging the truth of God.

When God created mankind, He made one human being out of the dust of the earth and breathed into that person the breath of life (Gen. 2:7). With a little reflection it should be clear that all the elements of maleness and femaleness (at least mentally and emotionally) were present in the first created human being (Adam) even though he was physically and outwardly a male. Eve was not made separately out of the dust as Adam was, but was carefully separated out from within Adam's body by God (Gen. 2:21-22). It is an interesting fact of science that every man and every woman in the world has both male and female hormones in his or her body.

It should be evident from the creation of Eve that in the heart of God there must be all the essential non-physical elements of both maleness and femaleness, since mankind (as male and female) was made in the image of God. For example, men in general tend to be more objective and more decisive than women. They tend to be leaders more than followers. They tend to be more authoritative and less submissive than women. They tend to be less sensitive and less emotional than women. By contrast, women in general tend to be more compassionate, more gentle, more sensitive and more emotional than men. There will always be exceptions but these general tendencies are common in many parts of the world. The interesting fact is that we see all of these qualities joined together in the character of God.

Consider the revelation of God in Jesus Christ. We see the awesome power of God displayed in Jesus Christ (John 11:43-44) but we also see His loving gentleness (Isa. 42:3, Mark 5:40-41). We see the absolute authority of God over all things (Matt. 8:26-27,

Matt. 28:18), but we also see His humility and submission before His accusers (Isa. 53:7, Matt. 26:62-63, Matt. 27:12-14). We see the wrath and judgment of God against sin (John 2:13-16) but we also see His compassion and pity for the helpless (Matt. 14:14). We see the strong and unchanging character of God (Heb. 13:8), but we also see Jesus shedding tears at the sorrow of Mary and Martha over the death of their brother Lazarus (John 11:33-35).

Much of the confusion in the secular world today and even in the church seems to come from a failure to understand the difference between the truth of the equal importance of men and women to God and the reality of God-given differences in responsibiity between men and women. It is obvious to everyone that men and women are physically different. What is not so obvious to most people is that they are also quite different emotionally and psychologically. God purposely made them different for good reasons. The Bible reveals to us the plan of God in creating women. We read in the creation story, "The LORD God said, "It is not good for the man to be alone. I will make a helper suitable for him" (Gen. 2:18). Later the story tells us, "For this reason a man will leave his father and mother and be united to his wife, and they will become one flesh" (Gen. 2:24).

The purpose of God in creating a woman was directly related to the physical, mental and emotional needs of the man He created.. The man needed a partner, a companion and a helper in life. The woman was created to be that partner, companion and helper. She was created to complete the man in every way, including the physical, mental, emotional and social parts of life. It is a basic fact of life that men need women and women need men. The Bible teaches this. In the words of the apostle Paul, "woman is not independent of man, nor is man independent of woman. For as woman came from man, so also man is born of woman" (1 Cor. 11:11-12). It was God who made it that way.

Christians will only have a biblical understanding of the relationship between men and women which God intended when they understand that God purposely planned creation so that men and women would be dependent on one another for the normal functions of life. This has many applications to everyday life. It also has application to the normal functions and well-being of the local church. Men are not better or more important than women. Women are not better or more important than men. They are both equally necessary and equally important to each other and to God. Any other view of the relationship between men and women is less than what the Bible teaches.

THE DIFFERENCES BETWEEN MEN AND WOMEN

Although men and women are equally important and precious to God, He did not make them exactly alike. God clearly made men and women for different responsibilities and for different purposes in life. If we try to change or distort these roles, we interfere with the plan of God. Concerning the marriage relationship, for example, the Bible says, "the husband is the head of the wife as Christ is the head of the church" (Eph.5:23). This is not a statement of the importance or value of men in relation to women. It is a statement of order in the home. If a culture were to insist that women should have final authority in the home, such a culture would violate the purposes of God.

Equality of value and importance to God is not the same thing as equality of roles in life. It is a reflection on mankind's failure to understand God's creation of men and women to insist that men and women must have the same roles and do the same work in all aspects of life as some people in the West insist today. No man has ever given birth to a baby or nursed a baby at his breast. God gave that function to women. No woman ever created a sperm cell to fertilize the egg cell in her body. God gave that function to men. These physical functions also have an application to the emotional and social parts of life because of the physical, chemical and psychological differences between men and women.

There are exceptions, but women in general are better suited to the gentleness and emotional sensitivity needed to care for babies and very small children. There are exceptions, but men in general are better suited to sustained hard work or to withstand the emotional stress and responsibilities of leadership. That does not mean that it is wrong for a man to care for a baby. It does not mean that it is wrong for a woman to be in a position of leadership. It simply reflects the natural difference which God created

A government health publication in Ethiopia lists ten severe problems resulting from female genital mutilation.[4] These include (1) severe pain (2) serious bleeding (3) shock (4) general infection (5) urine retention (6) tetanus infection (7) pain and laceration with sexual intercourse (8) the possibility of AIDS infection (9) urinary tract infection and (10) pelvic infection. In addition to these problems, women who have been subjected to female genital mutilation will experience considerably greater pain and difficulty in childbirth, sometimes resulting in death to either the mother or the child, or both. As a very minimum, the wife will not be able to experience a normal, fulfilling sexual relationship with her husband.

Female genital mutilation is a cultural practice followed even by some Christians. It is a serious violation of the body of every female who has been forced to endure this practice. It is a great evil which needs to exposed and removed from the society. If Christian men have agreed to this practice for their own daughters they need to repent of it as a sin and renounce it from their lives, because a Christian girl's body is the temple of God (1 Cor. 6:19-20). If they do not renounce this practice, they will invite God's wrath on themselves for destroying the temple of God (1 Cor. 3:17). The practice of female circumcision needs to be exposed and rejected from all cultures in the world as a barbaric, uncivilized abuse of the body of a female and a cause of permanent harm both to marriage and to childbirth. Because of the way it interferes with God's purposes for married women, it is probably demonic in origin.

Another form of abuse of women is rape and other forms of sexual harassment by men. This is because men have more intense sexual desires than women. It is also partly because men are stronger than women. Most countries of the world have identified rape as a crime. Women, however, can greatly help to reduce the possibility of this kind of crime through modest dress, which is the will of God (1 Timothy 2:9).

THE NEEDS OF SINGLE WOMEN

There are an increasing number of women in Africa who do not marry. The problems of remaining single for a woman can be great. She may find it difficult to support herself. She may feel she is not attractive and develop a very low image of herself. She may feel that she has been denied the most important part of life in not being able to have a husband and children of her own. She may feel she is rejected by her community and people for being different from other women. She may be subject to temptation from men who want to use her as a prostitute. It is important, therefore, to consider how to meet some of the needs of single women. It is also helpful to consider some of the advantages of remaining single.

First and most important, the local church should take an active role in encouraging and helping single women find their place in life and in the community. The church may be in a position to provide some kind of employment, either part time or full time, to some single women. The church may be able to direct single women into a job or a ministry which involves caring for children. In this way the great desire felt by most women to have children of their own can be at least partly satisfied. The church should seek to provide a fellowship group (support group) where single women can find encouragement and support from other single women who are struggling with the same problems. Married people in the church should make a special effort to reach out to help and encourage single women, recognizing that they do have special needs that are hard to meet.

Some people have the idea that singleness is second best. That is not the view of Scripture. It is not a matter of singleness or marriage, but a matter of God's will. Jesus Himself never married. In a very interesting statement (Matt. 19:10-12), Jesus taught that singleness for the kingdom of God is a high and holy calling, but that it was reserved for specially called people. In this passage He said, "He who is able to receive this, let him receive it." This statement suggests that God has prepared certain people for a kind of ministry which involves remaining single. It also suggests that if God calls a person to a single life, He will give that person a special kind of grace to be fulfilled and spiritually fruitful in remaining single. Paul indicated that he had this special grace, and even wished that others could share his gift (1 Cor. 7:7).

Some of the greatest early missionaries of the Christian church were men and women whom God called to be single. Among single women were Mary Slessor, a Scotch lady, who was a pioneer missionary to Nigeria. Amy Carmichael, a single missionary woman to India, wrote 35 books in her lifetime. God still calls certain men and women today to remain single in order to fulfill a special calling.

WHAT ARE THE ADVANTAGES OF BEING SINGLE?

On a practical level, whether one is single for just a few years or for a lifetime, there are some advantages to being single. Single women should use these advantages to serve the Lord more effectively.

1. Freedom in the use of time. This is an area that single people rarely think about until they get married. When they marry they discover that life has changed and time is no longer their own.
2. Freedom to get further higher education without difficulty. It is not impossible to get higher education after you have a family but it can be very difficult. It can bring real stress to the marriage and the family.
3. Freedom to travel widely. This and other similar activities are usually not possible with a family.
4. The emotional risk of marriage. The most significant difference between being married and being single is the emotional risk a person takes when he gets married. Once you have committed yourself to the closest of all human relationships in having a husband and children, you create the possibility of being bitterly hurt for a lifetime if you lose your husband or your children. Most people don't think about that possibility but it does happen, and it happens more often than we would like to think. When it does happen it can cause a lifetime of emotional suffering.
5. Freedom to undertake ministries not possible for married people. There are ministries in the Lord's work which would probably not be done if there were no single women. One of these is the ministry of operating orphanages. Most of the orphanages in the world have been established by single women.

Surely such women have a great reward waiting for them in Heaven from the God who cares for the orphan and the widow (Deut. 24:19-21, Isa. 1:17). One of those rewards is having a great many "children" of her own (Isaiah 54:1).

SUMMARY

Christians should be careful to avoid the extreme attitudes toward women which are the result of cultural pressure. On the one hand, there is an unhealthy and unbiblical attitude in the West of trying to force women to do all that men do in the name of equality. God loves men and women equally but we must remember that He created them differently. We do well to respect those differences. On the other hand, there is a tendency among some men in Africa to regard women as less important and of less value than men. This attitude has no support in the Bible and certainly dishonors and displeases God who created both men and women in His own image. Let us then have God's viewpoint concerning the importance of the female half of the human race. Let the leaders of the local church seek to use all of the gifts and abilities of the women in their congregation so that the church of Jesus Christ may be built up for the glory of God. The church should speak out strongly against the various forms of abuse of women. The church should also take an active role in helping single women to meet their needs.

QUESTIONS FOR REVIEW, REFLECTION AND GROUP DISCUSSION

1. What was God's purpose in His creation of women, according to the Bible? In what ways would single Christian women today fit into these purposes of God?
2. In what way is the attitude of many African men toward women contrary to the will of God as revealed in the Bible?
3. In what ways is the western movement called feminism contrary to the will of God in His creation of women?

4. What are some of the differences in the roles of men and women as revealed by the physical, mental and emotional differences between men and women?
5. In what ways can women be used in the local church?
6. Are there any spiritual gifts which the Bible says are limited to men?
7. What are some forms of abuse of women which are practiced even by some Christian men in Africa? What is the solution to these evil practices?
8. List some of the ways in which a local church can help the single women in the congregation.

END NOTES

1. Kore, Danfulani. Culture And The Christian Home. Jos, Nigeria: Africa Christian Textbooks, 1989. p. 2.
2. Ibid. p. 3.
3. Ibid. pp. 3-4.
4. Leaflet Number 2. Female Genital Mutilation. Addis Ababa: National Committee on Traditional Practices of Ethiiopia.

CHAPTER 11

THE CHALLENGE OF YOUTH IN MODERN AFRICA

Modern Africa is increasingly shifting to a younger population every year. In many African countries more than 60 percent of the population is under 21 years of age. In spite of this population shift many cultures in Africa reflect an attitude of indifference toward children and youth. In some places youth are almost completely disregarded until they marry or reach marriageable age. Instead of seeing youth as the source of leadership for the next generation, many African leaders see them as a threat to their own leadership and therefore spend their time struggling to hold on to their positions even when their leadership is no longer appreciated or has become ineffective. This tendency is found both in public office and in church leadership. This failure to take a wise and mature view of the importance of youth in the culture is a major cultural problem. It is a major problem for the future good of Africa.

In this chapter we will examine the characteristics of youth, the challenge of an increasingly youthful population in Africa and the importance of approaching this challenge in the right way. We will also consider the generational problem (the "generation gap") as it is found in Africa today. We will discover how God would have us resolve this age-old problem.

A. WHAT ARE THE CHARACTERISTICS OF YOUTH?

1. The most obvious fact about youth is that today's youth are the future of the next generation, whether in the nation, in the local society or in the church. There is no one in the culture more important to influence, train, encourage and disciple for the Lord than the youth of a nation. There is no one in the world who is more important for a Christian father to dis-

ciple for the Lord than his own child. Yet many African cultures are almost totally indifferent to the opportunities, needs and problems of youth today. Many cultures consider young people of no importance until they reach adulthood. Many African church leaders are totally occupied with meetings and ministry to other adults while their own children are left to follow the ways of the world.

2. A young child's mind is like a blank exercise book. Everything he or she hears or sees is written on the pages of that book. The experiences of childhood become the basis for adult behavior and adult values. A young child's mind is like wet cement. It is easy to make a mark in wet cement and even to change the marks immediately after they are made. After a while the cement hardens and changes can only be made with great difficulty. The impressions made on children during childhood and youth will determine the direction they will follow in life. They are like marks made in cement. For this reason the Bible has a lot to say about the correct way to train and instruct children and youth.
3. Enthusiasm, energy and physical strength are qualities of youth (Prov. 20:29). This energy and enthusiasm needs to be given the right guidance. There is an urgent need to train, educate and guide young people. We faithfully educate our children in secular schools but we often neglect the more important matter of their moral and spiritual training. Christian training for youth will have a lasting impact on their lives and turn them in the right direction to serve God while their young hearts are still open to serving Him. Over 60 years ago a certain young girl memorized many verses of Scripture in a mission boarding school. Now, a lifetime later, these treasures of the Word of God are still firmly planted in the heart and mind of this woman. More important, the effect of this early Christian training moved her heart to serve Christ for a lifetime as a missionary. God says, "Train up a child in the way he should go: and when he is old, he will not depart from it" (Prov. 22:6).

4. Youth are always looking for new ideas and excitement. They are easily influenced to change in ways that adults would nev-

er consider. This has both secular and religious implications. In the secular world, young people quickly adapt to cultural change if they think it is exciting or modern or if they think it will make them more popular. Thus it is the youth in the cities of Africa who are most rapidly adopting western cultural values and western behavior. It is the youth who are most affected by the influences of modernity. It is the youth who are most permanently changed by western video, western music, western education and western technology. In the religious area, it is young people who will most quickly follow new and unusual religious movements, cults or self-proclaimed prophets of whom Africa has many. It is interesting that Jesus chose young men under 30 years old to be His apostles. This fact alone shows how important it is to God to guide and train young people in the right way while they are still young.

This fact has an urgent application to the ministry of the church. Whose voice will young people hear first? To which voice will they respond? The application of this truth is extremely important to the future of Africa and to the future of the church. If youth do not hear the voice of the Lord calling them, who will they follow? If the church does not change its emphasis to a serious ministry directed toward young people, they are going to lose the present generation of youth. If they lose the present generation of youth they are going to lose Africa.

The church urgently needs to direct its primary evangelistic and discipleship effort to win the youth in their community instead of planning the majority of its ministry around older people. The church needs to train and employ youth pastors and youth leaders whose entire job is working with the young people in the church. It is youth who are by far the most open to the gospel of Christ. Billy Graham's evangelistic organization has found that more than 70 percent of all the people who turn to Christ come from young people under 25 years old.

We can learn something from the communists. When communism takes control of a country, the first thing they do is to set up indoctrination programs for children and youth. Communists clearly understand that when they convert the youth of the country to their ideas they can control the future of that country. Yet some churches in Africa seems blind to this truth. The church needs to wake up and learn from its enemies!

Older pastors and church leaders need to concentrate their time and attention on training, discipling and preparing young people for future leadership rather than struggling to hold on to their own positions of leadership. If Jesus had not spent the main part of His three year public ministry training 12 young men to carry on His work after He was gone, there would be no church on earth today.

5. Because youth are interested in excitement and new ideas, they are also looking for an example to follow. Many of those God called into the ministry followed the example of an older leader. God called them when they were young people. Take the example of King David. God called David when he was a youth caring for his father's sheep (1 Sam. 16:10-13, 1 Sam. 17:42). Take the example of Jeremiah the prophet. God called him when he was a boy (Jer. 1:6-7). Take the example of Jesus' disciples. They were all young men. If that is the importance God has placed on youth then the church needs to learn a lesson. God called most missionaries and evangelists to serve him before they were 25 years old. The church could raise up a mighty army of dedicated workers for God if it would learn to disciple its youth.

   Unfortunately many churches are so out of touch with the younger generation that young people are bored by the church and disinterested in its activities. There is an urgent need for the church to study the young generation and to find ways to appeal to the youth. Churches need to put time, effort, money, skill and the best trained people they can find into youth ministry and youth work. They need to promote youth Bible studies, Sunday School for young people, youth rallies, youth conferences, youth camps, youth training programs, music, drama and sports programs for young people directed toward winning, training and discipling their young people. If the church fails in this area it has failed the most critical part of its responsibility to God. Its elders will live to weep tears of grief over the consequences of their failure. The Bible says, "A foolish son brings grief to his father and bitterness to the one who bore him" (Prov. 17:25).

6. In general, youth lack mature wisdom and judgment. This emphasizes the need for the church to have training programs for young people so that they may gain the wisdom they need for godly living. Consider the following true story of one young leader in the Bible who lacked wisdom and good judgment. The result of this man's foolish decision cost the nation of Israel great pain and the loss of many lives.

   "Rehoboam went to Shechem, for all the Israelites had gone there to make him king. . . So they sent for Jeroboam, and he and the whole assembly of Israel went to Rehoboam and said to him: "Your father put a heavy yoke on us, but now lighten the harsh labor and the heavy yoke he put on us, and we will serve you." Rehoboam answered, "Go away for three days and then come back to me." So the people went away. Then King Rehoboam consulted the elders who had served his father Solomon during his lifetime. "How would you advise me to answer these people?" he asked. They replied, "If today you will be a servant to these people and serve them and give them a favorable answer, they will always be your servants." But Rehoboam rejected the advice the elders gave him and consulted the young men who had grown up with him and were serving him. He asked them, "What is your advice? . . . The young men who had grown up with him replied, "Tell these people . . .'My little finger is thicker than my father's waist. My father laid on you a heavy yoke; I will make it even heavier. My father scourged you with whips; I will scourge you with scorpions.'" Three days later Jeroboam and all the people returned to Rehoboam, as the king had said, "Come back to me in three days." The king answered the people harshly. Rejecting the advice given him by the elders, he followed the advice of the young men . . .

When all Israel saw that the king refused to listen to them, they answered the king: "What share do we have in David, what part in Jesse's son? To your tents, O Israel! Look after your own house, O David!" So the Israelites went home. But as for the Israelites who were living in the towns of Judah, Rehoboam still ruled over them. King Rehoboam sent out Adoniram, who was in charge of forced labor, but all Israel stoned him to death. King Rehoboam, however, managed to get into his chariot and escape to Jerusalem. So Israel has been in rebellion against the house of David to this day" (1 Kings 12:1-19).

This story reveals the lack of wisdom found among many young people. Young Rehoboam was given good advice by his elders but he chose to listen to the impulsive and foolish ideas of his young friends. This foolish decision brought conflict, war and death to the nation of Israel for 400 years.

B. HOW SHOULD THE CHURCH DEAL WITH THE "GENERATION GAP?"

The generation gap could be defined as the great difference in attitude and mentality between the younger generation and the older generation. Younger people tend to be critical of older people. In the minds of young people, old people are out of touch with the present world and the present generation. They see old people as slow, uninteresting and unable to change. Many times young people want to see things change quickly. Young people tend to be impatient and hasty in their decisions but those decisions are often unwise, as the story of Rehoboam demonstrates.

Old people are often equally critical of young people. They see young people as foolish, impulsive, shallow and immature in their thinking. Old people fear that young people will change things which the old people like and want to keep. Hence old people tend to feel threatened and annoyed with the ideas and behavior of young people. Each group tends to be critical of the other group and impatient with the other. The old feel threatened by the young and the young feel restricted and hindered by the old.

This results not only in a barrier between them but in significant conflict between the two groups. A recent incident in an urban African church illustrates this point.

Twenty five years ago the denomination of this local church had a doctrinal statement which was non-charismatic. Events of the past twenty years in the country, however, brought Pentecostal and non-Pentecostal Christians close together. Christians of every group had to stand together and support each other against anti-Christian persecution by the government. As a result, many of the younger people in this church made close friends among the Pentecostals and began to adopt the practices of their Pentecostal friends, especially speaking in tongues.

The older leadership of the church did not agree with this practice but it spread rapidly among the young people anyway. The practice spread for some of the very reasons given in the analysis of youth at the beginning of this chapter. When some of the older men in the church began to preach against undisciplined speaking in tongues the young people reacted in anger and accused the older people of being spiritually dead and in need of revival. The controversy became so bitter that the young people finally threatened the church elders that if they spoke against the practice one more time, all the young people in the church would leave permanently. Since well over 75 percent of this church's membership were young people who supported the new practice, the threat of the youth became a major conflict which involved the very survival of this local church. It put a painful barrier between the older and younger people in the church which has seriously hurt the fellowship, unity and love within that church.

How can such generational barriers be overcome? Does the Bible give any advice which can remove or eliminate this problem? The answer is that the Bible does provide a clear solution. We will examine this solution in some detail. The biblical solution is critically important if the will of God is to be done to disciple the young people of this generation effectively to serve the Lord. Before we look at the biblical solution to the generation gap it is important to observe that God has been concerned about this problem for a long time.

When the future ministry of John the Baptist was prophesied in the Old Testament, the Bible says that one part of John's ministry would be that he would "turn the hearts of the fathers to their children, and the hearts of the children to their fathers" (Malachi 4:6). In other words, John's ministry would help to overcome the generational barriers of his day. The last part of the same verse contains a sober warning of what can happen if the generational problem is not overcome. God warns his people that if the generational barrier is not removed , "I will come and strike the land with a curse" (Malachi 4:6). It is therefore very important for us to understand how God wants the problem to be solved in our churches today.

We have seen some of the basic characteristics of youth. In order to understand the biblical solution to the generation gap, we also need to understand the characteristics of older people. Most of the characteristics of older people are the opposite of the characteristics of young people.

1. The future does not belong to the older generation. Many of them will not live to see the future arrive.
2. The "cement" in the thinking of older people hardened long ago. Older people tend to be set in their ways. They have fixed patterns of thinking and fixed habits of behavior. They feel uncomfortable with change. An English language proverb says, "You cannot teach an old dog new tricks."
3. Although older people may not have much energy or strength they generally have great wisdom. They have lost much of their youthful enthusiasm because they have lived through the sorrows and difficulties of life but they do have years of experience which has given them a mature perspective on life. Their decisions tend to be carefully thought through, based on many years of living. The Bible strongly urges young people to listen carefully to the advice of their parents (Prov. 1:8, Prov. 5:1-2). In the story of Rehoboam given above, it was the wise old men who counseled Rehoboam to deal gently and reasonably with the people of Israel in order to secure their cooperation. If Rehoboam had followed their advice, it would have avoided 400 years of bitter conflict, war and death.
4. Old people tend to be conservative. This means that they want to keep (conserve) the ways of the past in which they

feel secure. They are not inclined to adopt new ideas or to learn new skills. They would rather do things in the familiar traditional ways than to experiment with the uncertainty of new ideas and new practices. This conservatism can be both a good thing and a bad thing. Conservatism can be good in protecting a culture from harmful and impulsive change. It can be bad in hindering new ideas or new technology which can help the community.

C. WHAT IS GOD'S SOLUTION TO THE GENERATIONAL PROBLEM?

Briefly stated the solution is this. The old need to train and prepare the young to take their place. The young need to learn from the old and to submit to them so that God's will for future generations will be done. The old need the strength, enthusiasm and creative ideas of the young. The young need the wisdom, mature counsel, training and restraint of the old so that wrong decisions with painful consequences are not made. For this to happen there must a humble and right attitude on the part of both groups toward the other. The Bible says, "Young men, in the same way be submissive to those who are older. All of you, clothe yourselves with humility toward one another" (1 Peter 5:5). Let us look at some biblical examples where those of each generation had the right attitude and the right relationship toward the other.

Moses trained Joshua. Eli trained Samuel. Elijah trained Elisha. Jesus trained His disciples. Paul trained Timothy and Titus. Notice in each of these examples that the older and the younger did their part with the right attitude. The older men did not try to selfishly protect their positions of leadership but gave themselves fully to prepare those who would follow them in leadership. The younger men did not criticize or try to replace the older men but patiently learned from them with humility and respect. They patiently waited for God's time to assume the leadership God had prepared for them.

Even in the case of corrupt older leaders we see a different pattern in the Bible than we do in the generational conflict today. King Saul was anointed by God for his leadership (1 Sam. 10:1) but

Saul became corrupt and rebellious toward God. Saul relentlessly pursued David to kill him because of his insane jealousy that David would take his place even though David had served Saul well. David served Saul both in his emotional needs (1 Sam. 16:14-23) and in battle (1 Samuel 17).

David had good reason to want to be rid of Saul. Yet twice when David could have easily killed Saul, he would not lift his hand against him (1 Samuel 24 and 1 Samuel 26) because he recognized that Saul was chosen by God. David knew that God had anointed David to be king (1 Sam. 16:13) but he was willing to wait patiently for God's time. He was willing to serve the one whom God had placed over him. Young people today need this attitude of humility which David displayed because of his love for God. Joshua displayed the same attitude of respect and submission to Moses (Ex. 33:11). Perhaps it is just because these young men took the position of submission and humility to those God had placed over them that God later gave them positions of leadership among His people.

In each case (except Saul), the older men did not try to jealously guard their position. They did not disregard the younger men God had given them. Instead, they diligently trained and prepared these younger men to take up the leadership God wanted them to have. There is a very great need for church leaders in Africa today to have the same attitude of diligent and unselfish preparation toward the younger generation in their churches. Concerning both the young and the old, Jesus said, "If anyone wants to be first, he must be the very last, and the servant of all" (Mark 9:35). There is a very great need in the church today for servant leadership. Jesus said, "the Son of Man did not come to be served, but to serve" (Mark 10:45). He also said, "Do you understand what I have done for you? . . . You call me 'Teacher' and 'Lord,' and rightly so, for that is what I am. Now that I, your Lord and Teacher, have washed your feet, you also should wash one another's feet. I have set you an example that you should do as I have done for you" (John 13:12-15).

SUMMARY

The majority population of Africa is becoming younger every year. Youth represent one of the greatest challenges and greatest unmet needs in the church today. Churches need to drastically change their programs in order to address the needs of youth or there will soon be a crisis in African churches.

The problem of conflict between the older and the younger generation is not new. The solution to the generational conflict in the church today is for both old and young to adopt the servant heart of Christ toward one another. Each group needs to recognize that they need one another to accomplish God's will. They need to humble themselves and to take on the attitude of Christ in learning to serve one another instead of criticizing and condemning one another. The old need to lovingly disciple, teach, train and prepare the young to take their places of leadership. The young need to respect and submit to their elders and patiently wait for God's time to give them leadership in the church.

QUESTIONS FOR REVIEW, REFLECTION AND GROUP DISCUSSION

1. What are the primary characteristics of youth?
2. Why do you think young people are so quick to follow new ideas?
3. What are some of the most important needs of young people?
4. Give some reasons why youth are so important to the future of the church.
5. Discuss the kind of programs which your local church could undertake which would minister to the needs of its youth.
6. What are the characteristics of older people compared with younger people?
7. What is the source of the conflict between the older generation and the younger generation?
8. What is the biblical solution to the conflict between the older and younger generation?

CHAPTER 12

THE NEED FOR BIBLICAL CHRISTIANITY IN MODERN AFRICA: THE PROBLEM OF WRONG TEACHING AND MISTAKEN PRACTICES IN THE CHURCH

There is a great need in modern Africa for biblical Christianity. As the earlier chapters of this book have suggested, the church urgently needs to take a biblical position on such issues as tribalism, poverty, injustice, sexual immorality, abortion, corruption in the church and in the government, responsible use of money, self-sustainable development, materialism, secularism, overpopulation, the needs of youth, family life teaching, women in the church and other matters related to modernity and urban life in Africa. The church needs to take a biblical and prophetic role on these issues and to be ready to offer solutions based on the Bible (Rom. 12:2, Titus 2:11-12, 1 John 2:15-17). The church is called to be salt and light in a corrupt and evil world (Matt. 5:13-14). Only when it does this will the church experience the full blessing and power of God on its ministry. Only then will the church see God's intervention in answer to its prayers.

In addition to the above issues, there is much that is accepted as Christianity in Africa today which is not biblical Christianity. There are many churches who claim they are the true church of Jesus Christ or the true apostolic church. There are many who call themselves prophets of God or apostles of Christ. How can a Christian know what is true Christianity and what is not? In this chapter we will examine a number of beliefs and practices which have come to be accepted in many churches but which are contrary to the Bible. We will evaluate these beliefs and practices in the light of the Word of God to see what is Christianity according to the Bible and what is not.

NOMINAL CHRISTIANS

The churches in Africa are full of nominal Christians. Nominal Christians are those who are Christians in name only. In any local church there are likely to be both true believers and false believers. The problem is that in most local churches there are true Christians who are spiritually joined to Christ living side by side with those who claim to be Christians but who are not joined to Christ. Everyone assumes that because people come to church they are true Christians. Nominal Christians usually consider themselves to be Christians because they go to church, or because they grew up in a Christian home, or because they have a Christian name or because they have been baptized or for some other reason, but they have no personal relationship with Christ. They have never been "born of the Spirit" (John 3:5-6).

A Christian is a person who has a personal, living relationship with God through Jesus Christ. Jesus said, "this is eternal life: that they may know you, the only true God, and Jesus Christ, whom you have sent" (John 17:3). Jesus defined eternal life as a personal relationship with Himself and God the Father. Jesus said, "I tell you the truth, no one can see the kingdom of God unless he is born again" (John 3:3). A true Christian is someone who has been born of the Holy Spirit (that is, he or she has made spiritually alive by the transforming power of the Holy Spirit). Through that work of renewal by the Holy Spirit, he or she has been joined to Christ in a vital personal relationship with God the Father through Jesus Christ. The Bible says, "He saved us through the washing of rebirth and renewal by the Holy Spirit, whom he poured out on us generously through Jesus Christ our Saviour" (Titus 3:5-6).

It is very important for the leaders of every local church to make clear to their people what it means to be a true, born-again Christian and how a person may become a true Christian. It is very important that people realize that they do not become true Christians just by attending church, or by having a Christian name or by being baptized or in some other way. A person becomes a true Christian by repenting from sin and by personally receiving Jesus Christ as his or her Lord and Saviour (John 1:12-13, Acts 20:21). When a person does this, the Holy Spirit gives that person a new spiritual life by joining him or her to Christ. In other words, it is the Holy Spirit who makes the person a part of the true Church (the body of Christ). The Bible says, "we were all baptized by one Spirit into one body--whether Jews or Greeks, slave or free--and we were all given the one Spirit to drink" (1 Cor. 12:13).

It would be a good thing for the pastor of every local church to give a clear message every few months on how people can be saved and become a part of the true church of Jesus Christ. It would also be good if the pastor gave an invitation at the end of such a service for people (including church members who have never done so) to publicly repent and receive Jesus Christ as their Lord and Saviour..

A few years ago a missionary did this in a strong evangelical church. To his surprise half of the congregation indicated a desire to receive Christ. The missionary assumed that the congregation did not understand what he said and he explained it all again. Again half the church responded. He still thought people did not understand so he explained it more carefully a third time. Again half the church responded. Later in the counseling room it became clear that none of these people had ever repented from their sin and personally received Christ even though some had been attending that church for many years. They considered themselves to be Christians for various reasons but they had never experienced a personal relationship with Jesus Christ. They were nominal Christians but that day they became true Christians with great joy and celebration.

FALSE MIRACLE WORKERS

Jesus spoke about another group of false believers. In a shocking statement Jesus said, "Not everyone who says to me, 'Lord, Lord,' will enter the kingdom of heaven, but only he who does the will of my Father who is in heaven. Many will say to me on that day, 'Lord, Lord, did we not prophesy in your name, and in your name drive out demons and perform many miracles?' Then I will tell them plainly, 'I never knew you. Away from me, you evildoers!' (Matt. 7:21-23).

This statement by Christ introduces us to one of the more difficult problems faced by the true church. There are those who claim to be true believers who have even performed miraculous signs and wonders. Jesus said they may have prophesied, they may have cast out demons and may even have performed miracles! This problem presents a great challenge to the true church.

It is common to assume that when there is a supernatural demonstration of power in the church, the person who performs such miraculous signs must be a true Christian or perhaps even a prophet or messenger of God. But Jesus made it clear that this is not always the case. The truth is, there are other spirits who are not from God who can enable human beings to perform supernatural signs and wonders. There are people in churches today who prophesy, who speak in tongues and who perform other supernatural wonders. The important question is, which spirit enables them to do these things? Some of these signs may be demonstrations of the gifts of the Holy Spirit (1 Cor. 12:10) but according to Jesus some of them are not. Jesus said some of these works are being done by those He called evildoers! There are people in the church today who can perform supernatural miracles and who claim to have the Spirit of God but they are not true Christians. Jesus called them wolves in sheep's clothing (Matt. 7:15)!

How can God's people know if a person who works miracles is a true believer or a wolf in sheep's clothing? Jesus answered this question when He said, "By their fruit you will recognize them. Do people pick grapes from thornbushes, or figs from thistles? Likewise every good tree bears good fruit, but a bad tree bears bad fruit" (Matt. 7:16-17). The evidence of a true Christian is the life he or she lives. True Christians can be recognized by the moral and spiritual fruit of their lives. The test of a true believer is Christian character produced by the Holy Spirit in that person's life (Eph. 2:10). Jesus said, "By this all men will know that you are My disciples, if you have love for one another" (John 13:35).

MODERN DAY PHARISEES

A third group of people in the church today who claim to be Christians are not only false but are dangerously false. This is the category we might call the religious hypocrites, or modern-day Pharisees. Sometimes these people are actually leaders in the church and sometimes they are the very top leaders! This is the way it was with the Pharisees of Jesus' day. It was the Pharisees who were the religious leaders of their day. They knew what the Bible said but they were not changed in their hearts. An example of this can be seen when King Herod called in the Jewish priests and teachers of the law to find out where the Messiah was to be born (Matt. 2:3-6). These Pharisees and priests accurately quoted the Old Testament and told Herod that the Messiah would be born in Bethlehem. But when this very Messiah came to them from Bethlehem they were the ones who demanded His crucifixion and death (Mark 15:11-13)!

Jesus condemned the Scribes and Pharisees more than any other group of people. Listen to these strong words of judgment. "Woe to you, teachers of the law and Pharisees, you hypocrites! You clean the outside of the cup and dish, but inside they are full of greed and self-indulgence. . . Woe to you, teachers of the law and Pharisees, you hypocrites! You are like whitewashed tombs, which look beautiful on the outside but on the inside are full of dead men's bones and everything unclean. In the same way, on the outside you appear to people as righteous but on the inside you are full of hypocrisy and wickedness" (Matt. 23:25-28). So great was Jesus' condemnation of religious hypocrisy that he said the Pharisees would go to hell! He said to them, "You snakes! You brood of vipers! How will you escape being condemned to hell?" (Matt. 23:33).

There are many examples of such hypocrites in the church today. A few years ago a church bishop in the state of California in the United States revealed himself to be such a person when he went on nationwide television in the United States to try to contact his dead son through a spiritist medium - an action which God condemns as an abomination (Deut. 18:10-12). If the true Christians in this man's denomination had been listening carefully to the words of this church leader, they would have learned even before this event that the man could not have been a true Christian. In his sermons the man had already denied the basic truths of the Christian faith such as the resurrection of Christ from the dead. People were deceived because the man was a bishop in the church.

In another recent example of modern-day Pharisees, two leaders in an African church district were so full of greed for development money and political power in their church that they took each other to civil court to have the other one imprisoned! At one point in this conflict, one of these leaders had guards with guns stationed at the entrance to a church compound to shoot members of the other faction who might try to enter! Let no one be deceived by such people. The fact that they may have authority or leadership in their church denomination means nothing. Their lives reveal their hypocrisy. Not only are they not true Christians but Jesus called them "ferocious wolves in sheep's clothing" (Matt. 7:15)!

As human beings we tend to think of sins with regard to money and sex as the worst sins. This is because these sins are obvious and our consciences convict us about these sins. The fact is that sins related to pride are far more serious, yet we tend to laugh about them and make light of them. The Bible says, "Pride goes before destruction" (Prov. 16:18). Jesus said to the Pharisees, "the tax collectors (those who cheated with money) and the prostitutes (those who sinned sexually) are entering the kingdom of God ahead of you" (Matt. 21:31)! Jesus was not excusing the love of money and sexual sin. Rather He was teaching that those involved in the sins of money and sex are more likely to repent and change whereas those who sin with pride will rarely humble themselves and change. Thus those who sin with regard to pride are in much greater danger of being lost forever. Those who sin because of pride often boast about it and even justify their behavior with no sense of guilt whatever. Yet pride will send people to hell just as the pride of Satan (1 Tim. 3:6) will send that fallen angel to hell (Matt. 23:33, Matt. 25:41, Rev. 20:10).

A specific sin related to pride and modern-day Pharisees is tribalism and favoritism by church leaders. This is just another form of religious hypocrisy. Tribalism is one of the greatest curses in the world, especially when it is found in the church. It is based on pride and selfishness which were the reasons for Satan's fall in the beginning (Isa. 14:12-14). Tribalism is not just a small problem or a human weakness. It is a great sin with eternal consequences (James 2:9-10).

In summary, true Christians must be aware that churches are often filled with false believers who can bring great confusion and trouble to the true people of God. Those who preach and teach the Word of God need to fearlessly expose and condemn those sins which God condemns. They need to be very clear about who is a true believer and how a person can become a true believer in Jesus Christ.

FALSE TEACHING AND WRONG IDEAS IN THE CHURCH

In addition to false believers, another major problem for the church today is false teaching and wrong ideas in the church. This is not something new. The epistle of Jude in the New Testament was written about this problem in the early days of the church (Jude 3-4). Others such as the Apostle Paul were also concerned about false teaching in their day (Gal. 1:6-7).

It would be impossible to analyze the many forms of false teaching found in churches and "Christian" cults around the world in a book such as this. The devil and his demons have been busy inventing false teaching for almost 2000 years! The apostle Paul also taught that false teaching would increase in the later years of the church. Paul wrote, "The Spirit clearly says that in later times some will abandon the faith and follow deceiving spirits and things taught by demons" (1 Tim. 4:1). This book will only briefly discuss a few wrong ideas which have become popular among some Christians in Africa in recent years.

1. SALVATION BY WORKS RATHER THAN BY FAITH

One form of false teaching which seems to occur in every new generation of the church is the idea that salvation is somehow the result of what we do for God rather than what God has done for us. This false idea is the basis for just about every non-Christian religion in the world. It was the false idea believed by the Galatian Christians in the very first century of the Christian church (Gal. 1:6-8, Gal. 3:1-3). Paul devoted most of his epistle to the Galatians to correct this wrong idea (Gal. 3:4-5:6). The issue of salvation by faith rather than by works was also one of the great issues of the Protestant Reformation when the Roman Catholic monk Martin Luther rediscovered (by studying the book of Galatians and the book of Romans) that salvation was indeed by grace through faith and not by good works a person may do. (Gal. 3:11, Rom. 3:20-24, Eph. 2:8-9).

In modern days the same false teaching continues to creep into the church in a variety of subtle ways. A commonly believed idea is that a person becomes a Christian by doing certain things. This can include a variety of practices such as attending church, taking a Christian name, giving money to the church, wearing clothes or wearing certain kinds of clothes, having a "Christian" wedding or even being baptized. Another popular teaching is the idea that to become a Christian a person must give up certain practices which are considered to be sinful by the Christians of that culture. These practices may include such things such as drinking alcoholic drinks, attending cinema, smoking cigarettes or Indian hemp, chewing cola nuts or chat, retaining polygamous wives, wearing certain kinds of clothes, eating certain foods and other culturally significant practices. The particular list of such practices which must be forsaken to become a "Christian" will vary from one culture to another.

The basic problem with each of these ideas is the same. The idea is clearly communicated to new believers that if they will simply do certain things or give up doing certain things, that this will make them Christians and bring them into the kingdom of God. In a subtle way the idea is communicated to these new believers that they have been saved by what they have done and not by what God has done for them by sending Christ to die for their sins on the cross.

It is certainly the will of God for Christians to put away sinful or questionable practices from their lives. It is one evidence of regeneration by the Holy Spirit. The apostle James wrote, "In the same way, faith by itself, if it is not accompanied by action, is dead. But someone will say, 'You have faith; I have deeds.' Show me your faith without deeds, and I will show you my faith by what I do" (James 2:17-18). These actions, however, are the result of salvation not the reason for salvation. Sometimes these changes may take place immediately but often they will not take place without considerable teaching from the Bible. More important, doing or not doing certain things is definitely not the biblical basis for man's salvation.

In summary, the idea that salvation is based on what a person does or does not do may not seem important but it will have serious long term consequences as the church begins to grow in that culture. Eventually it will result in a church based on false doctrine where one false idea will lead to another until the church in that place either turns into nominal Christianity or into a "Christian" cult. The widespread presence of nominal Christianity in the world is evidence of this form of false teaching in the church.

2. EMPHASIS ON SIGNS AND WONDERS INSTEAD OF HOLINESS OF LIFE

Another problem among many believers today is an emphasis on supernatural signs and wonders instead of holiness of life. Many Christians are very interested in supernatural manifestations of the Holy Spirit such as the gifts of tongues, prophecy, healing, miracles and other signs and wonders. It is common in some churches to find a great interest in such things without an equal or greater concern for holiness of life and obedience to the Word of God.

The Holy Spirit chooses to distribute spiritual gifts to build up the church (1 Cor. 12:7-11, Eph. 4:11-12). It is not wrong for Christians to desire spiritual gifts. This is what Paul taught in 1 Corinthians 14:1. The great emphasis of the Bible, however, is not that we should see supernatural manifestations of God, but that the holy image of God should be restored in human beings. Holiness is one of the most important points of emphasis in the entire Bible (Heb. 12:14, 1 Pet. 1:15-16) Why is this?

Holiness is the most basic moral attribute of God. Holiness is the moral purity and perfection of God. It includes all of His perfect character. It is clearly seen in the unconditional, unselfish and constantly compassionate love that God has for all of His creation (Psalm 145:9, 17). It was most unforgettably seen in the unselfish and perfect love of Jesus Christ for human beings in spite of the indifference, scorn, hatred, brutal torture and finally murder inflicted on Christ by sinful men.

Most Christians think of holiness only in terms of the absence of sin. But there is much more to the holiness of God. Holiness includes every part of God's glorious character, including His love, His goodness, His mercy, His kindness, His grace, His generosity, His faithfulness, His patience, His peace, His gentleness and His truth. It was these beautiful and attractive qualities which drew people to Christ during His life on earth. It is the same qualities of life which will draw people to Christ today through Christians. These qualities of life (the fruit of the Spirit) come from the sanctifying work of the Holy Spirit in Christians who give themselves to God (Gal. 5:22-23).

Holiness and obedience to God is a central theme of both the Old and the New Testament (Lev. 20:7, 1 Pet. 1:15-16). Adam was created in the moral image of God and was holy until he disobeyed God and fell into sin. The plan of God's redemption was not just to save mankind from the death penalty for sin but to restore the holy image of God which was lost in the fall. In Romans we are told, "those God foreknew he also predestined to be conformed to the likeness of his Son, that he might be the firstborn among many brothers" (Rom. 8:29).

A key passage which describes the reason why God saved us is given in Paul's epistle to Titus. These verses state, "For the grace of God that brings salvation has appeared to all men. It teaches us to say "No" to ungodliness and worldly passions, and to live self-controlled, upright and godly lives in this present age, while we wait for the blessed hope--the glorious appearing of our great God and Savior, Jesus Christ, WHO GAVE HIMSELF FOR US TO REDEEM US FROM ALL WICKEDNESS AND TO PURIFY FOR HIMSELF A PEOPLE THAT ARE HIS VERY OWN, EAGER TO DO WHAT IS GOOD" (Titus 2:11-14). In another passage we are taught, "we are God's workmanship, created in Christ Jesus to do good works, which God prepared in advance for us to do" (Eph. 2:10). It is clear in the Bible that the ultimate purpose for which God saves people is to change them into the likeness of Christ and to restore biblical holiness in their lives. It is clear that this should be the primary goal of a Christian's life if that Christian wants to know the fullness of God's blessing on his or her life.

God will grant signs and wonders to establish and expand His church. He will distribute gifts of His Spirit to strengthen and mature His church. But the thing which God wants more than everything else from His people is obedience and a desire to be like Christ. It is then that the people of God will give evidence of being "a chosen people, a royal priesthood, a holy nation, a people belonging to God, that you may declare the praises of him who called you out of darkness into his wonderful light" (1 Pet. 2:9). It is then that the Lord's people will experience the greatest blessing of God in their lives. Many verses in the Psalms teach this truth, such as Psalm 34:15,17, Psalm 37:26, 29, Psalm 72:7, Psalm 92:12 and Psalm 97:11. Perhaps they can be summarized in the simple words of Psalm 5:12: "For surely, O LORD, YOU BLESS THE RIGHTEOUS; you surround them with your favor as with a shield."

To summarize, the Bible says, "The fear of the LORD is the beginning of wisdom" (Prov. 9:10) and, "The fear of the LORD is to hate evil" (Prov. 8:13 - NASB). In other words, the beginning of godly wisdom is to hate evil and to pursue holiness of life. The person with godly wisdom is the one who makes Christlikeness the goal of his or her life. Such persons will probably also see evidence of God's supernatural power in their lives from time to time. God's blessing on their lives will not come from seeking signs and wonders but in seeking to obey the Lord and to pursue holiness of life.

3. CHRISTIAN TEACHING BASED ON PERSONAL EXPERIENCE OR THE BIBLE?

Another problem which is growing in the church is the tendency to base Christian belief on personal experience rather than on the teaching of the Bible. The tendency with some people is to believe that if something happened to them, their experience represents the real truth about God. Their experience becomes the basis for what they believe about God rather than what the Bible teaches. Some people go even further and believe that their experience should be normal for all Christians. There are many errors in these ideas.

The problem with basing spiritual belief on experience is that experiences can come from many sources which are not from God. There are as many different kinds of human experience as there are human beings. Different experiences may come from differences in culture, differences in interpretation of events based on differences in world view, psychological, emotional and physical differences between people, differences in personality, differences in genetic inheritance, differences in childhood experiences and sometimes experiences brought about by spirits other than the Spirit of God. Only God fully knows and understands the reasons for all human behavior.

What has been said is especially important concerning supernatural experiences. God is not the only one who can provide supernatural experiences. In the matter of the gifts of the Holy Spirit, for example, spirits other than the Holy Spirit can imitate some of the experiences given by the Holy Spirit, such as speaking in tongues, prophecy, healing, miracles, and other supernatural things.

God has given a book to mankind which reveals the truth for all people. That book is the Bible. The truth in the Bible is intended for all human beings of all cultures and all ages. Since it came from God and not from man, the Bible is the final authority for Christian truth. Whatever experiences a person may have must be measured against the truth of the Bible. If our experience disagrees with the Word of God, we can be sure that God is not the source of that experience.

One example of this are those who have had the experience of speaking in tongues. The Bible teaches that the Holy Spirit gives the gift of tongues to certain people as He chooses (1 Cor. 12:10). The Bible also warns us, "do not believe every spirit, but test the spirits to see whether they are from God, because many false prophets have gone out into the world" (1 John 4:1). Those who have studied anthropology are well aware that there are people in almost every traditional religion in the world who speak in tongues when they are controlled by spirits other than the Spirit of God. The fact that a person has the ability to speak in tongues does not guarantee that God is the source of that experience even if a person has prayed for the gift of tongues. The spirit producing the experience must be identified. How this can be done will be explained later in this chapter.

In another example of people who base their belief on their experience, consider the testimony of many people today who claim to have had an experience of death and have returned. Many of these people claim they have experienced what lies beyond death. In some cases, their stories agree with what the Bible reveals but in many cases their stories clearly disagree with what the Bible teaches about death.

People believe their own experiences. Those who have had near-death experiences believe they have discovered the real truth about what lies beyond death. The problem is, what or who is the source of their experience? Only God knows what really lies beyond death and He has revealed this to us in the Bible. Other spirits, our own minds and emotions, or even medical treatment and drugs can provide near-death experiences and other kinds of experiences which may seem completely real. But such experiences do not represent reality, because they do not necessarily come from God.

To summarize, it is evident that Christian truth can only be based upon the Bible. It cannot be based on the experience of any individual. The experiences of people may be very real to them but who is to know the true source of their experience except God? The Bible reveals God's truth to all people of all cultures. It is very important to compare our individual experiences with the revelation of God's Word. One of the greatest unmet needs in the church today is a thorough knowledge of the Bible and an application of its truth to daily life.

4. DELIVERANCE FROM SPIRITUAL BONDAGE THROUGH EXORCISM OR THROUGH RENOUNCING SIN?

Another common problem in many churches today is a wrong theology which accompanies the practice of casting out evil spirits. To their credit, many Christians recognize the activity of demons in the problems which some people have. Errors arise, however, when we believe that evil spirits are the cause of just about every difficulty. An even more serious error is the belief that problems can be solved simply by identifying and casting out the demons concerned.

The Bible teaches that sin is the root cause of most human problems. The Bible says, "the wages of sin is death" (Rom. 6:23). That is a comprehensive statement which includes every part of human existence. Physical death is just the final result of sin for every person. During the course of life the death penalty for sin touches every aspect of human behavior, human relationships, human institutions, human governments and almost everything in life. One early evidence long ago of the terrible results of sin was the fact that the first child ever born (Cain) grew up to be a murderer (Gen. 4:8)!

The Bible has much to say about sin and its consequences and just a little to say about demons and their activities. It is necessary to understand spiritual bondage and deliverance in the light of this fact. The problems of human beings are primarily problems of the sin nature of mankind (Rom. 7:14-20). What then is the role of demons in human problems? What is the relationship between sin and the activity of demons, especially in the lives of Christians?

There is disagreement among Christians on the question of how much control Satan can have in the life of a Christian. At one extreme there are those who believe that Satan can not touch a Christian under any circumstances. At the other extreme there are those who believe that Christians can be possessed by demons. Neither of these extreme ideas is taught in the Bible.

To understand this issue we need a biblical understanding of the difference between the ultimate ownership of a Christian's soul and the practical results of sin in a Christian's life. We also need to understand the relationship between sin and the activity of Satan.

On the question of ownership, here are the words of Jesus. "the one who comes to Me I will certainly not cast out " (John 6:37). "I tell you the truth, whoever hears my word and believes him who sent me has eternal life and will not be condemned; he has crossed over from death to life" (John 5:24). " I give them eternal life, and they shall never perish; no one can snatch them out of my hand. My Father, who has given them to me, is greater than all ; no one can snatch them out of my Father's hand" (John 10:28-29). These verses encourage us with the truth that being saved and remaining saved are not something which happen because of our human effort. They happen because of the power of God. The Bible says, "he has rescued us from the dominion of darkness and brought us into the kingdom of the Son he loves" (Col. 1:13).

The question is commonly asked - "Yes, we are saved when we repent and believe. But what happens when we knowingly sin against God?" The Bible tells us of a situation where this happened. The story is related in 1 Corinthians 5:1-5. There was a man in the Corinthian church who was involved in sexual sin with his father's wife (probably not his mother). The man knew what he was doing but he would not stop. What happened to this man? The answer to this question reveals something about who ultimately owns us and about what can happen to a Christian if he or she will not give up a particular sin.

The Bible says that because the man refused to turn away from his sin Paul delivered the man over to Satan for "the destruction of his flesh" [or sin nature] (1 Cor. 5:5). Concerning God's ownership of the man's soul, the Bible says he did not lose his eternal salvation. Here is Paul's statement. "I have decided to deliver such a one to Satan for the destruction of his flesh, that his spirit may be saved in the day of the Lord Jesus" (1 Cor. 5:5-NASB). We are not completely certain what actually happened to this man. According to 2 Cor. 2:5 -11, it seems that he may have repented after experiencing some of the consequences of his sin (2 Cor. 2:6). Without repentance the man could very well have lost his mind, his health or even his life. This can happen to Christians according to what Jesus taught in Matt. 18:21-35 and what Paul taught in 1 Cor. 11:27-30.

The Bible says Satan goes about, "like a roaring lion, seeking someone to devour" (1 Pet. 5:8-NASB). What does that mean for a Christian? Clearly, Christians can be tempted by Satan or his demons. Equally clearly, they can fall into such temptation and commit sin. What is not usually clear to many Christians is the result of willing participation in sin if it is not confessed and renounced.

Perhaps it is like a parent who has a rebellious child who refuses to obey his parents. The parent has no choice but to let the child discover for himself or herself the bitter and painful consequences of his or her rebellion. The child never stops being the child of the parents but he or she may go through a terrible experience of suffering in order to learn the bitter consequences of such rebellion. According to Heb. 12:5-6 this discipline and suffering is not rejection by God but the stern discipline of a loving but no-nonsense Holy Father.

The story in 1 Corinthians 5:1-5 may also cast light on why God allows Satan and his demons freedom to act in this world. It would seem that God may actually use Satan and his demons as one of His instruments of judgment or discipline on those who willingly participate in Satan's rebellion against God. It would be as if God were to say, "If you have decided to go back and participate in the works of darkness in Satan's kingdom, then I will let you experience the terrible consequences of that decision." Some of those consequences could be brutal torture by demons on the minds, bodies or families of rebellious Christians. Perhaps this explains why God allows such terrible things to happen to Christians in places where the sin of tribalism has involved Christians in bringing harm and even death to fellow Christians.

Fortunately, with God there is always the possibility of forgiveness and restoration of fellowship with God and others when there is true repentance from sin. This happened in the case of King David (Psalm 51:3-13). God's willingness to forgive sin is also seen in Jesus' story of the prodigal son (Luke 15:11-27).

It is important, however, not to confuse eternal forgiveness of sin with earthly consequences of sin. David was forgiven by God for his terrible sins of adultery and murder (2 Sam. 12:13) but his family life was greatly disturbed for the rest of his life by what he had done (2 Sam. 12:10-12). First of all, God allowed the child of Bathsheba, conceived by David's sin, to die in spite of David's prayer and fasting (2 Sam. 12:15-18). Later, one of David's own sons (Amnon) raped and disgraced one of his own daughters (Tamar - 2 Sam. 13:1-15). For this crime, Tamar's brother Absalom took revenge by having his brother, Amnon, murdered, (2 Sam. 13:23-31). Later Absalom disgraced his father by having sex with David's wives in plain view of the Israelites (2 Sam. 16:22). Besides all this, Absalom also overthrew his own father, David, as king of Israel (2 Sam. 15:1-14).

Some Christians may wonder if God really forgave David as He said He would after David's confession of his sin (2 Sam. 12:13 -14). God did forgive David for his sins (Romans 4:6-8, 1 John 1:9), but that did not change the fact that David had to suffer the earthly consequences for what he had done. A husband may beat his wife to death in a moment of rage and later repent with bitter tears of grief for what he has done. No degree of repentance, however, will bring his wife back to life. David's confession and repentance (Psalm 51:3-4) did not bring Uriah back to life or heal Bathsheba's broken heart. So also when we sin: There are harmful consequences to our words and actions. God will not remove these consequences but He will give us the grace and strength to live with them day by day.

The other important question we need to understand is this: Where does Satan get his power? What is the relationship between sin and Satan's power? We learn from Col. 2:15 that evil angels were "disarmed" when Jesus was crucified. How were they "armed" before the cross? The answer is given in Col. 2:14 where it says that Christ, "canceled out the certificate of debt consisting of decrees against us."

Like a trial lawyer before a judge, prepared with his case against the accused criminal, Satan and his demons were armed with a record of our sins against God (the "certificate of debt"). As the one who accuses people before God (Rev. 12: 10), the weapon of Satan against mankind is his demand that human beings be judged and punished by God's law for their sins. Satan knows we have earned God's judgment by breaking the laws of God. Col. 2:14 says the "certificate" consists of the laws of God which we have broken. The penalty for our sins prescribed in this certificate is death. The Bible says, "the wages of sin is death" (Rom. 6:23).

When Jesus came He took the death penalty for our sins on the cross (Heb. 2:9) so that, "through death, He might render powerless him who had the power of death, that is the devil" (Heb. 2:14-NASB). The basis for Satan's accusations against us was removed by Jesus' death on the cross for those who repent and believe in Him. That is why the Bible says, "They overcame him (Satan) by the blood of the lamb" (Rev. 12:11). Romans 8:1 says, "Therefore, there is now no condemnation for those who are in Christ Jesus." Those who have been joined to Christ by faith have been eternally purchased by the blood of Christ (Rev. 5:9).

However, because the realm of Satan's power is sin and rebellion against God, Satan can still gain "a foothold" in the life of a Christian through willing sin according to Ephesians 4:27. This "foothold" can come through a great variety of sins, such as unforgiveness, pride, tribalism, resentment, bitterness, anger, lust, lying and especially participation in pagan religious practices. Such pagan practices are an abomination to God according to Deuteronomy 7:25 and Deut. 18:10-14. God even forbids His people to have the objects of pagan religion in their houses (Deut. 7:26).

It is in the matter of traditional religion that many African Christians struggle with deep spiritual bondage because they refuse to totally renounce the beliefs and practices of their traditional religion, especially in times of personal crisis. The "foothold" of traditional beliefs and practices is one reason why so many African Christians cannot break free from the sin of tribalism and other sinful bondages. There is an urgent need for Christians to confess and renounce these and all other sins so that they can be forgiven by God and find deliverance from spiritual bondage, as stated in Prov. 28:13.

The key to understanding this is found in James 4:7 which says, "Submit yourselves, then, to God. Resist the devil and he will flee from you." The critical element is submission to God. We must obey God if we are to be able to resist Satan and his demons with God's authority.

The Lord Himself did this in His temptation by Satan in the wilderness. He first submitted Himself to God the Father by choosing to obey the Word of God rather than His own desires. That is why He repeatedly quoted the Old Testament and said, "It is written. . ." (Matt. 4:4, 7,10). It was after He had submitted His will to God that He was in a position to resist Satan and to order him to leave (Matt. 4:10). If that was true for our sinless Lord in His earthly life, how much more is that necessary for us? When we have unconditionally submitted to God and His Word, it is then that we have the delegated authority of Christ to resist Satan and his demons (Luke 10:19, Eph. 6:11-18). It is very important to understand that no exorcism will result in permanent deliverance until the persons concerned have unconditionally submitted themselves to God and turned away from their sins.

To summarize, the Bible teaches that Satan's power is directly related to willing rebellion against God. Although no man or angel can remove God's ownership of a true Christian, God may allow severe discipline in the life of a rebellious Christian (Heb. 12:5-6). This could include permitting mental, emotional or physical affliction by demons or even physical death if the person does not truly repent from his sin and renounce it from his life. Demon "possession" is the wrong term to use in the case of true Christians. Satan cannot own those whom God owns. God may allow suffering of various kinds as a result of willing sin, including demonic affliction or oppression, but God will never abandon His own child (Heb. 13:5-6). There is a good reason why the Bible makes a central theme of personal holiness of life. God loves us with an everlasting, unconditional love. But He will not tolerate sin.

5. PROSPERITY THEOLOGY

Another form of false teaching which is gaining a large following in Africa today can be defined as "Prosperity Theology." This is the teaching that God does not want any of His children to be poor or to lack anything they may desire. This teaching is usually based on passages found in the Old Testament where God promised His people material blessing. These passages would include statements such as Psalm 23:1, "The LORD is my shepherd, I shall not be in want" or Psalm 34:9, "Fear the LORD, you his saints, for those who fear him lack nothing." Longer passages which promised specific physical blessings are quoted, such as Deuteronomy 28:1-8.

In addition, Jesus' promises in the New Testament concerning prayer are often quoted, such as, "Ask and it will be given to you; . . . For everyone who asks receives" (Matt. 7:7-8), or Mark 11:24, "Therefore I tell you, whatever you ask for in prayer, believe that you have received it, and it will be yours." From these and other references it is taught that the way to have whatever you want is simply to "name it and then claim it by faith." Without careful investigation, this teaching seems to have good support in the Bible.

Prosperity theology, like the teaching of many cults, reveals an error of Bible interpretation which has been the source of many "Christian" cults. That error is either to quote verses out of their biblical context in order to prove an idea, or to quote just a few verses on a subject without considering all the verses on that subject found in the Bible. It is only when all the passages in the Bible on a particular subject are considered together that a person can correctly understand the teaching of the Bible on that subject. For example, the statements by Jesus on prayer quoted above must be balanced with other statements by Jesus on prayer and on the rest of the teaching in the Bible on prayer. There are other conditions to answered prayer beyond the condition of faith (Mark 11:24) emphasized in prosperity theology. These other statements present specific conditions for answered prayer. Here are some of those conditions.

1. Prayer must not be made for selfish purposes. This condition alone disproves the most basic assumption of prosperity theology. The Bible says, "When you ask, you do not receive, because you ask with wrong motives, that you may spend what you get on your pleasures. You adulterous people, don't you know that friendship with the world is hatred toward God?" (James 4:3-4). These are strong words of condemnation for the very foundation of prosperity theology.
2. Prayer must be made not according to our desires but according to the will of God. The Bible says, "This is the confidence we have in approaching God: that if we ask anything according to HIS WILL, he hears us" (1 John 5:14).
3. To receive answers to prayer our lives must be characterized by unconditional obedience to the will of God. The Bible

says, "we have confidence before God and receive from him anything we ask, because we obey his commands and do what pleases him" (1 John 3:21-22).

4. To receive answers to prayer, our personal lives must be free from known sin, especially the sin of unforgiveness toward others (Matt. 6:15, Mark 11:25). The Bible says, "Surely the arm of the LORD is not too short to save, nor his ear too dull to hear. But your iniquities have separated you from your God; your sins have hidden his face from you, so that he will not hear" (Isa. 59:1-2).
5. To receive answers to prayer we must abide in Christ and His Word must abide in us. In other words, our prayers must be made according to the Word of God, not according to our selfish desires. Jesus said, "If you remain in me and my words remain in you, ask whatever you wish, and it will be given you" (John 15:7).

There are also other problems with prosperity theology, such as the failure to understand the difference between the Old Testament revelation of God's will for the Israelites as a nation and the New Testament revelation of God's will for all mankind. Many Old Testament promises were limited in time and purpose to the earthly people of God of that time who were the believing Jews. If we want to understand the truth of God for Christians of the present age we must understand the Old Testament in the light of the full revelation of God's will in the New Testament. When we do that, we discover that God does promise to provide our needs (Philippians 4:19). He does not, however, promise to satisfy all our desires (James 4:3) which are corrupt because our sin nature (Rom. 7:18).

To summarize, prosperity theology is not biblical theology. It is based on incomplete and incorrect interpretation of what the Bible teaches. God wants us to pray and He even commands us to pray (Matt. 6:9, Eph. 6:18). He wants us to expect answers to our prayers (Mark 11:22-23). Many of Jesus' promises concerning prayer were given to strengthen our faith as we pray. But He wants us to pray for His will, not our will, to be done on earth (Matt. 6:10). He does not intend to answer prayers intended for selfish indulgence but rather prayers that will advance His kingdom in this world (Matt. 6:10)

6. THE WRONG USE OF THE NAME OF JESUS IN PRAYER.

Besides the wrong ideas of prosperity theology concerning prayer, there is another problem in regard to prayer which has to do with the wrong use of the name of Jesus as a power word. Names are very important in many African cultures. In some cases there is a traditional belief that the name of a person carries the power or influence of that person.

With some Christians there is a belief which is very close to the practice of African traditional religion that the use of the name of Jesus carries special spiritual power to make things happen. It is the idea that the name of Jesus by itself carries the power of God. This is the same idea as the traditional African belief in magic power through the use of the right power words spoken in the correct way. The practical result of this is that some Christians shout, "In the name of Jesus" over and over again in order to bring the power of Christ to bear on the matter about which they are praying. There is a subtle danger in this practice. What does it mean to pray in the name of Jesus?

pray in the name of Jesus and given promises of answers from God when we do pray in His name (John 14:13-14, John 15:16, John 16:23-24). These promises by Christ are made to those who have a personal relationship with God the Father through Christ. The use of the name of Jesus in prayer is an indication of that personal relationship. It is not because the name of Jesus has some kind of supernatural power by itself. In the book of Acts, we read of seven sons of a Jewish priest named Sceva who tried to use the name of Jesus as a supernatural power word in order to drive out demons (Acts 19:13-15). These men, however, did not have a personal relationship with Jesus. The result was that they were physically overpowered and beaten by the demons (Acts 19:16)!

We must be careful not to return to the beliefs of African traditional religion that certain words used in just the right way have a power of their own. This practice can easily result in the very wrong idea that we can somehow force God to act if we just use the name of Jesus rather than praying according to the will of God. As with other practices of ATR, it is an abomination to God to imitate the practices of pagan religion (Lev. 18:1-3, Deut. 12:31, Deut. 18:9-12).

God knows everything there is to know before we ever think of it or pray about it (Psalm 139:1-4). He also knows just what He is going to do in response to our prayers before we pray. It is a form of dishonor and unbelief concerning the omniscience of God to think that by shouting the right words in the right way that we can force God to act in a certain way. This was the kind of thing which the pagan priests of Baal did when they had a power encounter with the prophet Elijah on Mr. Carmel (1 Kings 18:26). Jesus warned us about the use of vain repetition in prayer (Matt. 6:7) and this surely includes the use of His own name in prayer.

In summary, prayer which seeks to cause our will to be done by the forceful use of the name of Jesus is a form of pagan belief which dishonors God. Prayer which God honors and answers is not an attempt to cause our will to be done. Biblical prayer is seeking to cause the will of God to be done on earth as it is done in Heaven (Matt. 6:10). When such prayer is humbly made in the name of Jesus by true believers there will be an answer from God.

7. THE SOURCES OF HEALING, TONGUES AND OTHER MIRACLES

Another problem in some meetings and some churches is the source of healings, prophecies, speaking in tongues and other supernatural occurences which take place. There are spiritual gifts of healing, tongues, prophecies and miracles from the Holy Spirit (1 Cor. 12:9-10). There are also other supernatural sources of these phenomena. In traditional religions throughout the world there are medicine men, traditional healers, witch doctors and specialists who can perform supernatural healings, prophesy, speak in tongues and perform other miracles. How are we to determine what is from God and what is not? The way to evaluate the situation is to ask certain questions such as the following: "What is the result of this healing, prophecy, tongues utterance or miracle?" "Does it draw people to repentance and faith in Christ?" "Does it draw them into a deeper relationship with Christ?" Or does it have some other result?

There are examples of miraculous imitation in the Bible. When Moses challenged the pagan magicians of Egypt with the rod of God, the magicians were able to duplicate the miracle which God gave Moses to perform by turning Moses' rod into a snake. The Bible says, "Moses and Aaron went to Pharaoh and did just as the LORD commanded. Aaron threw his staff down in front of Pharaoh and his officials, and it became a snake. Pharaoh then summoned wise men and sorcerers, and the Egyptian magicians also did the same things by their secret arts: Each one threw down his staff and it became a snake. But Aaron's staff swallowed up their staffs" (Exodus 7:10-13).

It is a well known fact that there are people from just about every traditional religion on earth who give prophetic messages or who speak in tongues when they are possessed by spirits. Prophetic messages during spirit possession is a common way for so called ancestral spirits (which are really demons) to communicate with the living. How then can a person know if the spirit enabling a person to prophesy or to speak in tongues is the Holy Spirit or another spirit? The Bible says we must not "believe every spirit, but test the spirits to see whether they are from God, because many false prophets have gone out into the world" (1 John 4:1). Does anyone in the church today bother to test the spirits who enable people to prophesy or to speak in tongues? What dishonor and disgrace does it bring to our Lord when Christians permit other spirits to bring deception and disruption into the worship of God?

There are at least two biblical tests for testing the spirits who give supernatural messages or who perform miracles. The Bible says, "This is how you can recognize the Spirit of God: Every spirit that acknowledges that Jesus Christ has come in the flesh is from God but every spirit that does not acknowledge Jesus is not from God." Notice that this test applies to the spirit who is manifesting its presence, not to the person himself. A second test is found in 1 Cor. 12:3. Here we are told that, "no one can say, 'Jesus is Lord,' except by the Holy Spirit." As in the first test, the question must be directed to the spirit who is manifesting its presence, not to the person. It can be done with questions such as the following. "Spirit bringing this manifestation, Who is Jesus?" and, "Spirit bringing this manifestation, did Jesus Christ come in the flesh?"

In summary it can be said that a miracle which does not draw people to Christ or deepen their personal relationship to Christ is not likely to be a miracle performed by God. Another question which may be asked is this: "Who receives the honor from what has been done?" Does the honor go to some human being or does it go to the Lord? If a miracle is from God, God will see that the honor does not go to man. The Bible says, "I am the LORD; that is my name! I will not give my glory to another" (Isa. 42:8).

8. THE EVIDENCE OF THE FULLNESS OF THE HOLY SPIRIT

A problem in some churches today is a wrong understanding of the fulness of the Holy Spirit. The Bible calls on Christians to be filled with the Holy Spirit (Eph. 5:18), but what is the evidence that this has taken place? How can a person know who is truly filled with the Holy Spirit and who is controlled by some other spirit? Consider the following true story.

A young man was sitting in a church service on a Sunday morning. The woman next to him fell to the floor and began rolling about, making strange noises. After the service the young man asked the pastor of the church what was happening to the woman. The pastor answered, "She was being filled with the Holy Spirit." The young man was troubled and went to one of his friends and told him about the incident. The reason he was troubled, he told his friend, was that he had grown up in a home where African traditional religion was practiced. His mother had practiced this traditional religion for many years before she came to Christ. The young man related how his mother would often become possessed with ancestral spirits. When she was possessed she would behave in the same way as the woman he had seen in church.

On the American frontier during the nineteenth century preachers used to hold camp meetings for the settlers and preach the gospel. Sometimes at these meetings people would begin to shake and roll on the ground, often making noises like animals. They would claim that they got "the spirit." But what spirit was producing this behavior? How are we to know what spirit is controlling a person? What is the evidence of being filled with the Holy Spirit?

The Bible gives several indications about the character of the lives of those who are controlled by the Holy Spirit. One of the primary indications is a life of boldness and power in witnessing to the gospel of Christ. Jesus said, "you will receive power when the Holy Spirit comes on you; and you will be my witnesses in Jerusalem, and in all Judea and Samaria, and to the ends of the earth" (Acts 1:8). Another important indication is an effective prayer life where there are many answers to prayer. Paul wrote, "the Spirit helps us in our weakness. We do not know what we ought to pray for, but the Spirit himself intercedes for us with groans that words cannot express. And he who searches our hearts knows the mind of the Spirit, because the Spirit intercedes for the saints in accordance with God's will" (Rom. 8:26-27). Concerning answers to prayer which is guided by the Holy Spirit, the apostle John wrote, "This is the confidence we have in approaching God: that if we ask anything according to his will, he hears us. And if we know that he hears us--whatever we ask--we know that we have what we asked of him" (1 John 5:14-15). When we are filled with the Spirit and we pray in the Spirit according to the will of God, there will be clear and powerful answers to our prayers.

Another evidence of the control of the Holy Spirit in a person's life is the fruit of the Spirit. The Bible says, "the fruit of the Spirit is love, joy, peace, patience, kindness, goodness, faithfulness, gentleness and self-control" (Gal. 5:22-23). Those who claim to be filled with the Holy Spirit but who show no evidence of these qualities of life are deceived. This can be seen by asking another very important question. The question is, "Who was the only person in history who was completely filled with the Holy Spirit throughout life"? The answer of course is Jesus Christ our Lord (John 1:32-34, John 3:34, Matt. 12:28).

In summary, if we want to know how a person will act if he or she is truly filled with the Holy Spirit we need to study the life, the actions and the words of Jesus Christ. We need to compare the life, actions and words of the person who claims he or she is filled with the Holy Spirit with the life, actions and words of Christ. This is the biblical example for being filled with the Holy Spirit.

THE NEED FOR LOVE AND UNITY IN THE CHURCH

The Church of Jesus Christ is the largest common community of human beings in the entire world. The Church reaches across national, cultural, racial, ethnic, age and all other barriers between people. Because of this, the Church could be the strongest force on earth for good and for God. If the Church acted together as one body, the Church would be able to do more good than any other organization in the world. With its present size and membership of more than a billion people on earth, the Church should be able to influence much of the world for God.

Why does that not happen? Simply because the Church does not act together as one Body even though the Church in reality is one Body, the earthly Body of Jesus Christ (1 Cor. 12:27). The Church is filled with division, disunity, disagreement and internal conflict. Jesus said, "Every kingdom divided against itself will be ruined, and every city or household divided against itself will not stand" (Matt. 12:25). So it is with the Church. Its influence for God has been deeply hurt by division. It cannot stand against the evil of the present world system because it is so busy tearing itself to pieces with church fights, church splits, petty jealousies, selfish disputes and a long list of sinful attitudes and actions.

The unity of the Church is so important that it was one of the main themes of the high priestly prayer of our Lord Jesus Christ shortly before He was taken to be crucified. Three times in this prayer Jesus pleaded with God the Father that His people would be united (John 17:11, 21, 22). Yet this prayer has never been fully answered because of the pride, selfishness, jealousy, immaturity, quarreling and disobedience of the Lord's people. One of the greatest needs of the Church today is for revival and renewal by the Spirit of God so that reconciliation, love and unity can replace the endless fighting, division and disunity which has hindered the answer to this prayer of Jesus for His people.

The history of the Church does not offer much encouragement for lasting unity. Historically, only the bitter pill of persecution has drawn God's people together to the extent that they begin to love one another as the Bible teaches. Jesus said, "By this all men will know that you are my disciples, if you love one another" (John 13:35).

Love is the most powerful force in the universe for good. Love has more power to change human lives and to overcome evil than anything else in the world. No government, no organization, no conference of world leaders, no education, no program and no plan of man has ever provided the power to permanently change people for good like the power of the love of God in Jesus Christ. 1 Corinthians 13:8 says, "Love never fails."

Love is the greatest thing there is in life. When people are loved, they are fulfilled, happy, encouraged, motivated, helped and blessed. But where can you get love? You cannot buy it in a shop even if you are the richest person in the world. You cannot make it in a factory, even if you are the most brilliant engineer in the world. You cannot find it anywhere on earth, even if you are the greatest explorer in history. The whole problem of mankind is just this: There is not enough love. Instead there is hatred, anger, selfishness, pride, tribalism, crime, cruelty, violence, fighting, fear, jealousy, betrayal and every other evidence of the fallen sinful nature of the human race. So where can a person find genuine, unselfish love?

The answer is, God is love (1 John 4:8) and God has made it available to mankind by a miracle. The Bible says, "God has poured out his love into our hearts by the Holy Spirit, whom he has given us" (Rom. 5:5). In other words, love is now available to this sick and sinful world through the hearts and hands of God's people, the Church of Jesus Christ. If the Lord's people would give themselves to God and allow Him to express His love through them, the people of this broken and bitter world would find what they want more than all else in life. They would find love. And if they found love, they would find the greatest thing a person can ever find; a personal relationship with the God who is love.

It is God's people alone who have the key to this love. It is God's people who have the Holy Spirit and therefore they are the only people in the world who can offer the love of God.

The greatest need in the church, then, is for a return to biblical Christianity. Biblical Christianity means a church that is alive with the love of God by the power of the Holy Spirit through people who have been born of the Spirit (Titus 3:5-6). It means a church where the members love each other so that people outside the church are drawn to Christ by what they see in the lives of Christians. It means a church where the members are united as Jesus prayed they would be. It means a loving, united community which can act together as a body to meet the needs of the poor, the homeless, the helpless, the handicapped, the hurting, the sick, the needy, the discouraged and the forgotten. It means a church which joyfully gives of its money, its resources and its people to be the instruments of the love of God to a sick and dying world so that hope and meaning can be restored to broken and bitter people. It means a church which can pray in such a way that its prayers will be answered (Matt. 18:19), so that the will of God can be done on earth as it is done in Heaven (Matt. 6:10).

The church in Africa and in the rest of the world urgently needs biblical Christianity. Where there is biblical Christianity there will be blessing from God. There will be love, peace, joy and hope. When there is biblical Christianity in the church of Jesus Christ, then the Scripture written long ago by the prophet Isaiah will be fulfilled.

"Then will all your people be righteous and they will possess the land forever. They are the shoot I have planted, the work of my hands, for the display of my splendor. The least of you will become a thousand, the smallest a mighty nation. I am the LORD; in its time I will do this swiftly. The Spirit of the Sovereign LORD . . . has sent me to bind up the brokenhearted, to proclaim freedom for the captives and release from darkness for the prisoners, to proclaim the year of the Lord's favor and the day of vengeance of our God, to comfort all who mourn, and provide for those who grieve in Zion-- to bestow on them a crown of beauty instead of ashes, the oil of gladness instead of mourning, and a garment of praise instead of a spirit of despair. . . . For I, the LORD, love justice; I hate robbery and iniquity. In my faithfulness I will reward them and make an everlasting covenant with them. Their descendants will be known among the nations and their offspring among the peoples. ALL WHO SEE THEM WILL ACKNOWLEDGE THAT THEY ARE A PEOPLE THE LORD HAS BLESSED" (Isaiah 60:21 - 61:9).

SUMMARY

The church in Africa urgently needs to return to biblical Christianity. Churches are plagued with nominal Christians, false miracle workers, modern day Pharisees and false teaching of many kinds. Marriages and families are in great need of family life teaching based on the Bible rather than culture. The church is consumed with conflict, denominationalism and division. All of this has kept the church from being the greatest force on earth for good and for God in a sick and sin-filled world. The church is in need of revival - a revival based on obedience to the Word of God that will bring reconciliation, love and unity to God's people. God's people need to pray for such a revival.

QUESTIONS FOR REVIEW, REFLECTION AND GROUP DISCUSSION

1. Today there are many churches and organizations in Africa which claim to be Christian. How can we know what is truly Christian and what is not?
2. What do we mean by nominal Christians? For what kind of reasons do many people think they are Christians?
3. What must a person do to become a true Christian?
4. What is the work of the Holy Spirit in making a person a part of the true Church?
5. Jesus said that some people who claim to be Christians may even perform miracles, but that does not prove they are not true Christians (Matt. 7:21-23). What did Jesus say is the way true Christians can be recognized? (Matt. 7:16-20, John 13:35).
6. What were the characteristics of the Pharisees in Jesus' time which made Jesus so strongly condemn them? Are there people like this in church membership and leadership today?

7. List some of the more common false "Christian" teachings being promoted in Africa today.
8. What is the relationship between sin in the life of a Christian and the possible activity of Satan or demons in his or her life?
9. What is the biblical error in the teaching called "prosperity theology?
10. How will a person act who is controlled by the Holy Spirit and filled with the Holy Spirit? Who is the perfect example for such a life?
11. What happens to the witness of the church when there is disunity and fighting within the church? What do God's people have to do in order to eliminate disunity
12. What is the greatest thing in life? What can happen when Christians are willing to share the love of God with those around them?

END NOTES

1. Kore, Danfulani. Culture And The Christian Home. Jos, Nigeria: Africa Christian Textbooks, 1995. p. 3-4.
2. Ibid. p. 3
3. Ibid. p.8